Lecture Notes
in Business Information Processing   **234**

Series Editors

Wil M. P. van der Aalst
  RWTH Aachen University, Aachen, Germany
John Mylopoulos
  University of Trento, Trento, Italy
Michael Rosemann
  Queensland University of Technology, Brisbane, QLD, Australia
Michael J. Shaw
  University of Illinois, Urbana-Champaign, IL, USA
Clemens Szyperski
  Microsoft Research, Redmond, WA, USA

More information about this series at http://www.springer.com/series/7911

Amin Beheshti · Mustafa Hashmi
Hai Dong · Wei Emma Zhang (Eds.)

Service Research and Innovation

5th and 6th Australasian Symposium, ASSRI 2015
and ASSRI 2017, Sydney, NSW, Australia
November 2–3, 2015, and October 19–20, 2017
Revised Selected Papers

 Springer

Editors
Amin Beheshti ⓘ
Macquarie University
Sydney, NSW
Australia

Hai Dong ⓘ
Royal Melbourne Institute of Technology
Melbourne, VIC
Australia

Mustafa Hashmi ⓘ
CSIRO Research Organisation
Dutton Park, QLD
Australia

Wei Emma Zhang ⓘ
Macquarie University
Sydney, NSW
Australia

ISSN 1865-1348   ISSN 1865-1356 (electronic)
Lecture Notes in Business Information Processing
ISBN 978-3-319-76586-0   ISBN 978-3-319-76587-7   (eBook)
https://doi.org/10.1007/978-3-319-76587-7

Library of Congress Control Number: 2018934348

Printed on acid-free paper

This Springer imprint is published by the registered company Springer International Publishing AG
part of Springer Nature
The registered company address is: Gewerbestrasse 11, 6330 Cham, Switzerland

Preface

Today's knowledge-, service-, and cloud-based business environment is extraordinarily competitive. Organizations that have successfully laid a foundation for continuous innovation and agility have been focusing on service research and innovation to respond rapidly to the never-ending and ever-changing demands of the business. The Australasian Symposium on Service Research and Innovation (ASSRI), in its sixth year in 2017, has clearly established itself as an important academic event in service research and innovation. It is a premium event for researchers, practitioners, and developers in service-oriented computing that is changing the way software applications are designed, delivered, and consumed.

We are pleased to present to you the proceedings of the 6th Australasian Symposium on Service Research and Innovation (ASSRI 2017), which was held in Sydney, Australia, during October 19–20, 2017. The papers selected for presentation and publication in this volume showcase fresh ideas from exciting and emerging topics in service-oriented computing and case studies in business process and supply change management.

In this volume, we have selected 11 high-quality papers from ASSRI 2017 submissions keeping the acceptance rate at around 40%. We have also included three papers from ASSRI 2015 ("Information Systems as a Service (ISaaS): Consumer Co-creation of Value", "Auction-Based Models for Composite Service Selection: A Design Framework," and "Relating SOA Governance to IT Governance and EA Governance") and one invited keynote paper ("Big Data Analytics Has Little to Do with Analytics") in this volume. Each paper was reviewed by a team comprising a senior Program Committee member and at least two regular Program Committee members who engage in a discussion phase after the initial reviews are prepared. The papers in this volume cover topics related to cloud service discovery, service recommendation, crowdsourcing services as well as trust and privacy challenges in web services.

We are grateful for the support of the Service Science Society Australia and the general chairs, Prof. Aditya Ghose (University of Wollongong, Australia) and Prof. Michael Sheng (Macquarie University, Australia). We very much hope you enjoy reading the papers in this volume.

December 2017

Amin Beheshti
Hai Dong
Mustafa Hashmi

Organization

General Chairs

Aditya Ghose   University of Wollongong, Australia
Michael Sheng   Macquarie University, Australia

Program Chairs

Amin Beheshti   UNSW Sydney, Australia
Hai Dong   RMIT, Australia
Mustafa Hashmi   Data61, CSIRO, Australia

Publicity Chairs

Ho-Pun Lam   Data61, CSIRO, Australia
Carlos Rodriguez   UNSW Sydney, Australia

Industry Chairs

Jay Daniel   UTS, Australia
Mohammadreza   University of Wollongong, Australia
  Mohaghegian
Lina Yao   UNSW Sydney, Australia

Publication Chair

Wei Emma Zhang   Macquarie University, Australia

Web Chair

Joel Kocherry   University of Wollongong, Australia

Program Committee

Renu Agarwal   UTS Sydney, Australia
Don Allen   CISCO Systems, USA
Ralph Badinelli   Virginia Tech, USA
Boualem Benatallah   UNSW Sydney, Australia
Charlie Bess   HP
Daniel Beverungen   University of Münster/European Research Center
  for Information Systems
Athman Bouguettaya   University of Sydney, Australia

Contents

Invited Talk

Big Data Analytics Has Little to Do with Analytics

Fethi Rabhi[1], Madhushi Bandara[1], Anahita Namvar[1], and Onur Demirors[1,2(✉)]

[1] School of Computer Science and Engineering,
The University of New South Wales, Sydney, 2052, Australia
`{f.rabhi,k.bandara,o.demirors}@unsw.edu.au,`
`anahita.namvar@gmail.com`
[2] Department of Computer Engineering, Izmir Institute of Technology, Izmir, Turkey

Abstract. As big data analytics is adapted across multitude of domains and applications there is a need for new platforms and architectures that support analytic solution engineering as a lean and iterative process. In this paper we discuss how different software development processes can be adapted to data analytic process engineering, incorporating service oriented architecture, scientific workflows, model driven engineering and semantic technology. Based on the experience obtained through ADAGE framework [1] and the findings of the survey on how semantic modeling is used for data analytic solution engineering [6], we propose two research directions - big data analytic development lifecycle and data analytic knowledge management for lean and flexible data analytic platforms.

Keywords: Data analytic process · Solution engineering · Knowledge modelling
Analytic life cycle

1 Introduction

Big data analytics can be defined as the process of extracting meaning from big data using specialized software systems. As the definition emphasises, it has three significant aspects: the nature of the data, the software utilized and the processes applied. The nature of big data refers to voluminous datasets often in the range of terabytes and petabytes whose size and characteristics extend beyond the ability of standard storage and computing capacity. Big data has distinct characteristics with respect to the *Volume:* the rate at which data is generated, *Velocity*: the rate at which data flows from different sources and the rate at which the produced data can be processed at maximizing its value, and *Variety*: the diversity in data types and their representation. Some challenges associated with big data can be listed as handling the massive amount of information streams generated from different sources, identifying information that is critical for decision-making, handling volatile business context and frequent changes in data and the ability to anticipate and respond on different trends.

In the context of this paper, we define the big data related environment as a combination of three systems: data source, a data publisher and value generator. It differs from the traditional data warehouse environment that always has a shared view

© Springer International Publishing AG, part of Springer Nature 2018
A. Beheshti et al. (Eds.): ASSRI 2015/2017, LNBIP 234, pp. 3–17, 2018.
https://doi.org/10.1007/978-3-319-76587-7_1

of data. Big data environments can have multiple data sources such as Internet of Things (IoT) systems, different software applications, and social networks. These sources generate data which is stored and disseminated through different data providers. Analysts can use the data published by data providers to conduct analysis and generate value out of them. The results can be used for a variety of purposes. If we take an example of the financial data eco system as shown in Fig. 1, financial institutions (e.g.- banks) and financial market systems (e.g.- Australian Stock Exchange) generate different data sets which are collected, stored and published by financial data providers such as Thomson Reuters. A data scientist can access the raw data, transform them and conduct analysis to derive insights on data useful for financial institutions in their decision making. The outcome of the analysis can also be published and shared again as a new data set through the data provider.

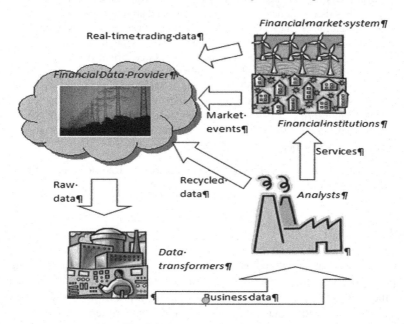

Fig. 1. Financial data eco system

Data analytics requires a complex process and involves multiple steps such as business understanding, data acquisition, cleaning and pre-processing, integration, pattern recognition, analyzing and interpreting results. As with the production of any service or artifact, cost, timeliness and quality determines the success of the analytics solution. Although it is depicted as an engineering solution, the analytics processes and the utilization of tools are frequently conducted in an ad-hoc fashion, based on the experience of individuals and have no traceability. Such an approach could have been feasible for the analytics problems of the last decade, but today the demand and criticality of the requirements have already gone far beyond what can be achieved with ad-hoc analytics models.

In this paper we provide our observations on how systematic approaches can improve the success rates of data analytics projects. In Sect. 2, we outline the role of the field of software engineering based on lessons learnt during the last 5 decades. Section 3 provides an overview of new and emerging tools, techniques and systematic approaches for handling unstructured problems as is the case for big data analytics. In the conclusion, we have summarized our observations in two aspects: analytic solution development lifecycle and better knowledge representation.

2   Why Software Engineering Matters

2.1   The Knowledge Silos Problem

To build a big data analytic solution, it is necessary for experts coming from different domains to be able to work together. One data analytic application may require application expert, social science expert, domain expert, big data specialist, statistical analytic and data mining specialists as well as a software engineer familiar with different platforms and programming techniques (see Fig. 2). On one hand there are domain experts who understand the context, purpose and business value of the analytics solution. On the other hand, analytic experts specializing in statistical modelling, machine learning and mathematics are needed. Deploying solutions on an IT infrastructure requires software engineering knowledge such as data modelling, algorithms, modular design and abstraction which domain experts and analysts do not possess.

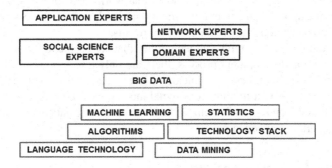

Fig. 2. Big data analytics expertise silos

There is no lack of software and tools to conduct a particular data analytic task. As an evidence, observe the data analytic software stack proposed by Milosevic et al. [22] in Fig. 3. There are sets of platforms suitable for different levels of data analysis and tools within one layer provide same or similar services.

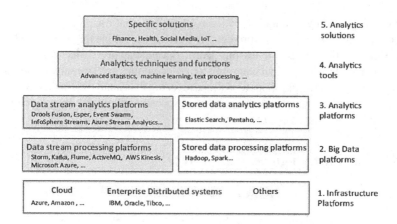

Fig. 3. Analytic software stack [22]

In many organizations, big data analytics practices are largely driven by analysts who tend to have expertise in using specific analysis or statistical modelling packages [e.g.- Weka, Tabula, SAS, Matlab]. Hence, the analysts are reluctant to design flexible analytics processes that align with organization's IT infrastructure, specific objectives, and to use a mix of data sources and software frameworks. Most organizations rely on a manual process to integrate different analytics tasks and data elements [7, 8] which are expensive and hard to maintain in the long term [7]. Moreover, according to No-Free-Lunch theorem [9], there is no one model that works best for every problem and depending on the application context and input data, analysts have to experiment with different analysis techniques to obtain optimum results.

Although there are many tools and techniques that are usable at different levels of the analytic solution development process, there are only few approaches that support the overall development process dynamically. Most research efforts concentrate in one area or domain such as text mining from social media or stock-market event analysis, but there is a lack of "end-to-end" methods for engineering big data analytics solutions, with proper separation of concerns.

2.2   Example of a Complex Analytics Process

To illustrate the challenges associated with data analytic processes, we exemplify a case related to predictive analytics. The process of predictive analytics aims to forecast future outcomes based on existing historical data to drive better decision [30]. In other words, it can help to identify unexpected opportunities and forecast problems before happening. In practice, predictive analytics can address business problems related to multiple disciplines from churn prediction to recommender systems. It can also anticipate when factory floor machines are likely to break down or figure out which customers are likely to default on a bank loan. Predictive analytics comprise a variety of statistical techniques and machine learning methods. Considering the inherent characteristics of predictive analytics in all domains the generic process is shown in Fig. 4, However, depend on application context and input data different techniques can be applied at each stage.

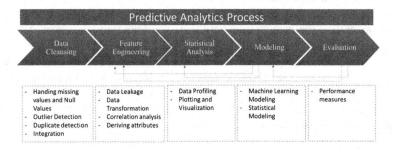

Fig. 4. Predictive analytic process

Table 1. Stages of credit risk prediction process

Predictive analytics process		Credit risk prediction
Data cleansing	Handling missing values	Removing missing values (empty, Null, N/A, none)
	Outlier detection	Removing outliers by applying IQR method
Feature engineering	Data leakage	Identification of features that are not available at the time of reviewing the applicant's request for a loan, and removing them from our analysis
	Data transformation	Encoding ordinal features to numeric feature Binarizing nominal features Log Transformation for features with high skewness Normalization and Standardization to have measurements to a standard scale
	Correlation analysis	Applying Pearson Correlation analysis for presenting the relationship of features (predictors) with respond variable (dependent variable) which is Loan Status Investigating significant difference in predictive features between the default and non-default borrowers
	Deriving attributes	Deriving different ratios by available features. According to classification result, defined ratios increased the classifier performance
Statistical analysis	Data profiling	Summarizing dataset through descriptive statistics such as mean, max, min, standard deviation and range
	Plotting and visualization	Depicting variables by presenting them on different plots and histograms
Modeling	Statistical modeling	Applying Linear Discriminant Analysis and Logistic Regression analysis for predicting borrower's status
	Machine learning modeling	Developing classification models such as Decision Tree Classifier and Random Forest for identification of default and non-default borrowers
Evaluation	Performance measures	Considering confusion matrix, performance metrics such as False positive rate, accuracy, sensitivity and specificity has been addressed, Also ROC curve and AUC has been employed

One such application of predictive analytics is Credit Risk Prediction, where the goal is to predict true creditworthiness of potential borrower. Table 1 depicts the general process that needs to be adapted for credit risk domain.

In practice, each of these analytic stages are conducted utilizing scripts or specific tools and integrating the data and analytic tools are done through scripts. Moreover, multiple experts should come together to understand and select data, to write software to clean and analyze them, to understand statistical and analytical models suitable for the task etc. This process is complex, time consuming and may have to go through multiple iterations before the model satisfies the evaluation criteria. Then the deployment and maintenance of the model in the bank environment should be conducted as a joint effort between system engineers, domain experts and analysts.

3   New and Emerging Software Engineering Approaches for Big Data Analytics

We discuss in this section some existing research areas in the software engineering space and their relevance in the field of big data analytics from different perspectives.

3.1   Development Processes

The best starting point for looking at the big data analytics processes from the lenses of a lean business is as an evolution of the software development life cycle models. Adapting an approach similar to Agile development can improve the analytic process by bringing a mixture of IT and business roles, providing rapid time to market strategy to model and evaluate analytic models, accepting failures and improving upon them and by challenging the existing practices. More specifically, the engineering of a big data analytics solution following an Agile method allows extensive collaboration, flexibility, and rapid development that fit with lean business practices.

We can identify three software engineering practices suitable for data analysis processes: business requirement analysis, solution design and implementation. Business requirement analysis focuses on capturing domain knowledge and acquiring requirements from different stakeholders and defining functional and non-functional requirements. Design enables the design of artifacts to be produced/discussed at a high level, with no commitment to any technology or platform. The implementation allows testing and refining the analytic solution and validating the quality. Figure 5 illustrates how different analytic expertise we discussed in Sect. 2 are involved in these three stages of a typical Agile iteration flow.

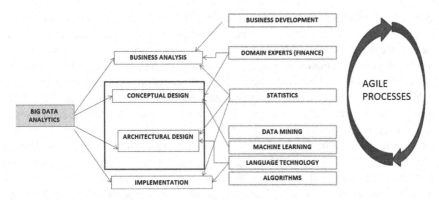

Fig. 5. How expert knowledge can be leveraged in different stages of agile big data analytics process

Agile methods are particularly suitable for big data analytics problems. As the problems cannot be formulated before the solution emerges, the early feedback loop between users and engineers are critical. The iterative nature of agile methods enables to establish a systematic engineering approach while at the same time keeping the bottom up feedback loop in place.

Literature such as such as CRISP-DM [2] and Domain-oriented data mining [3] is advocating the importance of considering practices related to analytics and establishing good understanding of data to build better analytic solutions more effectively. Significant limitations observed in data analytic solution engineering space are a lack of high-level architectural and data models to understand how to compose analytic pipelines, how data should flow between the different stages and how to create mappings between the stages and appropriate tools and data sets in the underlying infrastructure.

3.2 Architectural Design

Effectively designing, building and maintaining flexible data analytics processes from an architectural perspective remains to be a challenge. Service oriented architecture and scientific workflow techniques address the issue to a certain extent by providing modular, pluggable software components and a composition environment for them. Workflow technology as applied to big data analytics is generally called scientific workflow technology. It can assist in the composition of hundreds of distributed software components and data sources. Scientific workflow technology can be used to model scientists' analysis processes, where each step typically corresponds to an individual activity or task. If each task is performed by a component (or a service), then the composition of a set of components would be equivalent to performing a sequence of tasks, where the sequence is determined by the scientific workflow model. A scientific workflow system enables the definition, management and execution of scientific workflow models and allows scientists to automate the execution and management of complex sets of computations and data analyses, thereby enabling science at a large-scale.

Service-oriented architecture (SOA) is an architectural approach that advocates the creation of software components as autonomous, platform-independent, loosely coupled services that can be easily combined within and across enterprises to create new software applications to meet a business or scientific need [31]. Service-oriented technologies have a well-defined set of interfaces and consistent access protocols we can use to engineer data analytic solutions. In addition, business processes technologies can be used to provide an end-to-end analytic solution for the users by enabling automated or semi-automated service selection and composition. The concept of "data and analytics as a service" stems from a design paradigm of which design principles are governed by Service Oriented Architecture (SOA) [32]. This concept advocates accessing data and tools "where they live" – the actual platform on which the resource resides should not matter. Therefore, service-oriented design can play an important role in linking the analytic solution design to its implementation.

We identify two types of services we can leverage:

- Data services: hide data complexities and provide access to the data
- Analytics services: hide underlying technologies and conduct the model building and execution for the users

Although the use of SOA has improved interoperability, orchestration of web services into a workflow can be equally challenging for the end-user. Hence the literature emphasizes the necessity of better knowledge management in enterprise data analytic [2, 11] and scientific workflow [10] for better analytic platform development.

3.3 Integrated Frameworks

This section discusses integrated approaches for designing big data analytics processes. They generally fall under the category of model driven software development because they focus on models as central artifacts to provide an abstraction of a real-world application or system and apply model transformations to realise software systems from these models. Model Driven Engineering (MDE) is defined as the vision of constructing a model of a system that then can be transformed into a real artefact [24]. Use of MDE in the context of service-oriented architecture can deliver powerful software engineering methods [25].

One way to provide a platform for end-to-end data analytic solution development is to follow an MDE approach where knowledge related to data, mining algorithms and analytic services are captured through models which are leveraged to derive an analytic solution. There is ample literature emphasizing the advantage of using models [23, 28, 29], in analytic solution space to model data, analytic requirement or services etc. There are only a few studies in the literatures such as Rajbhoj et al. [26] and Ceri et al. [27] that explores the potential of applying MDE for big data analytics, but they are limited to particular analytic tool or technology such as Map-Reduce framework [26].

The ADAGE framework [1] specifically leverages the capabilities of service-oriented architectures and scientific workflow management systems into data analysis. The main idea is that the models used by analysts (i.e. workflow, service, and data models) contain concise information and instructions that can be viewed as an accurate record of the analytics process, become a useful artefact for provenance tracking and ensure reproducibility of such analytics processes. As shown in Fig. 6, the ADAGE framework consists a set of architectural patterns and operational guidelines.

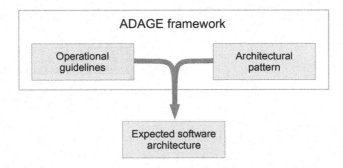

Fig. 6. Adage framework

ADAGE architecture patterns support the definition of analysis processes in a more convenient manner than using generic and conventional business processes. It uses a reference data model closely associated with a target domain to standardize the representation of datasets. Adage framework uses a set of services to process the datasets, so as to transform them into other datasets or information. Both the reference data model and the ADAGE services are embedded in a service-oriented architecture (SOA). Figure 7 represents a definition of an end-to-end data analytic process from importing data into dissemination of findings, defined using the ADAGE architectural pattern. Figure 8 represents an application of that analytic process for the analysis of financial market data.

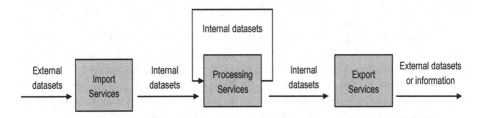

Fig. 7. Definition of an analytic process through the ADAGE architectural pattern

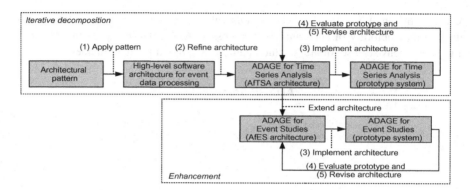

Fig. 8. Application to the analysis of financial market data

However, defining suitable data models to accurately represent complex business contexts associated with an analytic problem is not easy.

3.4   Knowledge Representation

The main critique of existing MDE approaches is that they often assume simple data reference models, which is unrealistic, hard to evolve and difficult to create and maintain when there are multiple stakeholders with conflicting viewpoints. Any analytic system has to recognize that different types of mental models can co-exist, each type of model can be particular to a community of practice, the mappings between concepts from different models can be subjective and the reference model needs to allow different interpretations of the data by different people. As an example, a financial data analysis system can have two types of models: event model and time-series model, two communities: computer science and statistics and it is not possible to always map between raw data and variables consistently.

Semantic technology, which is based on the vision of semantic web by Tim Berners-Lee is a new approach for modelling knowledge, data as well as their semantics and there is a well-developed set of standards and notations: RDF, RDSFS, OWL, supported by different tools for modelling, storing, querying, and inferencing the knowledge. Different communities have adapted semantic technologies to build standard ontologies related to their practices (e.g. ResMED for medical domain and FIBO in Finance).

The work in [21] summaries the value of semantic technology and ontologies from three angles. 1. Ontology is a way of clarifying meaning and reducing unnecessary complexity (e.g.- a precise technical jargon) 2. Ontology is a way to improve agility and flexibility, 3. Ontology is a way to improve interoperability and integration by representing information consistently across multiple domains and machines.

The main role of an ontology is to capture the domain knowledge, to evaluate constraints over domain data, to prove the consistency of domain data and to guide domain engineering while developing domain models [5]. Pan et al. [4] discuss in-depth about how a generic software development process can be enhanced with the use of ontologies as ontologies provide a representation of knowledge and the relationship between concepts they are good at tracking various kinds of software development arte-facts ranging from requirements to implementations code [4]. Such enhancements are important for the domain of data analytic where analyst have to deal with heterogeneous data sets, analytic models, and continuously changing requirements to derive different insights from big data sets.

Though there is multiple work done leveraging the semantic technology for analytics, they do not provide a complete solution that can address the challenges faced by analysts. Early work looked at how semantic web technology helps information inte-gration [12]. Moreover, there is a body of work that uses semantic web technologies for Exploratory OLAP [13], mainly to address the heterogeneity of data. There is a lot of work done on introducing semantics to scientific workflows such as SADI [17] and WINGS [18], to discover services that meet user requirements. Yet they do not discuss how the domain knowledge can be captured and how the whole process of the analytics can be automated and made user-driven. The existing work related to semantic web services (OWL-S, WSDL, WSMO etc.) plays a prominent role in service composition, yet they look at the operation angle and does not support the incorporation of analytic domain concepts.

Many existing applications that apply semantic technology in data analytics are very limited to a single domain and it is difficult to generalize and adapt them to design reusable architectures. For example, [14, 15] are limited to urban data, [16] applies for agriculture domain. Largely these applications were designed and developed in isola-tion, specific to a particular need of an organization or entity. Moreover, the solutions are highly domain specific and extendibility for new use cases or adaptability of them in other domains are questionable.

Work of Barisson and Collard [19] and Kumara et al. [20] are focusing on using semantic technology for CRISP-DM [2] based data mining process. However, they lack the linkage between the domain knowledge and analytic tasks and proposed models are complex to understand, less generalizable and difficult to be used for end-to-end analytic process development.

4   Conclusions and Future Work

From the discussions in the previous section, we believe that software engineering has a lot to offer in improving big data analytics solution. We identify two key areas of research work:

- new big data analytic development lifecycle
- better knowledge representation for analytics.

4.1   Towards Big Data Analytics Development Lifecycle

First we advocate the creation of a new big data analytic development process that maps different stages of analytic process into those of software engineering such as require-ment analysis, design and implementation. This process is iterative and may follow multiple iterations to come up with the final solution. The activities followed under three stages are illustrated in Fig. 9.

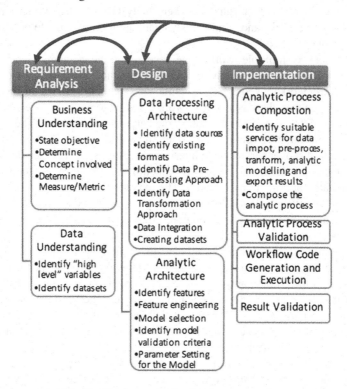

Fig. 9. Big data analytics development cycle

At the requirements analysis stage, analyst go through analyzing the problem; understanding the business domain and what is the context and nature of the data available. Design stage consists of two parts: data processing architecture design and analytic architecture design. These parts are interrelated as the nature of data influences the kind of model suitable for the analytic problem and also the data pre-processing and transformation should cater the input requirements and formats of the selected model.

At the implementation stage, we suggest to leverage service-oriented architecture and workflow modeling to conduct analytic process composition and execution.

4.2 Better Data Analytics Knowledge Management

We identify the need and propose a framework where analytic process, services and scientific workflows represented by semantic technology as well as domain knowledge fits together to provide efficient event data analytic platforms. To explore the state-of-art that use semantic technology for data analytic solution engineering and identify its potential, we conducted a systematic literature review that explores literature spread over three spheres: software engineering, semantic modelling and data analytics. A detailed discussion of this review findings is presented in [6].

Through the review we answered to the questions about what knowledge related to data analytic process is captured by existing work - we identified four classes of semantic concepts: Domain, Analytic Service and Intent. Then we study how this knowledge (semantic concepts) is applied in analytic process development process, related to different development tasks such as business understanding, data extraction, model selection and analytic process composition. Based on the limitations we found form the literature survey [6] we suggest future research directions in knowledge enabled analytics. Mainly, the analysts should consider leveraging intent related models that represent business requirements and goals, as only then the solution can address the core problem. Furthermore, model building should not be an isolated task of trial and error. Analysts can leverage different analytic models to understand available model building methods and instantiate them. Semantic models are useful in each stage of the analytic process, but state-of-art is limited to use them for a specific task such as data integration or model selection. Hence it is necessary to have good models that contain sufficient knowledge to help analysts throughout the development process.

The survey [6] provides evidence to the importance of service based approaches in analytic solution engineering and the SOA community has multitude of research regarding the service modelling, selection etc. which are useful for realizing the Agile based big data analytics development cycle. Furthermore, the work emphasizes the significance of model driven analytic solution engineering, which we try to cater through the big data analytics development lifecycle by introducing implementation as the third stage and facilitating process composition. Process composition and execution can be of model-driven fashion once the good models are in place, for incorporating SOA and workflow technologies. Data quality governance is a main concern that needs to be addressed when realizing model driven and service based analytic platforms. This can be the starting point for providing analytics as a service where expert knowledge is captured and provided for anyone to compose their own analytic solution.

Data analytics, domain expertise and software engineering communities need to work together to design ontologies that can support end-to-end data analytic solutions. Involvement of all three expert groups will result in better ontologies and it will aid to preserve the analytic related knowledge which exists in isolation today.

Finally, we emphasize the necessity of incorporating analytics as part of value chain of a business, rather than treating it as an isolated tool used by scientists. To realize this objective, analytic technologies should align well with the infrastructure of the organization and flexible to cater changing business values. We believe that the Agile lifecycle and the knowledge management strategies that we advocate can provide means to realize effective integration of business, IT and analytic environments within an organization.

References

1. Yao, L., Rabhi, F.A.: Building architectures for data-intensive science using the adage framework. Concurr. Comput. Pract. Exp. **27**(5), 1188–1206 (2015)

2. Chapman, P., Clinton, J., Kerber, R., Khabaza, T., Reinartz, T., Shearer, C., Wirth, R.: CRISP-DM 1.0 step-by-step data mining guide (2000)
3. Wang, G., Wang, Y.: 3DM: domain-oriented data-driven data mining. Fundamenta Informaticae **90**(4), 395–426 (2009)
4. Pan, J.Z., Staab, S., Aßmann, U., Ebert, J., Zhao, Y. (eds.): Ontology-Driven Software Development. Springer, Heidelberg (2012). https://doi.org/10.1007/978-3-642-31226-7
5. Baader, F., Calvanese, D., McGuinness, D.L., Nardi, D., Patel-Schneider, P.F. (eds.): The Description Logic Handbook: Theory, Implementation, and Applications. Cambridge University Press, Cambridge (2003). ISBN 0-521-78176-0
6. Bandara, M., Rabhi, F.: Semantic modelling for engineering data analytic solutions: a systematic survey (in review)
7. Espinosa, R., García-Saiz, D., Zorrilla, M., Zubcoff, J.J., Mazón, J.-N.: Enabling non-expert users to apply data mining for bridging the big data divide. In: Ceravolo, P., Accorsi, R., Cudre-Mauroux, P. (eds.) SIMPDA 2013. LNBIP, vol. 203, pp. 65–86. Springer, Heidelberg (2015). https://doi.org/10.1007/978-3-662-46436-6_4
8. Fisher, D., DeLine, R., Czerwinski, M., Drucker, S.: Interactions with big data analytics. Interactions **19**(3), 50–59 (2012)
9. Magdon-Ismail, M.: No free lunch for noise prediction. Neural Comput. **12**(3), 547–564 (2000)
10. Taylor, J.: Framing requirements for predictive analytic projects with decision modeling (2015)
11. Shumilov, S., Leng, Y., El-Gayyar, M., Cremers, A.B.: Distributed scientific workflow management for data-intensive applications, pp. 65–73 (2008)
12. Wache, H., Voegele, T., Visser, U., Stuckenschmidt, H., Schuster, G., Neumann, H., Hbner, S.: Ontology-based integration of information-a survey of existing approaches. In IJCAI 2001 Workshop: Ontologies and Information Sharing, vol. 2001, pp. 108–117 (2001)
13. Abell, A., Romero, O., Pedersen, T.B., Berlanga, R., Nebot, V., Aramburu, M.J., Simitsis, A.: Using semantic web technologies for exploratory OLAP: a survey. IEEE Trans. Knowl. Data Eng. **27**(2), 571–588 (2015)
14. Puiu, D., Barnaghi, P., Tonjes, R., Kumper, D., Ali, M.I., Mileo, A., et al.: CityPulse: large scale data analytics framework for smart cities. IEEE. Access **4**, 1086–1108 (2016)
15. Gao, F., Ali, M.I., Mileo, A.: Semantic discovery and integration of urban data streams. In: Proceedings of the Fifth International Conference on Semantics for Smarter Cities, vol. 1280, pp. 15–30 (2014)
16. Laliwala, Z., Sorathia, V., Chaudhary, S.: Semantic and rule based event-driven services-oriented agricultural recommendation system. In: 26th IEEE International Conference on Distributed Computing Systems Workshops, p. 24, IEEE 2006)
17. Withers, D., Kawas, E., McCarthy, L., Vandervalk, B., Wilkinson, M.: Semantically-guided workflow construction in Taverna: the SADI and BioMoby plug-ins. In: Margaria, T., Steffen, B. (eds.) ISoLA 2010. LNCS, vol. 6415, pp. 301–312. Springer, Heidelberg (2010). https://doi.org/10.1007/978-3-642-16558-0_26
18. Gil, Y., Ratnakar, V., Deelman, E., Mehta, G., Kim, J.: Wings for Pegasus: Creating large-scale scientific applications using semantic representations of computational workflows. In: Proceedings of the 19th National Conference on Innovative Applications of Artificial Intelligence, IAAI 2007, vol. 2, pp. 1767–1774. AAAI Press (2007)
19. Brisson, L., Collard, M.: An ontology driven data mining process. In: International Conference on Enterprise Information Systems, pp. 54–61 (2008)

20. Kumara, B.T., Paik, I., Zhang, J., Siriweera, T.H.A.S., Koswatte, K.R.: Ontology-based workflow generation for intelligent big data analytics. In: 2015 IEEE International Conference on Web Services (ICWS), pp. 495–502. IEEE (2015)
21. Uschold, M.: Making the case for ontology. Appl. Ontol. **6**(4), 377–385 (2011)
22. Milosevic, Z., Chen, W., Berry, A., Rabhi, F.A.: Real-time analytics (2016)
23. Taylor, J.: Framing analytic requirements (2017)
24. Mellor, S.J., Clark, T., Futagami, T.: Model-driven development: guest editors' introduction. IEEE Softw. **20**(5), 14–18 (2003)
25. Ameller, D., Burgues, X., Collell, O., Costal, D., Franch, X., Papazoglou, M.P.: Development of service-oriented architectures using model-driven development: A mapping study. Inf. Softw. Technol. **62**, 42–66 (2015)
26. Rajbhoj, A., Kulkarni, V., Bellarykar, N.: Early experience with model-driven development of map-reduce based big data application. In: 2014 21st Asia-Pacific Software Engineering Conference (APSEC), vol. 1, pp. 94–97. IEEE (2014)
27. Ceri, S., Della Valle, E., Pedreschi, D., Trasarti, R.: Mega-modeling for big data analytics. In: Atzeni, P., Cheung, D., Ram, S. (eds.) ER 2012. LNCS, vol. 7532, pp. 1–15. Springer, Heidelberg (2012). https://doi.org/10.1007/978-3-642-34002-4_1
28. Luján-Mora, S., Trujillo, J., Song, I.-Y.: A UML profile for multidimensional modeling in data warehouses. Data Knowl. Eng. **59**(3), 725–769 (2006)
29. Macià, H., Valero, V., Díaz, G., Boubeta-Puig, J., Ortiz, G.: Complex event processing modeling by prioritized colored petrinets. IEEE Access **4**, 7425–7439 (2016)
30. Gandomi, A., Haider, M.: Beyond the hype: big data concepts, methods, and analytics. Int. J. Inf. Manage. **35**(2), 137–144 (2015)
31. Papazoglou, M.P., Traverso, P., Dustdar, S., Leymann, F.: Service-oriented computing: state of the art and research challenges. Computer 38–45 (2007)
32. Thomas, E.: SOA Principles of Service Design, vol. 37, pp. 71–75. Prentice Hall, Boston (2007)

Modelling

Accommodating Information Priority Model in Cloudlet Environment

Teuku Aulia Geumpana[1](✉), Fethi Rabhi[1], and Liming Zhu[2]

[1] School of Computer Science and Engineering,
The University of New South Wales, Sydney, 2052, Australia
{t.geumpana,f.rabhi}@unsw.edu.au
[2] Data61 | CSIRO, Software and Computational Systems, Sydney, 2015, Australia
Liming.Zhu@data61.csiro.au

Abstract. Massive amounts of data during disaster situations require timely collection and analysis for the emergency team to mitigate the impact of the disaster under challenging social-technical conditions. The absence of Internet or its intermittent and bandwidth-constraint connection in disaster areas may exacerbate and disrupt the data collection process which may prevent some vital information to reach the control room in time for immediate response. Regardless the rare connection in the disaster area, there is a need to group information acquired during the response into a specific information model which accommodates different information priority levels. This is to establish a proper mechanism in transmitting higher prioritized information to the control room before other information. The purpose of this paper is to propose an information priority model and system architectures for data collection under challenging conditions in disaster areas.

Keywords: Information priority model · Adaption mechanism
Disaster response · Disaster Management Metamodel

1 Introduction

Major disasters and emergencies bring chaos and confusion. It is likely that information in the early stages of a disaster will be neither readily available nor very reliable. It is exacerbated by the breakdown of communication infrastructure which delays the transmission of the information from the disaster area. Regardless of the infrastructure breakdown, the emergency response teams still have to provide rapid and real-time communication using radio channels. Radio channels have become a global standard practice in emergency communication in order to have a real time communication [1]. Having a reliable communication is a fundamental requirement to support the communication during the emergency response. Nonetheless, the advancement of wireless mobile service communication and spatial information services can be considered as an essential solution to provide a quick support in difficult circumstances, especially in reaching remote areas or used in emergency situation. Both of these services may offer portability and flexibility in informing accurate location positioning of certain information around the disaster location. With these technologies, the team can quickly supply important data to the control room for crucial decision makings. Irrespective of the benefits it may offer, the wireless mobile service will not provide its best intended services upon the absence nor the unstable internet network within the disaster area. When most of the solutions to the network problem are coming from hardware level, we would like to find alternative solutions from examining the value in the information itself. We believe information can have different values for different information stakeholders and for this value, information can be treated differently. Identifying information urgency levels are difficult due to different definition of urgencies by different information stakeholders. Bear in mind that, in non-disaster situations, many disaster response stakeholders operate independently of each other. In a disaster situation, complexity arises from a variety of elements, systems, processes and actors, and it is hard to get a clear picture of the entire situation within the timeframe of a crisis. Information being generated during the emergency response is raw, unstructured, and uncertain. Yet, this massive information is meant to be treated importantly by different stakeholders to support their operations in saving lives, securing assets or preventing more damages caused by the disaster. For example, in a massive flood disaster, the emergency team needs to monitor the rise in the water level, the rain drop frequency and at the same time they have to decide carefully when to evacuate, which residential area will be affected, which power plants need to be secured and whether or not more resources are required. To make such decisions, the control room acquires nearly real-time information from the emergency teams on the disaster site. Assuming, the network within the disaster area is neither stable nor available, and then this information may take their journey to the control room in a long way.

The paper proposes three contributions: 1. Information priority model to improve communication between response team in unstable network environment during disaster response, 2. Novel cloudlet architecture for temporal information storage during data collection in disaster environment, 3. Adaptive mechanism to embed information priority model into the cloudlet architecture. This paper is structured into five sections. In the first section; we will briefly introduce the potential problem during the disaster emergency response. Then, we will show some related works to our solution in section two. Next in section three, we will present our proposed solution. In this section we will discuss the overview of information during the emergency operations to identify challenges and data collection requirements. Then, we determine priority dimension and we generate equation to determine priority weight. We will also discuss the mobile architecture and the adaptive mechanism that is used to facilitate the implementation of information model on the architecture. In section four, we elaborate our experiment and evaluation plan. We implement our solution in the form of simulation using discrete event simulation techniques to show which information should be prioritized based on the information flow datasets and structure provided. And last we conclude our paper in section five.

2 Related Works

Related work is divided into two areas; information model design for prioritization and information system development for disaster management. For the first area, the works in [2–5] is closely related to our research. The work in [2], presented a context information model for disaster response which adopted the *W4H* classification for the context data consisting a set of general classes, properties and relations. This model exploited five semantics dimensions: identity (*who*), location (*where*), time (*when*), activity (*what*) and device profiles (*how*). The work in [3], proposes an information model to examine the mechanism by which social capital contributes to information exchange in virtual communities in the context of a major natural disaster. This solution claimed to provide timely access to comprehensive, relevant, and reliable information that are critical for disaster management. Meanwhile, the work in [4], prioritizes information for resource allocation in the reconstruction phase. This work focused on identifying key information elements to better allocate resources for construction project using analytic hierarchical process (AHP). The procedure used in this solution generally involves dividing information based on its categories, split information into different phases of construction project and classify information with cross-combination of the above two steps. This work has no relation to disaster response but has shown a priority mechanism in classifying important information. Last but not least is the work in [5], proposed the bandwidth and energy efficient image sharing for real time situation awareness called BEES. This is based on the concept of Approximate Image Sharing (AIS), which explores and exploits approximate feature extraction, redundancy detection, and image uploading to trade the slightly low quality of computation results in content-based redundancy elimination for higher bandwidth and energy efficiency. BEES aims to provide efficient image sharing in disaster.

The second related work area consists of existing methods and frameworks that have been used to support information system development for disaster response. We found the works in [6, 7] address the process of modelling information during the emergency response. [6] is a dynamic emergency response management information system (DERMIS) framework which is presented for the system design and development that addresses the communication and information needs of first responders as well as the decision making needs of command and control personnel. The framework also incorporates thinking about the value of insights and information from communities of geographically dispersed experts and suggests how that such expertise can be brought to bear on crisis decision making. DERMIS framework has four major design components; design premises, conceptual design, general design principles and supporting design consideration prior to developing functionality requirements that the software needs for planning and executing the emergency response management function. The framework can be used to base the initial foundation of the information model. Meanwhile, [7] proposed a framework to analyze emergency response coordination patterns. The pattern included information as one of the five basic elements of the emergency response coordination life cycle. Information element is observed from three phases of response; pre-incident, during incident and recovery.

In the first related works area, we identified several gaps in response to our proposed solution. Those gaps include the absence of priority values in the model, the overlooked analysis on how to handle the information exchange failure causes, and the unsuitable context for disaster situation. Meanwhile, the gaps from the second related works area, existing works also did not accommodate the possibility of having intermittent connection and discounted the prioritization approach from the offered solution. Having studied the related works in [2–7], we could not find any solutions that resemble our proposed solution. Those solutions differ to our proposed solution in several ways; we assigned values to weight the information and create priority level from the information acquired, our solution will respond to network instability by creating an ad-hoc network utilizing nearby smartphones within the disaster area, we also assigned a temporal storage such as cloudlet to store acquired information from the response team to speed up the transmission process to the remote cloud server. To achieve all of these features, we integrate the proposed information model into a new system architecture design solution for disaster management response.

3   Proposed Solution

In this section, we will elaborate our proposed solution. First we will discuss the process that shows the information flow during disaster management response. Next, we will discuss an information model that we adapted in order to base our proposed priority model. Last we discuss about how to implement the priority model in the cloudlet environment.

3.1   Process Model

Generally, during the emergency response, there are four interconnected phases being carried throughout the process: emergency preparedness, crisis monitoring and early warning, emergency response, and the last is recovery and reconstruction [8]. The most vulnerable phase among all is the phase of emergency response. This is when disaster just broke out and infrastructure may not function as usual. Despite of its vulnerability, any information being acquired during this emergency phase can be highly important as it may be used to save one's life or prevent casualties from getting worse. Different agencies may acquire different information from each phase. Knowing the phases in disaster response is important to our research as we need to understand the environment from where information is generated.

Being in the most vulnerable phase, there are massive amounts of information to be collected during the disaster emergency response which are essential to the decision-making process. To supply accurate information, we believe that knowing the origins and the destinations of information are equally important and we depict the information flow into a process model which is illustrated in Fig. 1. The process shows the main components in a disaster management response which are; hazard, assets, support, environment, dataset, network nodes, cloudlet, remote server and control room.

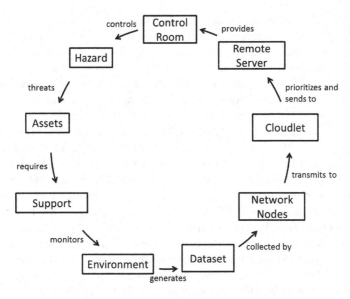

Fig. 1. Process model

This process model also shows how information is being exchanged in a continuous cycle. The cycle is formed by several interrelated entities and these entities will later be grouped into several components. To understand the cycle we may begin from the Hazard entities; in which hazards pose threats to surrounding assets like schools, hospitals, public transport stations or even to a living assets like human and nearby bio ecosystem. To reduce or overcome the threats, it is required to have proper support from nearby emergency response agencies. These supports can be given by monitoring the surrounding environments that may affect the spread of the threats such as wind velocity, heat temperature, rain drop rate, humidity level and others.

This act of monitoring will generate datasets which are collected through mobile devices which also act as the network nodes in a temporal network environment. These nodes are transmitting the collected data to the nearby cloudlet as a shared storage between devices. Cloudlet will later re-transmitted the collected data to the remote server to be consumed by the authority who resides in the control room to make decision making. The decisions being made in the control room will be used to control the hazards which will re-iterate the whole process until the hazards are diminished or vanished.

3.2 Information Model

3.2.1 Metamodel Used

Our information model is based on the Disaster Management Metamodel (DMM) [9]. This metamodeling works, study the characteristics of the response works on disaster area through evaluating disaster management documents like reports, manuals and standard operating procedures from different resources [10, 11]. These resources are different standards in running emergency responses in different countries and are generally developed by the national agency for disaster management of the country.

Disaster Management Metamodel (DMM) is developed by applying Meta Object Facility (MOF) framework to denote disaster management domain in several modelling layers. This process is to exploit the abstraction of disaster management knowledge domain. Before applying the priority over DMM framework, we will briefly elaborate the principal concept of how the DMM is being used in disaster management. As discussed in [9], we understood that DMM is being built using the Meta Object Facility (MOF) Framework. MOF framework represents DM knowledge domain in three abstraction layers; M0, M1 and M2. M0 represents the real world object which describes how knowledge related to tactical activities is structured. Meanwhile, M1 describes the model for policy and planning context and M2 is the metamodel itself in which the knowledge is abstracted in the conceptual model. The lower layer of MOF is an instance of the higher layer. This means; a model in a higher abstraction layer will represent language to be expressed for the model in the lower layer. For our research we are only looking for the layer M0 which deals with the knowledge domain in the tactical response. Based on the DMM abstraction and concept relationship in [12] we chose to only adapt the metamodel that is related to response phase; incident, aid and rescue.

3.2.2   Dimension Used in Information Priority Model

Knowing the tasks, agencies involved and dataset types, we identify several dimensions which determine data priority upon others. By taking into account dataset being generated in a task, the agencies that will be interested in the dataset, and the dimension created by the dataset; important dimensions of a data will be generated which later be used as the determination factors in assigning priority of information in the model. The generated dimensions classify several dimensions that may give different weight to an information package in hierarchical tree shape. The tree has three groups; information category group, information attributes group and network attributes group. All of these groups will contribute to the weight of the information package differently.

Information Group Category. This group classifies information according into five categories:

Asset (As) Category. Under this category, all valuable goods or living bodies will be considered as assets. This will include humans, government buildings, public buildings, business or individual properties. Some examples are like number of population within the disaster area, location of residential, logistic center, water dam, offices and schools.

Hazard (Ha) Category. In hazard category, an information will only be related to the disaster status, damaged caused by disasters, and potential escalation of the current hazard to create another hazards. Some examples from this category are like the flood status or the fire status whether are in danger, risky or safe. The contaminated areas due to the chemical leak, smokes from bushfire or volcanic ashes can also be grouped under this category.

Action (Ac) Category. The action category contains information related to actions required by response team when providing emergency response towards disaster victims. These actions may include search and rescue information, evacuation information, extinguishing effort on forest fire, water gate control to anticipate hard rain or medical decisions on disaster survivors.

Support (Su) Category. The support category includes all information about providing and allocating support towards the response team who are serving the victims of disasters. This kind of information can be seen in back up request on additional resources. For example, the request to get more firefighters to put off fires, the request to provide medical personnel to standby in the arrival of the victims, the request on basic live support; food, water, shelters, medicines and the request to provide transportation or guard the transportation of people to the refugee camps.

Environment (En) Category. Any information related to disaster surrounding can be grouped under this category. Information on the surroundings can help the response team to analyze nearby resources or make decisions when performing their operation. For example, knowing the nearby river or water source can help decide the location for temporary shelters or reporting the wind speed and its direction can help the fireman predicts the fire spread pattern.

3.2.3 Priority Weight

To determine the priority weight of information, we first use the naïve approach which accommodates basic equation on weight formulation. We define datasets and dimensions as the set of input to the equation. We define Ds as a set of datasets and D as a set of dimensions. Next, we defined W as a function to determine the *weight* of a dimension with respect to a particular dataset. Then, we define V as a function to determine the *value* of a dimension with respect to a particular dataset. Last, we take all defined entities to compute the priority through the function P. So, P is a function to calculate the priority value of a dataset, i.e. $Ds_j \mapsto \mathbb{R}$ as seen below:

$$P(Ds_j) = \sum_{i=1}^{n} W(D_i, Ds_j) \cdot V(D_i, Ds_j),$$
$$\text{where } D_i \in D \text{ and } Ds_j \in Ds. \tag{1}$$

3.3 Enabling Mobile Application Architecture

3.3.1 Overall Structure

Traditionally, cloudlet architecture concerns about offloading data received from mobile devices into its server. Cloudlet offloading mechanism unloads application package, client application metadata, VM overlay and server provisioning script onto the cloudlet server upon discovering the nearby cloudlet [13–17]. Cloudlet host will exchange information using its application server with mobile application client.

Based on the above existing architecture, we extended the function of cloudlet by adding new modules onto it. Our proposed mobile application architecture as it is shown in Fig. 2 includes three environments; mobile, cloudlet and remote cloud. Our mobile environment will retain components for locating position service, report and retrieve data and also pair up with its neighboring device to establish mobile ad-hoc network.

Data that will traverse in between devices will follow predefined policy to gain the best time in reaching the nearest cloudlet.

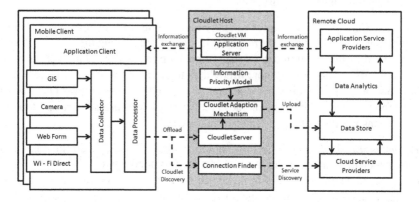

Fig. 2. Proposed mobile architecture for disaster emergency response

Meanwhile in our cloudlet configuration environment, apart from enabling connection finder, our cloudlet host will have the priority model embedded through the adaption mechanism module we created. The priority model is aimed to determine which information should be received first considering the priority values gained by each information package. Not only for priority determination, is the model also aimed to rule the data transmission from cloudlet to the cloud service providers considering intermittent connectivity between cloudlet and base station.

3.3.2   Cloudlet Adaption Mechanism

From our proposed Mobile Application Architecture before, we introduced two new modules in the cloudlet host; the priority model and the adaption mechanism. The information priority model is the model that we have defined earlier in Sect. 3.1. However,

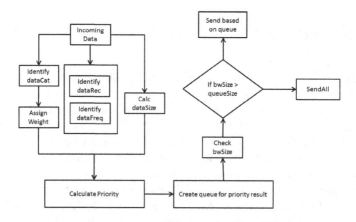

Fig. 3. Cloudlet adaption mechanism

this model needs to be embedded into the existing cloudlet architecture to serve its purposes. To do that, we created an adaption mechanism which facilitates the interaction between the priority model and the cloudlet. Figure 3 below showed how the interaction is orchestrated in data flow diagram.

If we observed the above adaption mechanism, we can see that incoming data are received at the cloudlet and has to go through processes to acquire certain information prior to priority calculation. The mechanism has the responsibility to extract metadata from the received information in determining its category, data size, data recentness, data frequency and then assign weight accordingly. Once all weights for each variable are ready, then the process goes to priority model to assign its priority value. Based on the priority values acquired, the information will be placed in the queue to wait the confirmation from the bandwidth size check. If the bandwidth size checked is larger than the queue size than all information should be sent if not then the information will be send according to its queue.

4   Experiment and Evaluation Plan

Our experiment is to represent data traversal in multi-hop mobile devices to reach the nearest cloudlet and embed information priority model into the cloudlet configuration to determine information priority level of each data collected before transmission. To do the experiment we will use simulation approach. For that, we define our scenario in two possible settings:

1. The scenario that accommodates the unweighted data flow from multi-hop mobile devices considering sufficient bandwidth.
2. The scenario that accommodates the unweighted data flow from multi-hop mobile devices considering insufficient bandwidth.
3. The scenario that accommodates the weighted data flow from multi-hop mobile devices considering sufficient bandwidth.
4. The scenario that accommodates the weighted data flow from multi-hop mobile devices considering insufficient bandwidth.

To set up an ad-hoc network through mobile smartphones, we choose Wi-Fi Direct technique because it has about 60–70 m range of radius. This is better than Bluetooth and ZigBee which can only cover 10–15 m. A policy will be introduced in the each hop to ensure the data traverse from each hops will reach the nearest cloudlet and the data offloaded can be available immediately to other devices.

4.1   Motivating Scenario: Case Study

Evacuation notice played a critical role in helping the residents to make quick decisions to evacuate. In the absence of network infrastructure, if each personnel from police and fire brigade are spread evenly around the disaster area, a temporal network can be established using the Wi-Fi Direct technique and create about 79.2 ha of mobile ad-hoc network coverage or almost equal to the size of 80 rugby fields. Ad hoc network can be used to create local temporal network between mobile devices to overcome the condition of no connectivity within the area or when the connectivity is presence but intermittent. Both of the conditions offer particular challenges. The first challenge happens when there is no available connection in the area and the ground response team has to continue collecting and sharing disaster situation data in real time. Another challenge happens when the connection existed but unstable or intermittent. The intermittence creates limited bandwidth for the collected data to be shared with other team members on the ground or with the decision makers in the control room. With the assumption that the data should continue to transmit, will force certain mechanism to take place in which only highest priority data will occupy the bandwidth. For this reason, there is a need to apply information priority model that was discussed in the previous section to assign level of importance of each data.

4.2 Information Abstraction

Based on the above scenario we developed information abstraction based on early disaster assessment. We assume potential information that may be used during the emergency response. Each of information carries details from different categories and attributes. We created Table 1 below to better visualize the category and attribute of the information (not all categories are shown in the table):

Table 1. Information abstraction

DATA	SUB INFO/DETAILS		CAT	DTYPE	ESIZE
Hazard status	- Danger - Risky - Safe		Hz	.txt, .jpg, .mp3, .mpeg	600 KB–2.5 MB
Population	- Casualties/Injured - Elderly/Babies - Survivors/Need shelters		As	.txt, .jpg	600–900 KB
Transportation network details	- Air - Sea	- Road/ Bridges	Sp	.txt, .jpg	600–900 KB

Looking at the above abstraction table, we can see that majority of data estimated sizes are between 600–900 KB which they may include different type of formats (text, voices, images). Based on ad-hoc network measurement guideline published in [18], to transfer 600–900 KB data size in a regular even nodes network having 140 kbps/flow capacity, we will get a successful data transfer in 4.3–6.4 s. Meanwhile, if we are sending those data in random uneven nodes network with 46.7 Kbps/flow capacity, we will manage to send it successfully after 12.85–19.3 s. So if we have about 20 nodes sending the data with similar sizes as above at the same time, our calculation indicates that we need to bear a longer time to successfully send all data for about 1.25–2.8 min in regular even nodes and 4.3–6.4 min in random uneven nodes.

The above results are beyond the standard of acceptable time for upload and download operation. To reflect the acceptable time for upload and download time at disaster area we compare it to the acceptable time in the rural area. According to

[19], the acceptable upload operation time for internet bandwidth in rural area is between 30–55 s. Meanwhile, the acceptable time for download operation is between 6–11 s. For this reason, critical information acquired from disaster response area should be able to be transferred to the control room through an ad hoc network protocols within 55 s at maximum allowed upload time in rural area.

4.3   Evaluation Measures

As part of evaluation process we, performed initial evaluation on completeness and coverage of our dimensions against different datasets and we set the guideline to perform validation test to ensure that our goal on creating prioritization for information assures to accommodate a faster delivery of important information to the control room.

4.3.1   Completeness and Coverage

At this stage, we have performed our initial evaluation on our model through the completeness and coverage evaluation against various dataset. We retrieved three reports from different cases of bush fire in Australia. Those reports are The New South Wales (NSW) - Rural Fire Service (RFS) Annual report for 2014/15, The 2009 Victorian Bushfires Royal Commission Final report and the 2003 report of the Inquiry of Operational Response for Bushfire in Australian Capital Territory (ACT). Our initial evaluation completely cover different terms that was mentioned in aforementioned reports and able to identify alternate source of information in different report like ICON for Incident Reporting, BRIS for Brigade Incident Reporting System and EMOS for Emergency Management Operation System.

As mentioned earlier about using dimensions to determine the weight of our priority model, we need to ensure these dimensions are complete and cover major information that required in disaster response operation. Therefore, the evaluation on our dimensions completeness and coverage is important to be done against existing reports.

4.3.2   Internal Validity Test

We also conducted internal validity tests on the model that we developed. This is to prove that our Information Priority Model is the only cause to critical information to arrive faster at the control room. For this reason, we set our priority model as the independent variable and fast delivery of critical information to control room in limited bandwidth network as the dependent variable. Our Internal validity test is conducted by defining dataset attributes, the scenarios it will undergo and object evaluations. To define the dataset attributes we ensure that all information being used in the experiment are belong to the five groups we defined in the information categories; *assets, hazards, actions, support, and environment*. Dataset should also have all attributes of *data type, data size, frequency, recentness* and entails attribute of *average distance between hubs* and *bandwidth size*.

We then configure the test setup to ensure that all predefined scenarios are followed accordingly. For this we define two groups of datasets which contain all dataset attributes above. Then, the test will run on the four scenarios we determined earlier at the beginning of this section. In which, both normal and weighted datasets will be transmitted in the normal and limited bandwidth settings. Every result from the test will be recorded in the dataset table of impact. Important observation as a result from this evaluation are; how latency delays being impacted upon applying priority model, how each groups differs in average transfer time, what are the dimension impact ratio upon the delivery of dataset, what impact would each data give upon arrival and how resource utilization is consumed.

4.3.3   Experimental Measures

To help us measure the effectiveness result of our proposed model and architecture, we use AnyLogic simulation modelling software as our tool. Our motivation to use simulation modelling as our experimental tool is because simulation may present key characteristics, behaviors and functions from the real-world disaster response process in a cheaper and safer way. In many cases, getting real objects or being at the real situation to find the right solutions can be too expensive or dangerous. For our solution we will be using Discrete Event Modelling technique; the reason we pick Discrete Event Simulation (DES) is because we view the flow of information during disaster response as sequence of processes and operations which may include delays, multiple resources or even limited resources.

As our initial work, the simulation we built is specifically aimed to model the information traversal during the bushfire disaster response. The model will allow the user to define the information and network attributes through interactive panels. We created multiple panel interfaces for the simulation in 2D and 3D formats to ease the user understand the control and supply the required input.

For the input interface, we separate two panels to accept different inputs from the users. The first panel is dedicated to accept input on infrastructure and environmental setup. Those data that user can input for environmental input are like wind speed and wind direction. Meanwhile, at the infrastructure setup input, the user can key in data related to the property of ad hoc network and cloudlet; like number of cloudlet in the area, number of hubs or nodes around the cloudlet, bandwidth size, and distance between nodes. User can also determine whether or not to allow random disruption during the simulation to see different performance impact on the result.

Under the information attributes panel, we group the information to be delivered only into three types of information; information related to fire status, information related to threats and information related to victims. For information related to fire status, user can determine how frequent information is updated and how much recentness of information required. User can also choose different types of the data; .txt, .jpeg, .mp3 or .mpeg by ticking the selection box provided. Similarly goes to the other two groups of information; threats and victims.

Our simulation model can also be viewed in 3D and animated format. By showing this option, we expect users can better visualize the process of information traversal from each node when reach the cloudlet. And if there is a delay happens during the information exchange, the user should be able to see only prioritized information is able to reach the cloudlet upon the transmission. The result per simulation will also be shown in an interactive way which consists of animated graph and texted summaries.

5 Conclusion

Critical information during emergency response works is highly important for decision makers to support the rescue tasks. Its presents at the control room at the right time can help the response team to make the correct decisions to save lives and prevent more casualties. However, different challenges from network instabilities to uncertain information model on determining its urgencies present in disaster area to hinder the expected information to reach the control room in time.

This paper proposes a solution of applying information priority model on the collected information when cloudlet is used as part of the information gathering infrastructure during the disaster response and ad-hoc network is used to create the temporal network within the disaster area. There are many works proposing information models for disaster situation but are lacking in properly incorporating information priority designs and that can be adapted to different contexts, plus difficulties in incorporating such information models as part of the operational architecture. The paper addresses these gaps by proposing information model that can perform analysis to determine information priority which adapts to multiple contexts, along with a novel cloudlet architecture that leverages the model during disaster operations. The proposal is being tested for realistic scenarios (fire rescue) and a simulator helps determine the effectiveness of the proposed approach as well as the impact of fine tuning some parameters.

Further works still need to be done to improve the proposed solution. The existing information analysis is very basic and needs to be further fine-tuned for different disaster contexts to achieve its goal. The simulator is to be completed and made into an environment in which the user can take control of setting the parameters that help the information analysis. More test scenarios representing different contexts need to be determined in collaboration with other organizations.

Existing approach leverages state of the arts technologies that are being used in disaster situations such as the ad hoc networks and Cloudlets. The overall benefits of our approach are the use of information priority model which enables flexible architectures to be designed and adapted in multiple contexts, involving the user/expert in refining the information model and setting the parameters helps in fine tuning the system.

Acknowledgements. We would like to thank the anonymous reviewers for their comments and suggestions that help us improve the paper. Special thanks to Architecture & Analytics Platforms (AAP) team of Data61 I CSIRO for helping us shape up the initial direction of this research. This work is partly funded through top up scholarships from Data61 I CSIRO and the Australia's Cooperative Research Centre Program for Spatial Information (CRCSI).

References

1. Smith, M.: NSW RFS Communication Model, March 2016. Geumpana, T. (ed.)
2. Truong, H.-L., Manzoor, A., Dustdar, S.: On modeling, collecting and utilizing context information for disaster responses in pervasive environments. In: Proceedings of the First International Workshop on Context-Aware Software Technology and Applications, pp. 25–28. ACM, Amsterdam (2009)

3. Lu, Y., Yang, D.: Information exchange in virtual communities under extreme disaster conditions. Decis. Support Syst. **50**(2), 529–538 (2011)
4. Cheng, E.W.L., Li, H.: Information priority-setting for better resource allocation using analytic hierarchy process (AHP). Inf. Manage. Comput. Secur. **9**(2), 61–70 (2001)
5. Zuo, P., et al.: BEES: bandwidth-and energy-efficient image sharing for real-time situation awareness. In: 2017 IEEE 37th International Conference on Distributed Computing Systems (ICDCS). IEEE (2017)
6. Turoff, M., et al.: The design of a dynamic emergency response management information system (DERMIS). JITTA: J. Inf. Technol. Theory Appl. **5**(4), 1 (2004)
7. Chen, R., et al.: Coordination in emergency response management. Commun. ACM **51**(5), 66–73 (2008)
8. Zhang, Z., et al.: Modelling the information flows during emergency response. In: 2011 19th International Conference on Geoinformatics. IEEE (2011)
9. Inan, D.I., Beydoun, G., Opper, S.: Agent-based knowledge analysis framework in disaster management. Inf. Syst. Frontiers, 1–20 (2017)
10. Barrantes, S.A., Rodriguez, M., Pérez, R.: Information Management and Communication in Emergencies and Disasters. Pan American Health Organization (2009)
11. Kusumasari, W., et al.: Technical guidelines for health crisis responses on disaster. In: Guidelines for Health Workers Involved in Health Crisis Responses on Disaster in Indonesia, p. 228. The Ministry of Health of Republic of Indonesia, Jakarta (2011)
12. Othman, S.H., Beydoun, G., Sugumaran, V.: Development and validation of a Disaster Management Metamodel (DMM). Inf. Process. Manage. **50**(2), 235–271 (2014)
13. Shaukat, U., et al.: Cloudlet deployment in local wireless networks: motivation, architectures, applications, and open challenges. J. Network Comput. Appl. **62**, 18–40 (2016)
14. Chen, M., et al.: On the computation offloading at ad hoc cloudlet: architecture and service modes. IEEE Commun. Mag. **53**(6), 18–24 (2015)
15. Bahtovski, A., Gusev, M.: Cloudlet Challenges. Procedia Eng. **69**, 704–711 (2014)
16. Simanta, S., Ha, K., Lewis, G., Morris, E., Satyanarayanan, M.: A reference architecture for mobile code offload in hostile environments. In: Uhler, D., Mehta, K., Wong, J.L. (eds.) MobiCASE 2012. LNICST, vol. 110, pp. 274–293. Springer, Heidelberg (2013). https://doi.org/10.1007/978-3-642-36632-1_16
17. Mahadev, S., et al.: The case for VM-based cloudlets in mobile computing. IEEE Pervasive Comput. **8**(4), 14–23 (2009)
18. Li, J., et al.: Capacity of ad hoc wireless networks. In: Proceedings of the 7th Annual International Conference on Mobile Computing and Networking. ACM (2001)
19. Reynisson, J.Á.: Performance of mobile GIS in conjunction with internet bandwidth in rural areas (2015)

Learning Planning Model for Semantic Process Compensation

Ahmad Alelaimat[(⊠)], Metta Santipuri, Yingzhi Gou, and Aditya Ghose

Decision Systems Lab, School of Computing and Information Technology,
University of Wollongong, Wollongong, NSW 2522, Australia
{aama963,ms804,yg4524,adity}@uow.edu.au

Abstract. Recent advancements in business process conformance analysis have shown that the detection of non-conformance states can be learned with discovering inconsistencies between process models and their historical execution logs, despite their real behaviour. A key challenge in managing business processes is compensating non-conformance states. The concentration of this work is on the hardest aspect of the challenge, where the process might be structurally conformant, but it does not achieve an effect conform to what is required by design. In this work, we propose learning and planning model to address the compensation of *semantically non-conformance states*. Our work departs from the integration of two well-known AI paradigms, Machine Learning (ML) and Automated Planning (AP). Learning model is divided into two models to address two planning problems: learning predictive model that provides the planner with the ability to respond to violation points during the execution of the process model, and instance-based learning model that provides the planer with a compensation based on the nearest class when there are no compensations perfectly fit to the violation point.

Keywords: Semantic process compensation · Learning model
Automated planning

1 Introduction

The problem of business process monitoring has received considerable recent attention in the literature. Much of the work done on process monitoring involves conformance checking, which seeks to ensure that the task sequence being executed is, in fact, a task sequence mandated by the operative process model. We shall refer to this conception of conformance as *structural conformance*. This paper builds on a more sophisticated notion of conformance *semantic conformance* [1] that seeks to ensure that the observed effects of a process at every step correspond to the expected post-conditions at those steps.

To provide comprehensive support for exception handling and run-time adaptation in executing process instances, this paper addresses the question of what can be done to "fix" non-conformant process instances. The notion of conformance used here is semantic non-conformance, but that notion subsumes structural non-conformance. When a process instance is found to be non-conformant, two possible strategies might be adopted: (1) aborting the process instance and starting again from scratch and (2) continuing the execution of the process instance by deploying an appropriate "fix". The former strategy can be problematic, since some of the transactions involved might be impossible to roll back. Our focus, therefore, is on the latter strategy. We shall refer to the "fix" as a *compensation*, i.e., a suffix of the current task sequence that is distinct to the one originally mandated by the process design that (eventually) restores to the process instance to a conformant state.

We offer a novel technique for computing compensations in this paper. Computing a compensation can be viewed, in the first instance, as a planning problem. We know the current state of the process, and we also have a specification of the goals of the process (and hence, a goal state). The planning operators [2] are the enterprise capabilities that appear as tasks either in the currently deployed process design, or in other designs in the organization's process repository. The output generated by a planner will therefore be a task sequence that will restore the process to a conformant state, or, at the very least, a goal-satisfying state.

The planning problem is not as straightforward as the account above suggests. There are trade-offs involved in terms of choosing between compensations that achieve full goal-compliance but delayed restoration of conformance (i.e., the process executes for a period of time in a non-conformant fashion). There might be a gap between *violation time*, when the non-conformance is detected, and *compensation time*, when the compensation is deployed. This raises questions about the trade-off between deliberation and action.

The paper innovates further by viewing the computation of compensations as a *learning* problem [3]. Given a history of past executions, it is possible to learn from past instances of non-conformance the compensations that were deployed and how effective they were. The problem can be viewed, for instance, as an instance-based learning problem [4], where we search for the most similar past instance and then deploy the compensation used in that case.

In the reminder of this paper, we describe learning planning semantic process compensation, which extends the idea of semantic monitoring and compensation in socio-technical processes [1]. The rest of the paper is structured as follows. In Sect. 2, we introduce some preliminaries. Section 3 represents learning planning semantic process compensation model. We describe the implementation and empirical evaluation of this model in Sect. 4. Then, in Sect. 5 we present some related literature about learning planning models and semantic process compensation. We conclude the work in Sect. 6.

2   Preliminaries

This section introduces the key concepts used in the reminder of this paper. First, we introduce process model notations, then we outline annotated strategies for computing semantic process compensation [1].

Definition 1. A semantically annotated process model $\mathcal{P}$ **is a process** model in which each activity or event is associated with a set of effect scenarios.

Each effect scenario es is a 4-tuple $\langle ID, S, Pre, Succ \rangle$, where S is a set of sentences in the background language, ID is a unique identification for each effect scenario, Pre is a set of IDs of effect scenarios that can be valid predecessors in $\mathcal{P}$ of the current effect scenario, while $Succ$ is a set of IDs of effect scenarios that can be valid successors in $\mathcal{P}$ of the current effect scenario.

Normally, business process models are associated with a set of **normative traces** [1], each normative trace nt represents one possible way in which the process might be executed. However, the actual execution of process models is not necessarily be normative. Thus, we introduce **semantic execution trace** to semantically annotate the execution of process model $\mathcal{P}$ at run time.

Definition 2. A normative trace nt is a sequence $\langle \tau_1, es_1, \tau_2, ...es_{n-1}, \tau_n, es_n \rangle$, where

- $es_i, ..., es_n$ are effect scenarios, and for each $es_i = \langle ID_i, S_i, Pre_i, Succ_i \rangle$, $i \in [2, .., n]$, it is always the case that $ID_{i-1} \in Pre_i$ and $ID_i \in Succ_{i-1}$;
- $es_n = \langle ID_n, S_n, Pre_n, \emptyset \rangle$ is the final effect scenario, normally associated with the end event of the process;
- $es_1 = \langle ID_1, S_1, \emptyset, Succ_1 \rangle$ is the initial effect scenario, normally associated with the start event of the process;
- Each of $\tau_1, \tau_2, ..., \tau_n$ is either an event or an activity in the process.

We shall refer to the sequence $\langle \tau_1, \tau_2, ..., \tau_n \rangle$ as the identity of the trace nt.

To simplify the presentation later on, the es in the trace, from now, refers to S in the 4-tuple $\langle ID, S, Pre, Succ \rangle$ because ID, Pre, and $Succ$ are meta information used only to construct normative traces.

Definition 3. A semantic execution trace of a process $\mathcal{P}$ is a sequence $et = \langle \tau_1, o_1, \tau_2, o_2, ..., \tau_m, o_m \rangle$, where each τ_i is either a task or an event, and o_i is a set of sentences in the background language that we shall refer to as an observation that describes the process context after each τ_i. We shall refer to the sequence $\langle \tau_1, \tau_2, ..., \tau_m \rangle$ as the identity of the execution trace.

Definition 4. Semantic non-conformance execution trace an execution trace $et = \langle \tau_1, o_1, ..., \tau_m, o_m \rangle$ is said to be **non-conformant** with respect to a semantically annotated process $\mathcal{P}$ if and only if any of the following hold: (1) there exists an o_i in et such that for all normative traces $nt' = \langle \tau_1', es_1, \tau_2', ... \rangle$ for which the identity of $\langle \tau_1, o_1, ..., \tau_i, o_i \rangle$ is a prefix of its identity and $o_j \models es_j$ for each $j = 1, ..., i - 1$, $o_i \not\models es_i$ (we shall refer to this as weak semantic non-conformance). (2) If we replace non-entailment with inconsistency in condition (1) above, i.e., $o_i \cup es_i \models \perp$, we obtain strong semantic non-conformance. In each case, we shall refer to τ_i as the violation point in the process.

Definition 5. Semantically compensated instance is a process instance $et = \langle \tau_1, o_1, ..., \tau_m, o_m \rangle$ will be referred to as a semantically compensated instance of a (semantically annotated) process $\mathcal{P}$ if there exist τ_i and τ_j in et, with $i < j$, such that τ_i is a violation point, and there exists a normative trace

$nt = \langle \tau_1, es_1, \tau_2, ...es_{h-1}, \tau_h, es_h, ..., \tau_n, es_n \rangle$ of $\mathcal{P}$ with an identity for which $\langle \tau_1, ..., \tau_{j-1} \rangle$ serves as a prefix, such that $o_k \models es_l$ for $k = j, ..., m$ and $l = h, ..., n$. As well, it must be the case that $o_m \models g$. We shall refer to τ_j as the compensation point. The compensation point must be a task and not an event.

Definition 6. A compensation given a semantically compensated process instance $et = \langle \tau_1, o_1, ..., \tau_m, o_m \rangle$ of $\mathcal{P}$ with a compensation point τ_j, a **compensation** is a process design $\mathcal{P}'$ for which the completion of τ_{j-1} serves as the start event and $\langle \tau_j, o_j, ..., \tau_m, o_m \rangle$ is a valid normative trace. Every normative trace associated with $\mathcal{P}'$ must end in an effect scenario es such that $es \models g$, where g is the goal associated with the original process $\mathcal{P}$.

3   Learning Planning Semantic Process Compensation

Constructing semantically compensated instance with learning planning model is described in term of data mining. This model aims to describe a way in which process model returns to a semantically conformant state after the occurrence of a violation point. The first part of the learning model is compensation description algorithm, where a semantic solution suggested to fix semantic non-conformance state. Given a process execution log, normative trace, and execution trace holds a violation point, compensation description algorithm will be able to produce compensated process instances. Compensation description algorithm generates compensated process instances based on three features: execution violation point, normative desired effect, and goal associated with the original process $\mathcal{P}$.

The learning model is divided into two models to address two planning problems. The first problem is prediction problem [5], where predictive model provides the planner with the ability to respond to violation point during the execution of the process model [6]. In the predictive model, the predicted target is an instance; one way in which the detected violation point might be compensated. The second problem is instance-based problem [4], where instance-based learning model provides the planner with experiences that are solved with the same compensation, thereby violation points can be compensated based on their classification. The reason behinds using instance-based learning model is to provide planers with a compensation based on the nearest class when there are no compensations fit exactly to the violation point. Figure 1 shows the detailed framework of learning planning semantic process compensation.

In Fig. 1, process execution log, normative traces and execution log are model inputs. Compensation description algorithm takes the role of selecting relevant features [7] for data modeling which are violation point, compensation point, and process association goal. The output of compensation description algorithm is a set of descriptions that illustrate potential fixes of the detected violation point. Data modeling generates a prediction or classification classes based on selecting relevant criteria. When all was said and done, automated planning befits from the learned knowledge through the using of exploitation learned knowledge algorithm, where it relies on employing the learned knowledge in planning problem description.

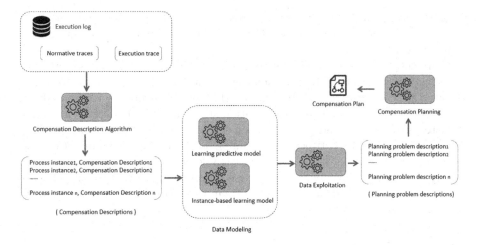

Fig. 1. Learning planning semantic process compensation model

3.1   Compensation Description

Compensation description algorithm is an algorithm-based software that has been designed to describe semantic compensation instances. Compensation description algorithm takes execution log, normative traces, execution trace, and a goal associated with the original process $\mathcal{P}$ as inputs. Standing on Definitions 5 and 6, compensation description algorithm produces semantic process compensation. Algorithm outputs illustrate selecting relevant features [7],

---

Compensation Description Algorithm

1: $EL \leftarrow execution\_log$ Data set
2: $nt \leftarrow normative\_trace$ Array
3: $et \leftarrow semantic\_execution\_trace$ Array
4: $de \leftarrow desired\_effect$ String
5: $g \leftarrow associated\_goal$ String
6: $V_p \leftarrow violation\_point$ String
7: *for* j=1 to size(nt)
8: **if** $similar(V_p, nt[j]) == 1$ **then**
9:      $de \leftarrow nt[j+1]$
10: *end for*
11: *for* k=1 to size(EL)
12: **if** (EL[k,end] != g) **then**
13:      **continue**
14: **if** $ismember(EL(k), et) == 1$ **&&** $ismember(EL(k), de) == 1$ **then**
15:      $Compensation \leftarrow EL(k, index(V_p) : index(end))$
16:      **else**
17:      $Print(No\ compensation\ found)$
18: *end for*

---

where the output might be singular task or sequence of tasks that describes how to execute the rest of the process model in which such violation point can be compensated.

Compensation description algorithm starts with discovering an $es \in nt$ that serves as a desired effect to the violation point (τ_i, o_i). A semantically compensated process instance is an instance that holds an observation entails g, (τ_i, o_i) such violation point and observation such the desired effect. When relevant process instance found, compensation description algorithm starts recording all activities positioned between (τ_i, o_i) and g. Thus, compensation might be singular task or sequence of tasks. Compensation description algorithm can be seen as a pre-processing phase, where each description will be used as nominal class [8] appended at the end of its instance, that way learning models are able to learn only from relevant experiences.

3.2   Data Modeling

Data modeling is divided into two models to address two planning problems. First problem is prediction problem, where the learning predictive model provides the planner with the ability to respond to violation points during the execution of the process model [6]. In the predictive model, the predicted compensation is one way in which the violation point might be compensated. The second problem is instance-based problem, where instance-based learning model provides the planner with experiences that are solved with the same compensation, thereby violation points can be compensated based on their classification.

The predictive model is a decision tree created using J48 prediction algorithm [5]. In an abstract sense, a compensation can be seen as a prediction of a singular task or a sequence of tasks that returns the process model to semantically conformant state. After the occurrence of a violation point, J48 prediction algorithm predicts a compensation based on compensation description algorithm.

Instance-based learning model is a description of instances generality created using IBK classification algorithm [4]. The reason behind selecting IBK is to design a learning model that is able to provide planers with a compensation based on the nearest class when there are no compensations fit exactly to the violation point. modeling of J48 prediction algorithm and IBK classifier has been implemented using Waikato Environment for Knowledge Analysis (WEKA) [9].

3.3   Data Exploitation

Exploitation of the learned knowledge [3] can be leveraged in two orientations: (1) an execution trace that has process compensation instance in EL can be planned using the predictive model. (2) an execution trace that has no process compensation instance in EL can be planned using instance-based learning model. The following shows exploitation of the learned knowledge algorithm.

In term of automated planning [2], semantic process compensation problem description consists of (:init state that represents the structural design of the

Exploitation of the learned knowledge

1: (:initial ← violation point
2: *predicted compensation* ← predicted compensation based on J48
3: *nearest compensation* ← nearest compensation based on IBK
4: **if** (∃ *compensation* ∈ *EL* | *compensation is relevant to (: initial*) **then**
5:    (:goal ← *predicted compensation*
6:    **else**
7:    (:goal ← *nearest compensation*

process and the violation point, and (:goal state represents what is the fact that we would to be true.

3.4 Semantic Process Compensation Planning

In the context of automated planning representation, exploited knowledge has been achieved using Planning Domain Definition Language (PDDL) [10]. PDDL domain has been designed based on the logic of Petri-net [11]. In an abstract sense, the EXECUTE of τ_i enables the transition of data flow from the current Event into an Event satisfies both Output function and Input function. In PDDL problem domain, detecting (:initial state and reasoning about (:goal state are considered in exploitation of the learned knowledge. Figure 2 shows PDDL representation for action EXECUTE from emergency department process example [12].

```
(:action EXECUTE
 :parameters (?exe - Task ?eve - Event)
 :precondition (forall (?e - Event)
              (imply (input_function ?exe ?e)(> (Patient_at ?e) 0)))
 :effect (and (forall (?e - Event)
              (when (input_function ?exe ?e)(decrease (Patient_at ?e) 1)))
              (forall (?e - Event) (when (output_function ?exe ?e)
              (increase (Patient_at ?e) 1)))
```

Fig. 2. PDDL representation for EXECUTE action

In order to solve semantic process planning problem, off-the-shelve domain independent planner has been used. SGPlan6 planning system [13] used to solve the problem domain shown in the running example (Sect. 4.1) through the plan shown in Fig. 2.

4 Implementation and Evaluation

In this section, we outline an implementation of learning planning semantic process model described previously and present empirical results. The implementation of proposed model starts with compensation description, running in

Matlab. It is useful to note, that we omit some details but these can be found in [12]. On the other hand, we use a machinery to semantically simulate process instances. After compensation description, process instances is tagged with a tag that represents nominal class (i.e., discrete class) [8], in which it serves as a target for prediction and classification.

As indicated in advance, modeling of J48 prediction algorithm and IBK classifier has been implemented using WEKA [9]. Predictive and instance-based models take tagged process instances as an input. Learning predictive model employed after the generation of compensation descriptions based on compensation description algorithm (see Sect. 3.1), while instance-based mode employed when we need to capture the nearest way in which such violation point could be compensated. In term of relevance measurement, the ideal k-*nearest neighbors* is $k = 3$.

In term of automated planning, we used PDDL to illustrate the running example in the following section. Planning starts with an off-the-shelf planner to plan a compensation for 5 randomly-chosen process instances base on compensation description algorithm and learning predictive model. In order to solve the given problem, SGPlan6 [13] has been used.

4.1   Running Example

Figure 3 illustrates a process from health care domain. The figure exemplifies the motivation of learning planing semantic process compensation. In a process model taken by [12], at a hospital equipped with a process-aware information system, when patients arrive they assigned a triage priority (i.e., an assignment of urgency degrees), registered and then assigned to a responsible nurse. The assigned nurse checks patient condition in parallel, but not simultaneous, with doctor visit, X-Ray and then Final visit. In the proposed example, there are set of possible observation of (check, X-Ray, visit, final visit) in which patient condition is represented and accordingly appropriate treatment.

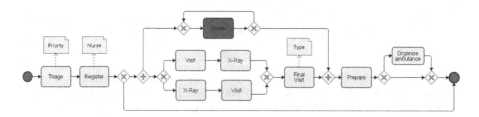

Fig. 3. A BPMN notation for emergency department process

For instance, a violation point appears when *observation(visit) = Patient blood pressure expected readings are lower* at execution trace holds *observation(check) = Patient pressure check reveals elevated readings*. Table 3 represents a fragment of execution trace terminated after the occurrence of a violation point.

Table 1. An execution trace of emergence department process holds a violation point

Execution trace			Observations	
Case	Activity	Timestamps	Observation	Timestamps
1000	Triage	02:17:00	Patient urgency degree is orange	02:19:00
1000	Register	02:25:00	Patient registered	02:28:00
1000	Visit	02:47:00	Patient blood pressure expected readings are lower	02:50:00
1000	Check	02:53:00	Patient pressure check reveals elevated readings	02:56:00

In Table 1, despite the structure of the execution trace until the violation point conforms to process model and vice versa, but it does not semantically. Non-conformance states might be much complicated and require deep models to detect them such as [14,15].

4.2 Learning Planning Model Evaluation

In this section, we aim to establish that the proposed model able to generate reliable throughput. Evaluation of learning model is helpful in achieving the following:

1. An accurate description of process instance compensations through compensation description algorithm.
2. A correct prediction of target variables based on learning predictive model.
3. An efficient generalization of process instances using instance-based learning model.

For learning model, we considered a synthetic process log consistences of 1000 instances. In Table 2, compensation description, learning predictive model, and instance-based learning model performance measures are illustrated.

Table 2. Learning model evaluation

Compensation description		Learning predictive model		Instance-based learning model	
# of instances	1000	Correctly classified	995	# of nearest neighbors	3
Precision	0.974	Precision	0.997	Precision	0.997
Recall	1.00	Recall	0.995	Recall	0.995
F-measure	0.986	F-measure	0.995	F-measure	0.995

In term of semantic process compensation planning, we evaluated five randomly-selected process instances, where they supplied first as a test set to the prediction algorithm. For comparison, we included two evaluation attribute: the number of required actions to reach to the compensation point and planning time.

Table 3. Compensation plans of five randomly selected process instances

Process instance ID	Process compensation plan	# of actions	Planning time
1	0.001: (EXECUTE X-RAY 2) [1]	4	0.019
	1.002: (EXECUTE VISIT 2) [1]		
	2.003: (EXECUTE FINAL VISIT) [1]		
	3.004: (EXECUTE PREPARE) [1]		
2	0.001: (EXECUTE CHECK) [1]	6	0.017
	1.002: (EXECUTE X-RAY 1) [1]		
	2.003: (EXECUTE VISIT 1) [1]		
	3.004: (EXECUTE FINAL VISIT) [1]		
	4.005: (EXECUTE PREPARE) [1]		
	5.006: (EXECUTE ORGANIZE AMBULANCE) [1]		
3	1.002: (EXECUTE X-RAY 1) [1]	5	0.015
	2.003: (EXECUTE CHECK) [1]		
	3.004: (EXECUTE VISIT 1) [1]		
	4.005: (EXECUTE FINAL VISIT) [1]		
	5.006: (EXECUTE PREPARE) [1]		
4	0.001: (EXECUTE FINAL_VISIT) [1]	3	0.014
	1.002: (EXECUTE PREPARE) [1]		
	2.003: (EXECUTE ORGANIZE AMBULANCE) [1]		
5	0.001: (EXECUTE CHECK) [1]	3	0.015
	1.002: (EXECUTE FINAL_VISIT) [1]		
	2.003: (EXECUTE PREPARE) [1]		

Table 3 represents a modest evaluation. An off-the-shelf classical planner used to generate compensation plans according to five different scenarios. The rightmost column shows the required time to compute the plan. Computing number of actions is important to identify where the earliest compensation is possible [1].

The evaluation of learning model shows that: compensation description algorithm able to produce an accurate description of semantic process compensation, learning predictive model is able to predict correct target variables, and instance-based learning model is able to generalize process instances correctly. The results obtained from the planning model are reasonable and encouraging. As a result, learning planning semantic process model is able to compute an accurate and correct compensation plan. Moreover, it beneficial in computing where the earliest compensation is possible.

5   Related Work

As far as we know, there are no literature illustrated the use of learning planning models as an aid for semantic process compensation. Thus, related work is divided into two subsections: learning planning models and semantic process compensation.

5.1   Learning Planning Models

The nearest research of departure for our work is learning planning portfolio [16], this model uses two shapes of machine learning: classification model (J48 decision tree) to solve the selection strategy based on planner ability to solve the problem, and classification model (IBK) to find the required time to compute the best plan. In [17], case-based planning approach for retrieve planning cases based on heuristically matching function is proposed, where similar reuse candidates can be chosen from plan libraries to solve similar planning problems in the future. Different from [16,17], compensation description algorithm reduces learning cost through allowing the learner to learn only from relevant experiences. The model taken in [18], provides rational learning to capture suitable action in different planing domains. The relational decision tree used as a guidance for ordering node evolutions which helps in limiting search tree, such guidance improves planner performance through controlling search knowledge. In [19], an architecture for integrating planning execution and learning (PELA) is presented, where PELA states the learning task with upgrading PDDL domain model which is executed initially with no prior sense of real life uncertainty. Relational learning task represents action performance patterns that can be compiled based on metric or probabilistic representation. When a decision has to be made, our model considers not only predictions, but also classifications.

5.2   Semantic Process Compensation

Learning planning semantic process compensation is strongly inspired by semantic monitoring and compensation [1]. The proposed approach in [1] introduces semantically annotated solution to detect and compensate semantically non-conformant state in socio-technical processes. In [20], compensation orchestrating for the semantics of long-running transaction is proposed. On the other side, [21] propose a framework for web services error-handling choreography. Many literature discussed semantic model checking. For example, [14] introduce semantic model checking algorithm to reason about web services behavior. In a similar way, [15] present semantic model checking for discovering bugs in cloud systems. Our approach is an assistance to these approaches, because learning past compensations allows to obtain effective plans to compensate semantically non-conformant states.

6   Conclusion

This research represents two primary contribution. First, we designed an algorithm to select relevant features that helps learning model to discover potential compensations. Second, we showed how to exploit and employ learned knowledge for planning semantic process compensations. We have shown that learning planning model can be competitive with state-of-the-art process compensation models. As far as we know, no prior learning planning model has employed to handle semantic process compensation issue. A key challenge in applying semantic process compensations based on learning planning model is to accurately deal with choosing a robust fix among available compensations. One natural extension to the semantic process compensation introduced in this research is to consider the trade-off between compensation search-time and tolerable delays in terms of choosing between compensations.

References

1. Gou, Y., Ghose, A., Chang, C.-F., Dam, H.K., Miller, A.: Semantic monitoring and compensation in socio-technical processes. In: Indulska, M., Purao, S. (eds.) ER 2014. LNCS, vol. 8823, pp. 117–126. Springer, Cham (2014). https://doi.org/10.1007/978-3-319-12256-4_12
2. Ghallab, M., Nau, D., Traverso, P.: Automated Planning: Theory and Practice. Elsevier, Amsterdam (2004)
3. Jimnez, S., De La Rosa, T., Fernindez, S., Fernindez, F., Borrajo, D.: A review of machine learning for automated planning. Knowl. Eng. Rev. **27**(4), 433–467 (2012)
4. Aha, D.W., Kibler, D., Albert, M.K.: Instance-based learning algorithms. Mach. Learn. **6**(1), 37–66 (1991)
5. Quinlan, J.R.: Learning with continuous classes. In: 5th Australian Joint Conference on Artificial Intelligence, vol. 92, pp. 343–348 (1992)
6. Weber, B.G., Mateas, M., Jhala, A.: Learning from demonstration for goal-driven autonomy. In: AAAI (2012)
7. Blum, A.L., Langley, P.: Selection of relevant features and examples in machine learning. Artif. Intell. **97**(1), 245–271 (1997)
8. Kirkby, R., Frank, E., Reutemann, P.: Weka explorer user guide for version 3-5-8. University of Waikato (2007)
9. Witten, I.H., Frank, E., Hall, M.A., Pal, C.J.: Data Mining: Practical Machine Learning Tools and Techniques. Morgan Kaufmann, San Francisco (2016)
10. McDermott, D., Ghallab, M., Howe, A., Knoblock, C., Ram, A., Veloso, M., Weld, D., Wilkins, D.: PDDL-the planning domain definition language (1998)
11. Peterson, J.L.: Petri Net Theory and the Modeling of Systems. Prentice Hall, Englewood Cliffs (1981)
12. Mannhardt, F., de Leoni, M., Reijers, H.A., van der Aalst, W.M.P.: Data-driven process discovery - revealing conditional infrequent behavior from event logs. In: Dubois, E., Pohl, K. (eds.) CAiSE 2017. LNCS, vol. 10253, pp. 545–560. Springer, Cham (2017). https://doi.org/10.1007/978-3-319-59536-8_34
13. Hsu, C.W., Wah, B.W.: The SGPlan planning system in IPC-6. In: Proceedings of IPC, September 2008

14. Di Pietro, I., Pagliarecci, F., Spalazzi, L.: Model checking semantically annotated services. IEEE Trans. Softw. Eng. **38**(3), 592–608 (2012)
15. Leesatapornwongsa, T., Hao, M., Joshi, P., Lukman, J.F., Gunawi, H.S.: SAMC: semantic-aware model checking for fast discovery of deep bugs in cloud systems. In: OSDI, pp. 399–414 (2014)
16. Cenamor, I., De La Rosa, T., Fernindez, F.: Learning predictive models to configure planning portfolios. In: Proceedings of the 4th Workshop on Planning and Learning, ICAPS-PAL, pp. 14–22, June 2013
17. Serina, I.: Kernel functions for case-based planning. Artif. Intell. **174**(16), 1369–1406 (2010)
18. De La Rosa, T., Celorrio, S.J., Borrajo, D.: Learning relational decision trees for guiding heuristic planning. In: ICAPS, pp. 60–67 (2008)
19. Jimnez, S., Fernindez, F., Borrajo, D.: The PELA architecture: integrating planning and learning to improve execution. In: National Conference on Artificial Intelligence (2008)
20. Butler, M., Hoare, T., Ferreira, C.: A trace semantics for long-running transactions. In: Abdallah, A.E., Jones, C.B., Sanders, J.W. (eds.) Communicating Sequential Processes. The First 25 Years. LNCS, vol. 3525, pp. 133–150. Springer, Heidelberg (2005). https://doi.org/10.1007/11423348_8
21. Mazzara, M., Lucchi, R.: A framework for generic error handling in business processes. Electron. Not. Theoret. Comput. Sci. **105**, 133–145 (2004)

Design

Information Systems as a Service (ISaaS): Consumer Co-creation of Value

Saradhi Motamarri[✉]

School of Management, Operations and Marketing,
University of Wollongong, Wollongong, NSW 2522, Australia
sm951@uowmail.edu.au

Abstract. The exchange of goods and services is an essential and intertwined aspect of human activity. Consumer co-creation of value is an important premise of *Service-Dominant Logic* (SDL). An interesting contrast is that *Socio-Technical Design* (STD) is shifting its focus towards incompletion of design where consumer complements design in-use. Furthermore, eminent scholars reflecting on the trajectory of the IS field, propose that *Complex Adaptive Systems* (CAS) and co-evolution as promising avenues to provide a conceptual basis for IS. Ultimately, service is what a consumer seeks from an IS. What distinguishes an IS from other technologies is its dual nature in fulfilling human needs: a direct service provider or mediator for an end-technology. In summary, this research posits that great synergies can be accrued by considering *IS as a Service* (ISaaS). This discussion while highlighting consumer co-creation of value, strengthens our theoretical understanding of both IS and Service Science disciplines.

Keywords: Information Systems as a Service (ISaaS) · Co-creation
Permanent beta · Service Dominant Logic (SDL)
Socio-Technical Design (STD) · Complex Adaptive Systems (CAS)

1 Introduction

Co-creation is a collaborative endeavour between a consumer and the service she/he receives. Service, in the context of this paper, may include a product as an appliance (Vargo and Lusch 2004). While technological innovation is not a new phenomenon, *Information Technology* (IT) has contributed to a new realm of collaboration and enabled globalisation of service. IT itself has benefited from the movements of collaborative open source developments of the earlier generations of Ethernet, Unix, X-Windows, Java, Linux and of course, *Service Oriented Architecture* (SOA). The antecedents to this technological progress are the evolving societal needs. In that evolution, the computer is an ingenious human creation (Motamarri 1992a). It is no doubt that humans have created technology, but the technology in turn altered societal work patterns and life styles (Silverman 1968; Toffler 1984a; b). These phenomena have motivated the author to take an integral view on *Socio-Technical Design* (STD) (Cecez-Kecmanovic et al. 2014; Erickson 2009; Mumford 2006), open innovation (Chesbrough 2011; Chesbrough

© Springer International Publishing AG, part of Springer Nature 2018
A. Beheshti et al. (Eds.): ASSRI 2015/2017, LNBIP 234, pp. 51–64, 2018.
https://doi.org/10.1007/978-3-319-76587-7_4

and Spohrer 2006; Oliveira and von Hippel 2011; von Hippel 1988, 2005) and *Service-Dominant Logic* (SDL) (Vargo and Lusch 2004). A hermeneutic dialogue (Boell and Cecez-Kecmanovic 2014; Jennex 2015) with the extant literature has provided interesting insights on the transformative shifts taking place in the realms of STD and SDL towards co-creation. This transformative convergence is dealt with in a separate paper (Motamarri 2015). From both social and technological fronts, consumers have been actively co-creating value with the services they consume (Oliveira and von Hippel 2011).

With the increasing penetration of IS into personal space (including social media), there ought to be a distinction among the roles played by individuals as (business) users, customers and consumers (Baskerville 2011; Tuunanen et al. 2010). However, for ease, in the context of this paper, the terms: user, customer and consumer are used interchangeably, to mean an individual like you or I.

1.1 Research Questions

Continuing that quest, this research, while relying on co-creation, argues that the time has come to treat *Information Systems* (IS) themselves as a services. We can premise that such a treatment will strengthen our theoretical understanding of both IS and *Service Science* (SS) disciplines. In one way or another, consumers ought to interact with (hard or soft) technologies. These interactions are in essence the services they receive. These interactions are socio-technical in nature (Boell and Cecez-Kecmanovic 2015; Cecez-Kecmanovic et al. 2014). The apparent convergence to co-creation from both social and technological fronts (Motamarri 2015) brings up the following questions:

1. Why can't IS be considered as a service? And if so,
2. How can we depict *IS as a Service* (ISaaS)?

1.2 Organisation of the Paper

The rest of the paper focuses on elaborating the inductive reasoning behind this motivation and presents a response to these research questions. The paper is organised as follows: section two synthesises relevant streams of extant literature: SDL, STD, value studies and IS strategy, and inductively concludes the need for a novel perspective to visualise IS; section three briefly presents the apparent convergence of SDL and STD perspectives to co-creation; section four proposes a conceptual model to visualise ISaaS, and finally section five summarises the discussion with contributions and limitations of this work.

2 Some Lessons from the Extant Literature

Figure 1 provides a pictorial representation of the extant literature streams, STD, SDL, value research and IS that have contributed to the inductive proposition of the conceptual model for ISaaS. The IT industry has embraced this transformation, re-orienting their businesses from product-centric to services-centric as pioneered by IBM in 1990s

(Gerstner Jr. 2002), though it may not have been addressed in the same terminology. Since then, the IT industry has become predominantly an exchange of service. The hitherto treatment of hardware and software as products has waned, giving rise to *cloud computing* portfolios like: *Hardware as a Service* (HaaS), *Software as a Service* (SaaS), *Infrastructure as a Service* (IaaS), *Platform as a Service* (PasS) with many more forms of services probably emerging in the future.

Fig. 1. Concept of ISaaS: contributing literature streams

In this evolutionary context, there is a need to extend the conventional view of an IS (Boell and Cecez-Kecmanovic 2015), as an artefact created by one group of individuals for the consumption of others. The conventional IS research is riddled with incoherent and borrowed theories and decades of IS research has not produced any significant native treatment of IS based on its core purpose (Merali et al. 2012). Merali et al. (2012) while looking at the trajectory of IS over three decades, argue that a new perspective is warranted for the survival of the IS discipline although they haven't offered any concrete framework for the re-evaluation.

The foundational purpose of an information system is service (Motamarri 1992b), but somehow this core purpose is not well incorporated into IS theoretical foundations. We argue that the proposed perspective of viewing *IS as a Service* (ISaaS), provides valuable mechanisms to innately position IS in the rapidly altering complex world. In the IS literature users are conceptualised as mostly business users with rigid focus on their effectiveness and efficiency (due to the emphasis on business side), whereas consumers seek a balance between utilitarian and hedonic utility (Kim and Han 2011; Tuunanen et al. 2010).

ISaaS implies that the value or utility of an IS does not depend on a frozen embedded value. It advocates *value-in-use* (Vargo and Lusch 2004) over value-in-*exchange*. Open innovation proponents also emphasise that the innovation happening in the individuals' domain far outweighs that of organisational context and it is undervalued (Oliveira and von Hippel 2011; von Hippel 1988, 2005). Thus, digressing main stream IS research focus on business value creation and innovation (Chau et al. 2007; Grover and Kohli 2012; Kohli and Grover 2008), this paper focuses on the consumer. This radical shift provides a strong footing for the theoretical foundations of IS.

2.1 SDL and Co-creation

Reflecting on the prominence of services over goods, Lusch and Vargo (2006), propose Service-Dominant Logic (SDL) as a paradigmatic change (Haase and Kleinaltenkamp 2013) in economic exchange and value creation. They view society as a macro-service provision institution. They argue that physical and mental skills are the two basic operant resources that all individuals possess (Vargo and Lusch 2004). The fact that not all humans have identical skills, has led to the art of specialisation and division of labour (Vargo and Lusch 2004). The increasing division of labour necessitated the connectedness among individuals, implying that the specialisation gives rise to interconnection with others, and the density of the connections network becomes a measure of division of labour in a society (Vargo and Lusch 2004). Thus, across the world we observe not only interacting entities but also at a macro level, completely dependent complex economies (for example, Australia on mining exports to China).

The pursuit of individuals/entities to do better over others contributes to adaptive systems. This emergence of division of labour is a *complex adaptive system* (CAS) (Vargo and Lusch 2004). Extension of micro specialisations from local, regional, national, and world economies is a direct consequence of creative learning and exchange. This spawns newer varieties of services (Vargo and Lusch 2004). Furthermore, Vargo and Lusch argue that though the *goods-dominant logic* (GDL) recognises the existence of informational flows, it is primarily concerned about the flow of goods in the value chain. A key foundational premise of SDL is that consumers co-create value through the exchange of service. Thus from a service perspective, while specialisation is the reason for service, co-creation of value is the ultimate outcome.

2.2 Socio-technical Design

Complex Adaptive Systems (CAS) (Merali et al. 2012; Nan 2011) visualise organisations as macro-social (*system of systems*), consisting of layers of inter-related systems with a complex pattern of interactions (Morris 2009). Consequently, where people and technologies are nested in a system of systems, design is no longer simple as it has to deal with complex socio-technical interactions. *Socio-Technical Design* (STD) is that branch of human endeavour concerned about the creation of artefacts that embed socio-technical elements (Erickson 2009). Here, design encompasses artefacts as well as the enabling work environment.

Design is a creative process whether it is the creation of physical objects or soft artefacts, for example, a service or an IS. Taking note of the works of von Hippel about consumer initiated innovations, Erickson in his prologue to the handbook on STD, states that: "Perhaps the notion that the end result of a design process is a stable product is old-fashioned. Perhaps we're headed towards a future of '*permanent beta*,' in which things are designed so that their design may continue during their use, where the leading edge of design resides not with the producers but with the users" (2009, p. 335). Thus, co-creation seems to be the unifying thread both for SDL and STD.

2.3 Value Research

The extant literature streams of both IS and Marketing have heavily considered value creation (Grover and Kohli 2012; Khalifa 2004; Kohli and Grover 2008; Schryen 2013). However, the measures considered for analysis are at the firm level (Schryen 2013), and as such are rooted in the context of organisations (Sherer 2014). There is no doubt that the role of technology is to enhance economic wellbeing, but it has a far more responsible role to enhance societal values, like quality of life (Motamarri 1992a). Societal values are inherently complex and intangible (Sherer 2014). Despite heavy scholarly investment, IT value research has not fully explained investments in technology and value (Schryen 2013; Sherer 2014).

Quite deviant from these issues of value, SDL overturns the concept of value-in-exchange and proposes the value-in-use as the crux of service. The SDL advocates that consumers co-create value in their own space during and after consumption of the service. Thus, in contrast to value-in-exchange, value-in-use is experiential and social, thereby focusing on the intangible. Khalifa (2004) provides an excellent model of value extending the conventional envelope of tangibility to include the intangible components of value creation. We emphasise that segment of value creation is an important element and the conventional IS has relegated it in its treatment.

2.4 Trends in IS (1980–2011)

In retrospectively analysing the progress and economic development and the role of technologies, Nelson (Nelson 2003a and b) makes an important distinction between *physical and social technologies*. Nelson (Nelson 2003b) observes that from the days of Adam Smith, economists recognised that the principal driving force for development has been either utilisation of more powerful ways of doing things or involving new products and services. He notes that in the past century, scholarship is concerned about how physical technologies advance over time. He reflects that there is limited and scattered scholarship that has focused on the development of social technologies, i.e., forms of business organisation, management practices, market mechanism and structures, public policies, legal and regulatory structures etc. His argument is that development of social technologies is prone to more frustration than society's ability to advance physical technologies.

It is no wonder that, Merali et al. (2012) consider Nelson's theory in understanding, the *'Information Systems Strategy: Past, Present, Future?'*. They made a thorough examination of *Strategic Information Systems* (SIS) research trajectory based on the publications in the reputed IS Journals: *MIS Quarterly* (MISQ), *Information Systems Research* (ISR) and the *Journal of Strategic Information Systems* (JSIS). Taking 33 years of IS research into perspective, by distilling 170 research articles, Merali et al. have summarised the SIS trajectory as shown in the Table 1. After this thorough examination of the IS extant literature, Merali et al. state that (2012, p. 126):

1. "We contribute to the extant literature by drawing on Nelson's (2003) theorisation of coevolution of Physical and Social Technologies to define the SIS domain as a

Complex Adaptive System for the coevolution of these technologies at all scales of organisation..." (emphasis is added)

2. "Second, we contribute to the emerging literature on the *need for a fundamental shift* for SIS research and practice in order *to deal with the increased turbulence, uncertainty and dynamism in the competitive landscape* (e.g. El Sawy et al. 2010; Nevo and Wade 2010; Pavlou and El Sawy 2006; Pavlou and El Sawy 2010; Tanriverdi et al. 2010)." (Note: references as per original, emphasis is added).

Table 1. Trajectory of strategic is over 34 years; Source: (Merali et al. 2012)

Dimension of change	1980s	1990s	2000s	2010+
Dominant alignment challenge	Aligning SIS with business strategy	Developing SIS for integration of SIS with business	Developing SIS for networks and resource-based competition (valuing relational, human and knowledge resources)	Developing SIS for complex, dynamic, distributed contexts
Integration focus	Systems	Process	Resource	"Global" socio-economic system architectures
Emergent/ adopted IT trends	Applications portfolios	Integrated systems	Enterprise architectures; service-oriented architectures and web-based services	Multi-scale ecologies; Cloud computing
		ERP and CRM systems	BI and knowledge management environments	Web 2.0 and Social media
Scope of strategic contextualisation	Internal	Industry-linked	Cross-industry value webs and networks	Wider global-local socio-economic context
Scope for business model innovations	Value chain	Extended enterprise	Value webs; Global reach	Distributed, socially relevant

Merali et al. (2012) advocate *for a fundamental shift* for IS research *to deal with the increased turbulence, uncertainty and dynamism of competitive landscape.* While these lessons sound logical, the big question still remains unanswered, which perspective makes IS relevant to the human race at a time when societies are transforming to complex service economies?

2.5 Information Systems Need a New Perspective

Synthesising the lessons of both IS strategic direction and value research and applying the SDL framework, we propose to treat *Information Systems as a Service*. This perspective will yield far more insights into the theoretical understanding of IS as the sole purpose of IS is to deliver a service to its consumer. It also implies that when an individual interacts with a computer or an IS artefact, the artefact itself is assumed to be the service provider. While decades of artificial intelligence research wanted to create systems that compete with a human being (or its own creator), IS research has not significantly leveraged that valuable body of extant literature (Motamarri 2014). Furthermore the ISaaS paradigm provides a means to understand how individuals co-create value in their space through their interactions with an IS artefact whether the context is organisational or personal.

The foregone discussion has shown that both STD and SDL are synergetic in saying that the coevolution/co-creation/co-innovation have much to offer in understanding socio-technical interactions. There is huge economic benefit as the ISaaS allows tackling the global trends of sustainability, doing more with less, market dynamism, and globalisation and outsourcing. Interestingly, but not surprisingly, while reflecting on the trajectory of IS and its future, Merali et al. (2012) came to the same recommendation that IS shall embrace CAS and its associated segments, co-creation/co-evolution so as to be a surviving discipline and to add value to both to academic and industry practice. Given this emergent realisation, the authors pose a question as to why SDL cannot be considered as a complementary lens to study IS, meaning viewing *IS as a Service* has something novel to offer compared to conventional IS theories.

The developed economies are facing significant challenges in service innovation (Chesbrough 2011). The product revenues are dwindling in the developed nations as manufacturing is progressively relocated to low cost countries like China. von Hippel (2005) proposes that by democratising innovation, i.e., consumers and producers working together in co-creating services, greater savings can be achieved and the future lies in such democratisation of service innovation.

In this context, STD has a significant role to play in *service design,* for technology and information are vital for service operation. From the perspective of Chesbrough (2011), at each interaction point between producers and consumers along the *service life cycle* (SLC) (Motamarri 2015), a systematic dialogue and exchange of knowledge are necessary. The STD principles provide invaluable insights in capturing the tacit knowledge and balancing the human perceptions with technology which shall help in achieving greater value through the exchange of services.

3 Convergence of SDL and SD Perspectives

As noted above, SDL envisages co-creation and STD foresees a permanent beta whereby consumers continue the design of a product/service in use. On the surface, these trends may sound different, but both anticipate significant involvement of the consumers in fulfilling their own needs through active participation in the production/experiential process. These strikingly converging notions of the emergent nature of service from the two different (SDL and STD) perspectives are portrayed in Fig. 2. In the pre-Industrial era, services were highly localised and custom made to the needs of the consumer and there existed a direct communication between a producer and consumer. The industrial revolution has profoundly altered this dimension with a progressive erosion of customised solutions to mass produced goods. From an STD perspective, this has led to automation at the cost of human factors. This induced the movement of STD as a response to counter neo-Taylorism.

A service inherently requires a customised response by the providers to the needs of the consumers, and consumer participation is essential in fulfilling the service. The providers are increasingly dependent on consumers as operant resources in the execution of services. The SDL, with its reliance on CAS theory, terms this emergent behaviour as co-creation. Starting from a different end, the socio-technical researchers are recognising the demise of big-bang design approaches in favour of delivery of incremental functionalities (agile) to services/systems where the developers and consumers co-create and co-evolve the IS (Alaa and Fitzgerald 2013; Babb and Keith 2012; Merali et al. 2012; Richard and Simon 2006). It has been a norm in the industry that consumers seek a complete solution. However, the convergence to co-creation indicates that consumers, while seeking a complete solution from the provider, also look for avenues to expand the solution to create value on their own. This is an important insight for not only services marketing and IS, but also for services management in general. Incidentally, Rust and Huang (2014) starting from a different end of analysis come to the conclusion that IT revolution and service revolution are two sides of the same coin.

4   Information Systems as a Service (ISaaS)

The previous sections have shown that both STD and SDL are synergetic in saying that co-creation has much to offer, and there is huge economic benefit in tackling the global trends of sustainability, doing more with less, market dynamism, globalisation and outsourcing (Benbya and McKelvey 2006, Oliveira and von Hippel 2011, von Hippel

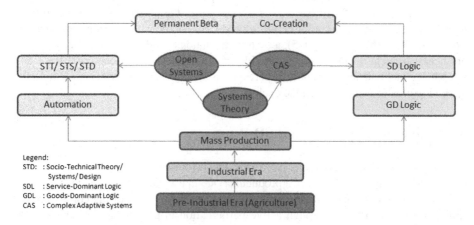

Fig. 2. The convergence of STD and SDL perspectives to co-creation; Source: (Motamarri 2015)

2005). von Hippel also posits that consumer created co-creation is under reported. Interestingly, but not surprisingly, portraying the trajectory (past, present and future) of IS, Merali et al. (2012) came to the same recommendation that IS shall embrace CAS and its associated segments, co-evolution in order to remain relevant and value-add to both academia and practice.

What distinguishes an IS from other technologies is its dual nature in fulfilling human needs: a direct service provider or mediator for an end-technology. This requires some explanation. Taking the case of an IS dedicated to a specific purpose, like an online banking application. If a consumer wants to settle a utility bill, he/she can utilise a payment service provided by the bank. While this direct utility of the IS has tremendously altered the human work patterns and contributed to phenomenal efficiencies (Motamarri 1992a). In its latter mode, an IS acts as a moderator for getting service from other technologies, for example, activating a machine through a soft instruction from an IS.

With these motivations, we premise that great synergies can be accrued by viewing *'IS as a Service'* (ISaaS). As noted earlier, ISaaS is not to be confused with IasS, PasS and SaaS. The primary idea of this research is to visualise consumer interaction with the IS towards co-creation of value. To this end, it is helpful to go back to the fundamental constituents of IS prior to charting the interactions. An axiomatically derived schematic to visualise ISaaS is shown in Fig. 3.

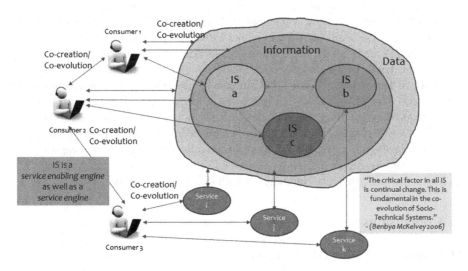

Fig. 3. Visualising information systems as a service (ISaaS)

Data is the fundamental constituent of an IS (Motamarri 1993). Data is not necessarily structured and as such, data is shown with a hazy boundary. Information is a derivative of data and it is organised in some fashion (functional division) whereby it is structured and is therefore shown with a clear boundary. While an IS operates on a segment of information, it is mostly dedicated to a specific purpose, for example: student enrolments or human resources. Organisations typically operate on several such IS depending on the complexity, scale and volume of their operations.

Figure 3 also conveys a hierarchical relation among data, information, and information systems. The recent industry wave of big data analytics (BDA) is referring to such a huge collection of data as a *data lake*. The refined segment of data is depicted as Information which predominantly consists of structured information likely agglomerated for a functional division of a business. The information pools may represent a data warehouse (DW) where information from several IS are collated to facilitate cross-functional as well as time-dimensional analysis which is infeasible by looking at a single system like Sales for either reasons of its limited data set or archival of past data from live IS.

The value of BDA comes from the services it renders to its consumers. The level of insight delivered and/or gained by consumers depends on the IS climate and level of access granted to consumers. For example, a consumer (Consumer 1) may directly interact with the data layer, or information layer or an IS layer. Similarly, a consumer (Consumer 3) may indirectly interact with the data, information and IS layers through services. Consumer co-creation is not only limited to his/her interaction with the IS, but also includes interaction with peers, for example, co-learning. From the perspective of ISaaS, three different categories of services are shown in Fig. 3, depending on the layer at which the raw interaction occurs. To interpret, Consumer 3 receives Service i, which directly interfaces the data layer, something similar to the current industry buzz, big data; Service j interacts at information layer, an agglomeration of refined data, similar to a Data Warehouse or Business Intelligence Database; and lastly, Service k is a type of service/transactions supported by IS b, like withdrawing money from an ATM.

In reality, IS are needed to manage service, service systems and SLC (OGC 2007). On the other hand, IS itself is a service where the consumer and the organisational repository of knowledge (codified and structured information/tacit knowledge), and transactional data of organisational processes work together in executing business processes resulting in co-creation of value. It is far more illuminating to visualise that the co-creation of consumers and IS provides intricate insights to the IS discipline. *The IS discipline can gain a broader and more sustainable foundation by viewing itself as a service enabling engine as well as a service engine.* Thus, this framework helps in advancing the theoretical underpinnings of both IS and SS disciplines.

5   Conclusions

5.1   Limitations/Future Opportunities

The argument for viewing ISaaS is not new as there is some body of literature (Alter 2010; Gable and Rai 2009; Hilman 2013) on this topic. It is important to note that the industry terminology of cloud services like: IaaS, PaaS and SaaS are different from the proposition of ISaaS. There is some scholarly work pertaining to IS and co-creation. This stream is predominantly conceptual or qualitative in nature. In time to come, we intend to combine these streams to analyse consumer co-creation of value with IS (Motamarri 2017).

We haven't been able to identify significant empirical work in relation to either IS value to consumers or consumer co-creation of value with IS from the lens of SDL. As co-creation of value is primarily studied in firm to firm context in IS, there is a vast opportunity to understand the value derived by individuals in the usage of IS (Baskerville 2011; McKenna et al. 2013; Tuunanen et al. 2010). A significant gap exists in literature for empirical studies on consumer co-creation of value with IS.

Empirical work in assessing co-creation (Sarker et al. 2012) is still at its infancy (Frow et al. 2012; Payne and Frow 2014). While this paper proposes an alternate view for IS, ISaaS, further studies are needed to conceptualise the model presented in Fig. 3. We expect that this article ignites some interest among IS and SS scholars to blend STD, SDL and open innovation. The emergence of diverse viewpoints will strengthen both IS and SS theoretical underpinnings.

5.2 Summary

The preceding sections presented the global economic shift towards service. Chesbrough (2011) contends that significant research is lacking on services, despite its disproportionate role in employing people (Sampson and Froehle 2006). The themes of von Hippel et al. (Oliveira and von Hippel 2011; von Hippel 1988; von Hippel 2005) and Prahalad and Ramaswamy (2004) stress the consumer value co-creation and open innovation. Vargo and Lusch conceptualise these transformational changes by proposing a ground-breaking S-D Logic to serve as a foundation for service and marketing theories (Vargo and Akaka 2009; Vargo and Lusch 2004). They advocate increasing significance of co-creation as greater diversity and differentiation occurs in service. STD, founded on the premise to balance the interplay of technology and human factors in work life (Erickson 2009; Mumford 2006), also foresees the evolution to incomplete design or permanent beta. While these concepts appear to be different, the emergence to co-creation seems to be identical.

Ultimately, service is what a consumer seeks from an IS. What distinguishes an IS from other technologies is its dual nature in fulfilling human needs: a direct service provider or mediator for an end-technology. These motivations are at the backdrop to propose an alternative perspective for IS, i.e., viewing information systems as a service, (ISaaS). In reality, an IS is needed to manage the life cycle of services. On the other hand, IS itself is a service where the user and the individual/organisational repository of knowledge (codified and structured information/tacit knowledge) and transactional data of individual/organisational processes work together in executing tasks resulting in the co-creation of value.

It is illuminating to recognise that the socio-technical interaction between consumer and IS culminates in co-creation of value. A deeper analysis of this phenomenon provides a rightful assessment of IS and consumer created innovation. As noted by Merali et al. (2012), IS need to shift their focus, so as to gain a broader and more sustainable foundation, and ISaaS framework has that potential. Such a perspective strengthens theoretical underpinnings of both information systems and service science disciplines.

Acknowledgements. This research is supported by an Australian Government Research Training Program.

References

Alaa, G., Fitzgerald, G.: Re-conceptualizing agile information systems development using complex adaptive systems theory. Emergence Complexity Organ. **15**(3), 1–23 (2013)

Alter, S.: Viewing systems as services: a fresh approach in the IS field. Commun. Assoc. Inf. Syst. **26**, 195–224 (2010). Article no. 11

Babb Jr., J.S., Keith, M.: Co-creating value in systems development: a shift towards service-dominant logic. J. Inf. Syst. Appl. Res. (JISAR) **1**(1), 4–15 (2012)

Baskerville, R.: Design theorizing individual information systems. In: PACIS 2011 (2011)

Benbya, H., McKelvey, B.: Toward a complexity theory of information systems development. Inf. Technol. People **19**(1), 12–34 (2006)

Boell, S.K., Cecez-Kecmanovic, D.: A hermeneutic approach for conducting literature reviews and literature searches. Commun. Assoc. Inf. Syst. **34**, 257–286 (2014)

Boell, S.K., Cecez-Kecmanovic, D.: What is an information system? In: 48th Hawaii International Conference on System Sciences, pp. 4959–4968 (2015)

Cecez-Kecmanovic, D., Galliers, D.R., Henfridsson, O., Newell, S., Vidgen, R.: The sociomateriality of information systems: current status, future directions. MIS Q. **38**(3), 809–830 (2014)

Chau, P.Y., Kuan, K.K., Liang, T.: Research on it value: what we have done in Asia and Europe. Eur. J. Inf. Syst. **16**(3), 196 (2007)

Chesbrough, H.: Bringing open innovation to services. MIT Sloan Manag. Rev. **52**(2), 85–90 (2011)

Chesbrough, H., Spohrer, J.: A research manifesto for services science. Commun. ACM **49**(7), 35–40 (2006)

Erickson, T.: Socio-technical design. In: Whitworth, B., de Moor, A. (eds.) Handbook of Research on Socio-Technical Design and Social Networking Systems, pp. 334–335. Information Science Research (IGI Global), New York (2009)

Frow, P., Payne, A., Storbacka, K.: Evolving the concept of co-creation: new research propositions. In: Academy of Marketing Conference, Southampton (2012)

Gable, G., Rai, A.: Reconceptulising the information system as a service. In: 17th European Conference on Information Systems (2009)

Gerstner Jr., L.V.: Who Says Elephants Can't Dance? Leading a Great Enterprise through Dramatic Change. HarperCollins Publishers Inc., New York (2002)

Grover, V., Kohli, R.: Cocreating it value: new capabilities and metrics for multifirm environments. MIS Q. **36**(1), 225–232 (2012)

Haase, M., Kleinaltenkamp, M.: S-D logic as an example of non-cumulative scientific progress in the marketing discipline. Bus. Adm. Rev. (DBW) **73**(2), 95–112 (2013)

Hilman, M.H.: Information system as a service: issues and challenges. Jurnal Sistem Informasi **8**(2), 71–77 (2013)

Jennex, M.E.: Literature reviews and the review process: an editor-in-chief's perspective. Commun. Assoc. Inf. Syst. **36**, 139–146 (2015). Article no. 8

Khalifa, A.S.: Customer value: a review of recent literature and an integrative configuration. Manag. Decis. **42**(5), 645–666 (2004)

Kim, B., Han, I.: The role of utilitarian and hedonic values and their antecedents in a mobile data service environment. Expert Syst. Appl. **38**(3), 2311–2318 (2011)

Kohli, R., Grover, V.: Business value of it: an essay on expanding research directions to keep up with the times. J. Assoc. Inf. Syst. **9**(1), 23–39 (2008)

Lusch, R.F., Vargo, S.L.: Service-dominant logic: reactions, reflections and refinements. Mark. Theory **6**(3), pp. 281–288 (2006)

McKenna, B., Tuunanen, T., Gardner, L.: Consumers' adoption of information services. Inf. Manag. **50**(5), 248–257 (2013)

Merali, Y., Papadopoulos, T., Nadkarni, T.: Information systems strategy: past, present, future? J. Strateg. Inf. Syst. **21**(2), 125–153 (2012)

Morris, A.: Socio-technical systems in ICT: a comprehensive survey. DISI-09-054, University of Trento, p. 16 (2009)

Motamarri, S.: A diagnostic view on information technology. SIGSOFT Softw. Eng. Notes **17**(4), 68–70 (1992a)

Motamarri, S.: Systems modelling and description. SIGSOFT Softw. Eng. Notes **17**(2), 57–63 (1992b)

Motamarri, S.: Database conversion planning. SIGSOFT Softw. Eng. Notes **18**(1), 59–64 (1993)

Motamarri, S.: Reflections on artificial intelligence – a hermeneutic journey. In: The 25th Australasian Conference on Information Systems. Auckland University of Technology, ACIS, Auckland (2014)

Motamarri, S.: The convergence of SDL and STD towards co-creation. In: ANZMAC-2015, p. 7. UNSW, Sydney, Australia (2015)

Motamarri, S.: Consumers' co-creation of value in Mhealth service. J. Creating Value **3**(1), 1–14 (2017)

Mumford, E.: The story of socio-technical design: reflections on its successes, failures and potential. Inf. Syst. J. **16**(4), 317–342 (2006)

Nan, N.: Capturing bottom-up information technology use processes: a complex adaptive systems model. MIS Q. **35**(2), 505–507 (2011)

Nelson, R.R.: On the uneven evolution of human know-how. Res. Policy **32**(6), 909–922 (2003a)

Nelson, R.R.: Physical and Social Technologies and their Evolution. Laboratory of Economics and Management, Sant'Anna School of Advanced Studies, Pisa, Italy (2003b)

OGC: ITIL, Version 3. Office of Government Commerce, The Stationery Office, London (2007)

Oliveira, P., von Hippel, E.: Users as service innovators: the case of banking services. Res. Policy **40**(6), 806–818 (2011)

Payne, A., Frow, P.: Deconstructing the value proposition of an innovation exemplar. Eur. J. Mark. **48**(1), 237–270 (2014)

Prahalad, C.K., Ramaswamy, V.: Co-creating unique value with customers. Strategy Leadersh. **32**(3), 4–9 (2004)

Richard, M.K., Simon, M.K.: Interpreting socio-technical co-evolution applying complex adaptive systems to IS engagement. Inf. Technol. People **19**(1), 35–54 (2006)

Rust, R.T., Huang, M.H.: The service revolution and the transformation of marketing science. Mark. Sci. **33**(2), 206–221 (2014)

Sampson, S.E., Froehle, C.M.: Foundations and implications of a proposed unified services theory. Prod. Oper. Manag. **15**(2), 329–343 (2006)

Sarker, S., Sarker, S., Sahaym, A., Bjorn-Anderson, N.: Exploring value cocreation in relationships between an ERP vendor and its partners: a revelatory case study. MIS Q. **36**(1), 317–338 (2012)

Schryen, G.: Revisiting IS business value research: what we already know, what we still need to know, and how we can get there. Eur. J. Inf. Syst. **22**(2), 139–169 (2013)

Sherer, S.A.: Advocating for action design research on it value creation in healthcare. J. Assoc. Inf. Syst. **15**(12), 860–878 (2014)

Silverman, D.: Formal organizations or industrial sociology: towards a social action analysis of organizations. Sociology **2**, 221–238 (1968)

Toffler, A.: Future Shock. Bantam, New York (1984a)

Toffler, A.: The Third Wave. Bantam, New York (1984b)

Tuunanen, T., Myers, M., Cassab, H.: A conceptual framework for consumer information systems development. Pac. Asia J. Assoc. Inf. Syst. **2**(1), 47–66 (2010)

Vargo, S.L., Akaka, M.A.: Service-dominant logic as a foundation for service science: clarifications. Serv. Sci. **1**(1), 32–41 (2009)

Vargo, S.L., Lusch, R.F.: Evolving to a new dominant logic for marketing. J. Mark. **68**, 1–17 (2004)

von Hippel, E.: Sources of Innovation. Oxford University Press, New York (1988)

von Hippel, E.: Democratizing Innovation. MIT Press, Cambridge (2005)

Scalable Architecture for Personalized Healthcare Service Recommendation Using Big Data Lake

Sarathkumar Rangarajan[1(✉)], Huai Liu[1], Hua Wang[1,2],
and Chuan-Long Wang[2]

[1] Centre for Applied Informatics, Victoria University, Melbourne, Australia
sarathkumar.rangarajan@live.vu.edu.au, {Huai.Liu,Hua.Wang}@vu.edu.au
[2] Taiyuan Normal University, Taiyuan, Shanxi Province, China
clwang218@126.com

Abstract. The personalized health care service utilizes the relational patient data and big data analytics to tailor the medication recommendations. However, most of the health care data are in unstructured form and it consumes a lot of time and effort to pull them into relational form. This study proposes a novel data lake architecture to reduce the data ingestion time and improve the precision of healthcare analytics. It also removes the data silos and enhances the analytics by allowing the connectivity to the third-party data providers (such as clinical lab results, chemist, insurance company, etc.). The data lake architecture uses the Hadoop Distributed File System (HDFS) to provide the storage for both structured and unstructured data. This study uses K-means clustering algorithm to find the patient clusters with similar health conditions. Subsequently, it employs a support vector machine to find the most successful healthcare recommendations for the each cluster. Our experiment results demonstrate the ability of data lake to reduce the time for ingesting data from various data vendors regardless of its format. Moreover, it is evident that the data lake poses the potential to generate clusters of patients more precisely than the existing approaches. It is obvious that the data lake provides an unified storage location for the data in its native format. It can also improve the personalized healthcare medication recommendations by removing the data silos.

Keywords: Electronic Health Record · EHR · Data lake · Big data
Personalized medication

1 Introduction

In the last two decades, our living and working environments were greatly enriched by affordable smart and mobile devices, and digital services [1]. The interactions with digital services and devices will generate a huge amount of data [2]. Undoubtedly, the enormous growth in the amount of data collected and stored by organization's around the world over the past few decades is irrefutable. The ability to

© Springer International Publishing AG, part of Springer Nature 2018
A. Beheshti et al. (Eds.): ASSRI 2015/2017, LNBIP 234, pp. 65–79, 2018.
https://doi.org/10.1007/978-3-319-76587-7_5

access and analyze this data is rapidly becoming more and more important. On the other hand, the workflow for acquiring and analyzing the data and subsequently transferring them into actionable knowledge is complex.

1.1 Personalized Healthcare

Based on the recent research observations, the patients with the same diagnosis may respond to the same medication in different ways. A drug can be highly effective for one patient, whereas the same drug might not produce the expected results when given to another patient with the same diagnosis. Personalized medication means the prescription of precise treatments and therapeutics well suited for an individual taking into consideration of all the data that influence response to therapy [3]. Due to the enormous growth of Internet of Things, healthcare industry is equipped with the smart devices and applications. Consequently, the digitalization creates valuable data about the patients and medications, namely Electronic Health Records (EHR) [4]. EHR's availability in large scale allows the researchers to unearth the possibilities to move the healthcare organizations towards the personalized healthcare [5].

EHR consists of not only the structured data but it contains the semi and unstructured data as well. Only 20% of data is in a structured format which can be easily utilized by data scientist; but semi and unstructured production rate is 15 times higher than the structured one [6]. However, health IT research demands to process all kind of structured, semi and unstructured data to find the valuable insights [7]. Inevitably, an improved data management system would help the data scientists to provide the tailored medication. The contemporary IT infrastructure provides many data handling systems such as Enterprise Data Warehouse (EDW) [8]; but there is a lack of scalability because the EDW data management system is for well-known queries and clearly defined policies [9].

To pull the data into EDW for further processing, it should be gone through the procedure of data preprocessing namely Extract, Transform, Load (ETL) [10]. ETL process predominantly consumes notable cost and time. To provide custom-made medical intervention, data from diverse sources need to be processed [11,12]. However, EDW system is not so capable of handling the various sourced data. Another contention in healthcare analytics to adapt EDW is it's inability to coexist with the contemporary programming based query languages. If an EDW once designed properly for processing certain business rules then it is too difficult to redesign for the future needs. This paper proposes a novel method for the healthcare data architecture using data lake technology as an alternative data architecture.

1.2 Data Lake

An emerging concept that has gained increasing popularity is the data lake. A data lake uses a flat architecture to store data in their raw format [13]. Each data entity in the lake is associated with a unique identifier and a set of extended metadata. The consumers can use purpose-built schemas for query-relevant data, which will result in a smaller set of data that can be analysed to help answer a consumer's question. There are doubts and concerns about the possibility of data becoming incomprehensible due to a lack of schema or similar means of interpretation, and that could cause the lake to turn into a "data swamp" [14]. Therefore, a metadata repository that registers high-level information about data entities (type, time, creator etc.) is an essential component of a robust data lake structure. A data lake's flat structure stores data regardless of its format and places the responsibility for understanding the data elsewhere.

We are thus motivated to choose an alternative data architecture for the healthcare industry. Personal data lake system proposed by Walker and Alrehamy [15] gives a basis for designing our proposed approach. The promising properties of personal data lake architecture are as follows:

– It can provide a unified location for all the data from the different social network about a single user.
– It can improve the privacy and security by storing in a single location and the user is given the rights to design how to access their data.
– It also offers the Personal Lake Serialization Format (PLSF) approach for storing meta-data.

However, the original personal data lake proposed is restricted with structured and semi-structured data and it is not able to manage the unstructured data [15].

1.3   Role of Data Lake in Healthcare

This study proposes to adopt data lake architecture as a replacement for the traditional data management architecture in healthcare. Data lake possesses the following capabilities to address the aims of this research:

– It can store the data in its native format (structured/unstructured) as arrived without any pre-processing delay.
– Data lake can connect with trusted external sources (clinical lab, genomic centre, insurance payers, and social media) [16]. This will reduce the data silo across health care institution [17].
– It can support new types of data processing and improve the adaptability of the analytics system. It can store huge amount of data from a diverse source with less cost.

1.4   Contribution of the Research

Motivated by the above-mentioned needs and possibilities, we propose a scalable architecture for personalized healthcare recommendation. The main contributions of this study are:

– It introduces the data lake architecture in healthcare to crawl and ingest healthcare data from vendors without any data preprocessing delay.

– It enhances the data IT infrastructure in healthcare by accepting the connection from trusted third party data stakeholders.
– It accumulates the data with different formats and store it in the unified data lake to avoid the Data silos across the healthcare organizations.

2   Proposed Data Lake Architecture

The proposed data lake architecture for this research is plotted in Fig. 1. It has four layers, namely, data ingestion layer, data governance layer, security layer, analytics layer, which will be respectively discussed in the following four sections.

2.1   Data Ingestion Layer

Typically, data will be crawled from multitude sources with its raw format. More often, the data will be available as structured but sometimes it may also arrive as semi-structured and unstructured. Data lake can ingest all the available data without any ETL processing but it also needs a worthy Metadata management. Because data lake without a proper metadata management will make it as a data swamp. Metadata contains information about how, when and by whom it was collected, created, accessed, modified and how it is formatted [18]. Metadata can be categorised into technical, operational, and business metadata.

Data lake can be implemented using open source software named Apache Hadoop. It has a Hadoop Distributed File System (HDFS), which allows us

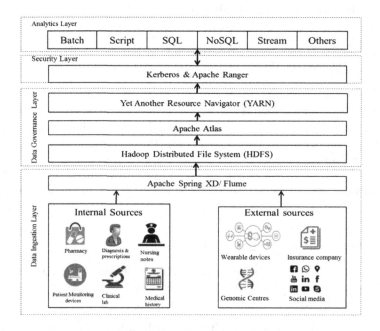

Fig. 1. Data lake architecture

to store structured, semi-structured and unstructured types of files. HDFS can store petabytes of data and can act as a single storage location. It is fault tolerant, scalable, and extremely simple to expand [6]. There are many tools available to ingest data to the HDFS from sources. In the healthcare industry, three basic types of data sources are available. The first type is the bulk size of data providers, such as genomic centres and biobanks. Next type of data sources is event-based data source, such as doctor appointment, pharmacy purchase, and clinical notes. The last data source type is trusted third party streaming data [19] providers such as clinical labs, X-ray centres, social media, wearable devices.

In our architecture, we have the following particular settings.

- Hadoop's Spring XD tool is used to transfer bulk data [20]. It also can create metadata information while the data ingested and loaded with the HDFS.
- Apache Flume is a distributed, reliable, and available service for efficiently collecting, aggregating, and moving large amounts of log data [21]. It has a simple and flexible architecture based on the data flows and it is robust and fault tolerant.
- To handle the stream of data and avoid data silos, we planned to utilise Hadoop spring XD tool. It can do data ingestion along with metadata information creation from multiple input sources into HDFS with high throughput.

2.2   Data Governance Layer

The main purpose of this layer to understand, organise, manage and provide access to all the data collected. This layer uses Apache Atlas, a tool for Hadoop to handle metadata framework and governance [21]. It has a set of basic governance services to meet the compatibility requirements for the HDFS. Atlas tool has four important features, namely data classification, centralised auditing, search and lineage, and security and policy engine.

Data Classification. It imports or defines data-oriented metadata from the data source state, interpret and understand the relationships between data sets and core elements including source, target, and ingestion processes.

Centralized Auditing. It makes a log registry for interaction with the data stored in HDFS for reporting.

Search and Lineage. It develops a well-defined path for data exploration by recording the information about the creation of data and metadata.

Security and Policy Engine. It defines and justifies the data access by role based access and protects data from tampering [22]. Data governance layer is also responsible for resource management and job scheduling. Data available in the data lake are not in the similar structure. Therefore, an efficient resource

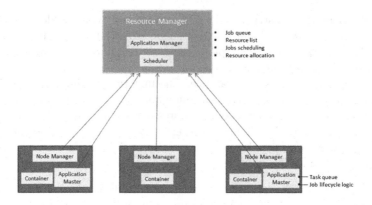

Fig. 2. Work flow of YARN

management is essential to make the negotiation of the data analytical programs easier. The existing healthcare analytics system uses Map Reduce methodology to schedule the CPU cycle and memory across the clusters in Hadoop to process the job [23]. However, MapReduce is not dealing with the scheduling of Data resource for the waiting jobs. Therefore, we utilise Apache Hadoop YARN (Yet Another Resource Negotiator) instead of MapReduce as a data operating system to let the data processing systems to interact with the data efficiently [24]. Unlike MapReduce, YARN handles data processing efficiently by splitting resource management and job scheduling into separate process [25]. The work flow of YARN is depicted in Fig. 2.

Application Master (AM), Node Manager (NM), Resource Manager (RM) are the major actors of YARN. These actors work as follows:

– Once a data processing engine request reached YARN, it allocates required resources to start AM. After starting up, AM will log its entry in RM.
– If any additional resource needed, then AM can negotiate with RM. Once the resource made available, AM will make the NM allocate the resources to the process.
– A vacuum created for the resources and the code to run within it. AM will get the execution status and it will be reported to RM too.
– The client can communicate with either AM or RM to get the status update. Once the code executed, AM for the respective job will remove itself from the RM and release all the allocated resources.

2.3   Security Layer

Obviously, the healthcare data needs highly secured environment because it contains information that is very sensitive [26,27]. Therefore, we plan to provide a more efficient security system for HDFS. Authentication and authorization are the two important processes for providing controlled access in HDFS [28,29].

- To provide authentication, we are going use Kerberos authentication protocol. Kerberos protocol will create a proxy server to receive a client request [30]. If the request is legitimate, then it will provide a ticket for the client with a timestamp.
- Apache Ranger is an efficient tool to provide the authorization [31]. It is a unified authorization model for HDFS. It enables the data lake leaders to create security policies and role-based access control for the data.

Whenever a client with a legitimate ticket enters into the system, Apache Ranger validates the ticket using its security policies. It has a very flexible user interface and is easy to deploy security policies for the huge amount of data storage.

2.4 Analytics Layer

While comparing with Data warehouse, Data Lake is very effective at utilizing the vast amount of data with data analytical algorithms to identify the valuable insights that will improve real-time decision analytics. Since the HDFS can be connected with many number of data analytics tools, Data Lake can be adapted for the future. To evaluate our system, we planned to make the clusters of patients with similar health conditions and drug acceptance based on their detail available in the EHR and other data sources. In particular,

- K-means clustering algorithm is used to do the clustering. K-means algorithm will be implemented using Matlab programming environment.
- The next step is to find the best medication practice for each cluster using Support Vector Machine (SVM).

SVM is a supervised machine-learning model associated with a learning algorithm [32]. Ideal medication training data to be used to train the SVM. Then the cluster will be processed by SVM and best efficient medication recommendation will be identified. Some sample data will be given to the SVM to validate its accuracy level. Once the SVM reaches 90% of accuracy then it will act as a recommender system for the future medication recommendations.

3 Experiments

We evaluated our methods via experiments on sample EMRs data. In this section, we first give a brief description of the research questions, and then explain the experimental setup to validate the usability of the proposed architecture.

3.1 Research Questions

We designed our experimental study to answer the following two research questions:

RQ1: Can the proposed architecture reduce the time for data ingesting and crawling from various internal and external data stakeholders? Compared with the traditional data warehouse, the data lake allows the storage of data as it comes without bounding with any schema. In addition, it uses HDFS file system, which can connect to any remote application using Apache tools. The time taken for the data architecture to load and store the data is represented as Data ingestion time. Apparently, the less the data ingestion time the better the data architecture for healthcare analytics. Therefore, if the proposed data lake architecture can reduce the data analytics processing time, it will also improve the healthcare recommendations.

RQ2: Can the data lake architecture able to avoid data silos? Due to the pre-defined data schema for data warehouse architecture, it is impossible to store the data of different types in a unified storage location. It leads to the creation of numerous data silos for the dataset about each patient. The precision of clustering is dependent on the perimeter of the data about the patients. The more data from various data stakeholders will help the data analytics to provide better results. Hence, if our proposed data lake architecture can handle the various data types in a unified location without the data swamp threat, it can improve the precision of the clustering significantly.

3.2   Variables and Objects

Independent Variables

Independent variable in the experiment is the technique under investigation. By nature, the proposed data lake architecture was selected for this variable. We focused on the patient clustering methodology in the architecture, as it is the vital process to identify the more suitable healthcare practice for the given patient pool. In addition, we selected the traditional data warehouse (DW) as the baseline technique for the evaluation and comparison of clustering precision.

Dependent Variables

Data Ingestion time: We used data ingestion time as a metric to validate the RQ1. The ingestion time is the time taken for the data architecture to load the data to its storage. The meta data log updated by Apache spring XD each time whenever there is a new data was entered in the data architecture. The timer started when the data reaches the data architecture and it stops when the data entry created in the meta-data log. Data ingestion time IT can be calculated by finding the difference between the meta log time and the arrival time. Formula (1) shows the calculation of data ingestion time for data k by subtracting the data arrival time of k from the meta data log entry time of k.

$$IT_k = MLtime_k - DAtime_k, \tag{1}$$

where IT_k refers to the data ingestion time of kth data, $MLtime_k$ represents the data log entry time for data k, and $DAtime_k$ is the data arrival time of data k.

Clustering precision: In pattern recognition studies, the importance goes to finding out the relevance between patterns falling in n-dimensional pattern space. To find out the relevance between the patterns, it is important to examine the characteristic distance between them. The characteristics distance between the patterns decides the unsupervised classification (clustering) criterion. As per the theory, we considered the Euclidean distance to evaluate the precision of the clustering [33].

$$\text{Euclidian distance } d = \sqrt{\sum_{i=1}^{n}(x_i - y_i)^2} \tag{2}$$

We used the Euclidian distance as a metric to for RQ2. For the same collection of patient records, the patients clustering need to created. The distance between two points can be calculated using Formula (2), where, x_i and y_i are the ith coordinates for points x and y, respectively, and d is the distance between x and y.

The clustering metric d was calculated for all the available clusters created by both DW architecture and proposed data lake architecture. The lower value of d indicates the higher precision of clustering. Obviously, the higher cluster precision implies a more effective data architecture for the healthcare recommendation system.

3.3   Objects

We made use of anonymized EHR [34] and its supporting data to evaluate our data lake architecture. We made use of UCI machine learning repository [35], which contains the data set of diabetes form 130 US hospitals during the years of 1999–2008. It has 10 years of inpatient encounters from 130 US hospitals and integrated delivery networks. It contains 50 features representing patient and hospital outcomes. The data contains such attributes as patient number, race, gender, age, admission type, time in hospital, medical specialty of admitting physician, number of lab test performed, HbA1c test result, diagnosis, number of medications, diabetic medications, as well as the number of outpatients, inpatients, and emergency visits in the year before the hospitalization, etc.

3.4   Empirical Environment

The data available in the data set was classified as internal sourced data and external sourced data. The internal source data was connected with HDFS system Apache spring XD and loaded into the data lake. The external sourced data was connected with data lake system by using Apache Flume. Apache atlas identified the metadata available with data from the source. Each data would be allocated with a unique identifier to easy access. K-means algorithm using

Matlab was performed on the available data to identify the available clusters. The identified cluster would contain the patients with similar health conditions. SVM trained with the training data from the data set. SVM run on each cluster to find the most successful medication recommendation. A new data would be given to the system after the authorization. The personalized recommendation for the new data have been identified from the SVM.

4   Experimental Results

This section describes the performance of proposed data lake architecture compared with the data warehouse.

4.1   Reduction of Data Ingestion Time

We collected the data arrival time and Meta data log entry time for all the data tuples from the dataset in both DW and our data lake architecture. We then calculated the data ingestion time based on Formula (1). The average values of the ingestion time for DW and the data lake architecture are plotted in Fig. 3. It is clearly shown that the data lake architecture has much lower average value of IT.

Answer to RQ1: The experimental results clearly show the proposed approach's ability to store the data even from those in the native form. The data ingestion time has been improved significantly by the data lake architecture. Since the proposed architecture makes use of the HDFS file system, it does not require the preprocessing stage for the data. By contrast, the DW technique involves the ETL process, which takes much more time to ingest the data into the data warehouse.

The Apache Flume has the ability to pull the data from the remote data vendors and to store successfully in the data lake environment. The Kerberos

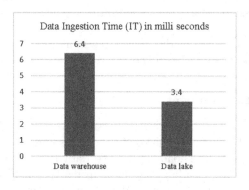

Fig. 3. Comparison of data ingestion time of DW and data lake

Table 1. Comparison of precision value d for DW and data lake

Euclidean distance	d value of data lake	d value of DW
Cluster 1	0.64	0.76
Cluster 2	0.71	0.87
Cluster 3	0.65	0.87
Cluster 4	0.88	0.99

engine creates an authentication ticket for each login, and the Apache Ranger tool verifies the authentication tickets and then provides the access rights to the remote login. These steps enable the third party data stakeholders to connect with the data lake architecture with security.

4.2 Removal of Data Silos

We compared the clustering algorithm based on the precision quality. We identified four clusters with maximum data points for each data architecture. The data points (namely, x and y) were further identified for the calculation of the precision value. In particular, the Euclidean distance d between x and y was calculated according to Formula (2). Table 1 summarises the values of d for each cluster. The results clearly show that the data lake architecture has smaller values of d for clustering than DW. In other words, the proposed data lake architecture has higher precision in the clustering.

Answer to RQ2: The precision of clustering normally increases as the amount of data becomes larger. However, due to its schema and organizational rules of DW, much vital information about patients will be lost during the ETL process. By contrast, the data lake architecture makes use of the schema-on-read method to load the data into the environment, which bring in the ability to connect with the third-party and external data stakeholders. The high availability of data about patients helps improve the precision of clustering. In a word, the data lake architecture delivers the ability to store a variety of data within the unified location. Thus, the clustering precision has been significantly improved.

5   Related Work

Undoubtedly, we are living in the world of smart devices, which create data for almost everything. Reuters predicted the global growth of data in 2020 will be nearly 35 ZB (one Zettabyte = one million petabytes) through all the electronified organizations. It is three times higher than the amount of data we produced in 2015.

Due to this enormous usage of data all over the world, the term "Big Data" is widespread and starting to be a part of every business process. Collecting and storing this vast scale of data is worth nothing without retrieving useful knowledge through processing and analysing it [17]. Unlike the traditional data generation models, big data contains a variety of data from the diverse sources with high velocity in huge volumes.

The evolution of Big Data created the conditions for transforming the Healthcare industry towards the Electronic Health Records (EHR) and managing computerized archives. The EHR may contain the information about various attributes of the patients, which could include demographic details, previous medication history, and allergies, vaccination status, laboratory test results, EMR scan reports, payer information, insurer details, a previous visit to hospitals and so on [36].

Therefore, it is obvious that the research on EHR and patient related auxiliary data will illuminate the improvised healthcare at the point of care. Inevitably, big data analytics on healthcare will enhance clinical operation by providing more relevant, efficient, error-free and cost effective diagnosis and medication. Since the availability of the data also shared with the patient, it will increase the transparency and reliability of the medical institutions [6].

The proactive, patient-centric and tailored healthcare medication recommendation to the individual based on the analysis of the corresponding person's EHR, genomic profile, laboratory data and other related supporting data [37].

The healthcare organisations create structured, semi-structured and unstructured data in the form of EHR. Even more importantly, only 20% data is in a structured format, which can be easily utilised by data scientist using the analytics machines but semi/unstructured production rate is 15 times higher than the structured one [6].

Naturally, the sources for the data also range from mobile devices, social media feeds wearable devices, Radio Frequency Identification (RFID) devices, sensors and monitoring devices attached to the patient and their bed [18]. Even though the health IT has seen tremendous technology development, it is challenging to manage this complex data flood.

Systems like CARE (Collaborative Assessment and Recommendation Engine), ICARE predicts the future disease risk of the patient by analysing patient's previous history [38]. HealthCare ND is also a system to predict the future disease risk of the patient [39]. However, it is an interactive system, which will get the health-related information from the patient and process the data with ICD-9-CM codes then return the results of the patient's future prediction. Abbas et al. proposed a system called Collaborative Filtering based Disease Risk Assessment (CFDRA) [22]. It is a cloud computing based risk assessment prediction system. In a system anticipated by Veeresh Patel et al., genomics and clinical data from patients EHR will be utilised to predict the cancer risk [25]. Physical therapy-as-a-service (PTaaS) application is a model designed to connect the sensors available in the patient's home and the therapist office computer [40].

The above said healthcare system are using the well defined bussiness rules and vocabularies. But, health IT systems need different type of data management architecture to address its particular challenges. Particularly, healthcare IT needs a late binding model, which is flexible, time efficient, scalable, and adaptable [41].

Blockchain data structures utilises the data lakes to support the data from variety of sources such as patients' mobile applications, wearable sensors, EMR's, documents and images [42]. Blockchain data structures utilises the data lakes to support the data from variety of sources such as patients' mobile applications, wearable sensors, EMR's, documents and images.

6 Conclusion

The traditional data warehouse (DW) technique is no longer suitable for healthcare analytics due to its schema on write nature and inability to handle data silos. In our study, an effective data lake system was proposed for the personalized healthcare data recommendations. The data lake is a flat, schema-on-read data architecture. We conducted experiments to evaluate and compare the proposed data lake architecture and DW on the dataset obtained from UCI repository. Our data lake architecture outperformed DW significantly in terms of data ingestion time: The time for loading and storing data in data lake architecture is nearly 50% less than that in DW. Moreover, the data lake architecture has higher precision in clustering than DW, mainly because of its ability to connect with more data sources. Briefly speaking, it was demonstrated that the data lake architecture can be an effective alternative to the existing health IT infrastructure. The proposed system can ingest all data in the unstructured, semi-structured, and structured formats. It can store data with low cost, taking advantages of HDFS. Hence, the data lake-based healthcare recommendation system will address the drawbacks of the traditional data architectures and provide additional capabilities for the future caliber of the data reusability.

References

1. Wang, H., Zhang, Z., Taleb, T.: Special issue on security and privacy of IoT. World Wide Web **21**(1), 1–6 (2017)
2. Wang, H., Jiang, X., Kambourakis, G.: Special issue on security, privacy and trust in network-based big data. Inf. Sci. Int. J. **318**(C), 48–50 (2015)
3. Jain, K.K., et al.: Textbook of Personalized Medicine. Springer, New York (2009). https://doi.org/10.1007/978-1-4419-0769-1
4. Zhang, Y., Qiu, M., Tsai, C.W., Hassan, M.M., Alamri, A.: Health-CPS: Healthcare cyber-physical system assisted by cloud and big data. IEEE Syst. J. **11**(1), 88–95 (2017)
5. Wang, H., Zhang, Y., et al.: Detection of motor imagery EEG signals employing naïve bayes based learning process. Measurement **86**, 148–158 (2016)
6. Feldman, B., Martin, E.M., Skotnes, T.: Big data in healthcare hype and hope, October 2012. Dr. Bonnie 360 (2012)
7. Chen, M., Mao, S., Liu, Y.: Big data: a survey. Mob. Netw. Appl. **19**(2), 171–209 (2014)

8. Inmon, W.H., Strauss, D., Neushloss, G.: DW 2.0: The Architecture for the Next Generation of Data Warehousing. Morgan Kaufmann, San Francisco (2010)

9. Devlin, B., Cote, L.D.: Data Warehouse: From Architecture to Implementation. Addison-Wesley Longman Publishing Co., Inc., Boston (1996)

10. Simitisis, A., Vassiliadis, P., Skiadopoulos, S., Sellis, T.: Data warehouse refreshment (2007)

11. Amine, A., Daoud, R.A., Bouikhalene, B.: Efficiency comparaison and evaluation between two ETL extraction tools. Indonesian J. Electr. Eng. Comput. Sci. **3**(1), 174–181 (2016)

12. Simitsis, A., Vassiliadis, P., Sellis, T.K.: Extraction-transformation-loading processes (2005)

13. Inmon, B.: Data Lake Architecture: Designing the Data Lake and Avoiding the Garbage Dump. Technics Publications (2016)

14. Hai, R., Geisler, S., Quix, C.: Constance: an intelligent data lake system. In: Proceedings of the 2016 International Conference on Management of Data, SIGMOD 2016, pp. 2097–2100. ACM, New York (2016)

15. Walker, C., Alrehamy, H.: Personal data lake with data gravity pull. In: 2015 IEEE Fifth International Conference on Big Data and Cloud Computing (BDCloud), pp. 160–167. IEEE (2015)

16. Vernon, M.M., Ulicny, B., Bennett, D.: An information provider's wish list for a next generation big data end-to-end information system. In: CIDR (2015)

17. Henry, R., Venkatraman, S.: Big data analytics the next big learning opportunity. J. Manage. Inf. Decis. Sci. **18**(2), 17 (2015)

18. Mathew, P.S., Pillai, A.S.: Big data challenges and solutions in healthcare: a survey. In: Snášel, V., Abraham, A., Krömer, P., Pant, M., Muda, A.K. (eds.) Innovations in Bio-Inspired Computing and Applications. AISC, vol. 424, pp. 543–553. Springer, Cham (2016). https://doi.org/10.1007/978-3-319-28031-8_48

19. Li, H., Wang, Y., Wang, H., Zhou, B.: Multi-window based ensemble learning for classification of imbalanced streaming data. World Wide Web **20**(6), 1–19 (2017)

20. Kamal, R., Shah, M.A., Hanif, A., Ahmad, J.: Real-time opinion mining of twitter data using spring XD and hadoop. In: 2017 23rd International Conference on Automation and Computing (ICAC), pp. 1–4. IEEE (2017)

21. Begum, N., Shankara, A.A.: Rectify and envision the server log data using apache flume. Int. J. Technol. Res. Eng. **3**(9) (2016)

22. Abbas, A., Ali, M., Khan, M.U.S., Khan, S.U.: Personalized healthcare cloud services for disease risk assessment and wellness management using social media. Pervasive Mobile Comput. **28**, 81–99 (2016)

23. Archenaa, J., Anita, E.M.: A survey of big data analytics in healthcare and government. Procedia Comput. Sci. **50**, 408–413 (2015)

24. Shaikh, S., Vora, D.: YARN versus MapReduce-a comparative study. In: 2016 3rd International Conference on Computing for Sustainable Global Development (INDIACom), pp. 1294–1297. IEEE (2016)

25. Patel, V., Adhil, M., Bhardwaj, T., Talukder, A.K.: Big data analytics of genomic and clinical data for diagnosis and prognosis of cancer. In: 2015 2nd International Conference on Computing for Sustainable Global Development (INDIACom), pp. 611–615. IEEE (2015)

26. Sun, L., Wang, H., Soar, J., Rong, C.: Purpose based access control for privacy protection in e-healthcare services. J. Softw. **7**(11), 2443–2449 (2012)

27. Li, J., Wang, H., Jin, H., Yong, J.: Current developments of k-anonymous data releasing. Electron. J. Health Inform. **3**(1), 6 (2008)

28. Sun, L., Wang, H., Yong, J., Wu, G.: Semantic access control for cloud computing based on e-healthcare. In: 2012 IEEE 16th International Conference on Computer Supported Cooperative Work in Design (CSCWD), pp. 512–518. IEEE (2012)
29. Wang, H., Cao, J., Zhang, Y.: A flexible payment scheme and its role-based access control. IEEE Trans. Knowl. Data Eng. **17**(3), 425–436 (2005)
30. Valliyappan, V., Singh, P.: Hap: protecting the apache hadoop clusters with hadoop authentication process using kerberos. In: Nagar, A., Mohapatra, D.P., Chaki, N. (eds.) Proceedings of 3rd International Conference on Advanced Computing, Networking and Informatics. SIST, vol. 43, pp. 151–161. Springer, New Delhi (2016). https://doi.org/10.1007/978-81-322-2538-6_16
31. Shaw, S., Vermeulen, A.F., Gupta, A., Kjerrumgaard, D.: Hive security. In: Practical Hive, pp. 233–243. Springer, New York (2016)
32. Weston, J.: Support vector machine. Tutorial http://www.cs.columbia.edu/~kathy/cs4701/documents/jason_svm_tutorial.pdf. Accessed 01 Aug 2017
33. Ghosh, S., Dubey, S.K.: Comparative analysis of K-means and fuzzy C-means algorithms. Int. J. Adv. Comput. Sci. Appl. **4**(4), 35–39 (2013)
34. Sun, X., Wang, H., Li, J., Zhang, Y.: Satisfying privacy requirements before data anonymization. Comput. J. **55**(4), 422–437 (2012)
35. Strack, B., DeShazo, J.P., Gennings, C., Olmo, J.L., Ventura, S., Cios, K.J., Clore, J.N.: Impact of HbA1c measurement on hospital readmission rates: analysis of 70,000 clinical database patient records. BioMed Res. Int. **2014**, 11 (2014)
36. Katehakis, D.G., Tsiknakis, M.: Electronic health record. In: Wiley Encyclopedia of Biomedical Engineering (2006)
37. Yoon, J., Davtyan, C., van der Schaar, M.: Discovery and clinical decision support for personalized healthcare. IEEE J. Biomed. Health Inform. **21**(4), 1133–1145 (2017)
38. Davis, D.A., Chawla, N.V., Blumm, N., Christakis, N., Barabási, A.L.: Predicting individual disease risk based on medical history. In: Proceedings of the 17th ACM Conference on Information and Knowledge Management, pp. 769–778. ACM (2008)
39. Dentino, B., Davis, D., Chawla, N.V.: HealthcareND: leveraging EHR and care for prospective healthcare. In: Proceedings of the 1st ACM International Health Informatics Symposium, pp. 841–844. ACM (2010)
40. Calyam, P., Mishra, A., Antequera, R.B., Chemodanov, D., Berryman, A., Zhu, K., Abbott, C., Skubic, M.: Synchronous big data analytics for personalized and remote physical therapy. Pervasive Mobile Comput. **28**, 3–20 (2016)
41. Barlow, S.: Comparing the three major approaches to healthcare data warehousing (2017)
42. Linn, L.A., Koo, M.B.: Blockchain for health data and its potential use in health it and health care related research. In: ONC/NIST Use of Blockchain for Healthcare and Research Workshop, Gaithersburg, Maryland, United States: ONC/NIST (2016)

Declarative Approaches for Compliance by Design

Francesco Olivieri[1]([⊠])(iD), Guido Governatori[1](iD), Nick van Beest[1](iD), and Nina Ghanbari Ghooshchi[2](iD)

[1] Data61, CSIRO, Dutton Park, Brisbane, Australia
{francesco.olivieri,guido.governatori,nick.vanbeest}@data61.csiro.au
[2] Griffith University, Brisbane, Australia
nina.ghanbari@griffithuni.edu.au

Abstract. The interest of scholars in devising automated methods to describe and analyse business processes has increased in the last decades due to the extreme interest of organisations in achieving their business objectives while remaining compliant with the relevant normative system. Adhering with norms and policies does not only help to avoid severe sanctions but also results in greater confidence by the consumers, and prestige for the organisation. Defining processes through the paradigm of *declarative specifications* is gaining momentum due to its intrinsic characteristic of being able to capture business as well as normative specifications within the same framework. We describe some of the state of the art techniques in the field of Business Process Compliance, focusing on pros and cons of such techniques, and advancing future lines of research.

1 Introduction

Business processes are used world-wide by organisations at every hierarchical level for diverse purposes. We can identify two causative reasons. First, they provide a good source of information about the activities and capabilities of an organisation. Second, such information is used to improve them. Business Process Management (BPM) can be described as a "process optimisation process". Being a holistic managerial approach, BPM considers processes as strategic means of an organisation that must be understood, analysed, and improved to continually furnish better and increasingly desirable products to clients. These processes are critical to any organisation as they often represent a significant proportion of costs.

For the benefits brought by BPM to be effective, suitable representations of business processes should be given. While an experienced programmer writes thousands of lines of code, a typical user (or process owner) does not want, or have the ability, to analyse complicated or convoluted formulas. They instead want simple, easy to understand representations. In this sense, Business Process Modelling technology emerged as a strong paradigm for the modelling, analysis, improvement, and automation of the day-to-day activities of organisations. The field is now a mature research area with widespread industry adoption. Business Process Modelling covers a wide variety of methodologies: from graphical modelling languages to ease the understanding of the stakeholders (e.g., YAWL [33],

© Springer International Publishing AG, part of Springer Nature 2018
A. Beheshti et al. (Eds.): ASSRI 2015/2017, LNBIP 234, pp. 80–97, 2018.
https://doi.org/10.1007/978-3-319-76587-7_6

EPC [38], BPMN[1]) to fully precise mathematical formalisms (e.g., Petri nets [37], π-calculus [24]) for formal analysis and automated process verification.

All the above mentioned formalisms and representations fall into the family of *imperative approaches*: they define a process model as a detailed specification of a step-by-step procedure that should be followed during the whole execution. In such a way, they strictly specify how the process will be executed. If from one side this procedural nature is their strength, it is also their main drawback. In fact, they suffer from some limitations. First, it is sometimes hard to obtain precise information about the order of the actions to be performed from the business requirements. Second, such a paradigm is not suitable to capture flexible business processes, i.e., processes whose internal structure and relationships among the various tasks is dynamic and with a large degree of variations (e.g., triage processes in hospital emergency rooms). Third, their imperative nature yields over-specified and highly-structured processes [39] where it is difficult to define relationships among the atoms. For instance, it is possible to model a simple statement as "activities A and B should never occur together" only through a detailed strategy to implement it.

In the opposing direction moves the school of modelling processes by *declarative specifications* [5,14,30]. Instead of specifying a process step by step, the focus in this approach being on defining relationships among the tasks to be executed to achieve a goal, as well as in understanding the behaviour of such "atoms". By shifting the focus from the whole process to its basic building blocks, you gain knowledge regarding which preconditions trigger the activation of a task (*inputs*), as well as what happens once a task completes its execution (*outputs*). It is indeed a common practice that organisations develop business rules manuals for their operations: such business rules may specify constraints that apply to their business processes (e.g., a customer has to be older than 18 in order to be eligible for a loan). As organisations grow, so do their processes and business rules. As a consequence, the number of business rules is generally very large [25].

Another important value of the declarative specification approach is that we can combine business specifications with normative specifications within a single framework. This is a crucial aspect of BPM for two reasons. From one side, the field of Business Process Compliance studies that the business practices are not in breach with the legislation regulating the organisational environment [19,34]. Worldwide scandals such as Societe Generale (France), Enron (USA) and HIH (Australia) forced governments and standard organisations to enact more restrictive regulatory mandates leading enterprises to massive investments in the market of compliance related software and services (over $30billion in 2008 [20]). Scholars have studied automated methods to establish whether a business process is compliant or not with the norms ruling the environment where the organisation acts in [16–18] and BPC deals with the problem of developing the above mentioned methods.

Secondly, compliance requirements are usually formulated as a set of rules that can be checked during, or after, the execution of the business process,

---

[1] http://www.bpmn.org.

called compliance by detection. If a non-compliant behaviour is detected, the business process needs to be redesigned. Alternatively, the rules can already be taken into account while modelling the business process. The result is a business process that is compliant by design. This technique, which goes under the name of *compliance by design*, has the advantage that a subsequent verification of compliance is not required. Automated tools able to generate *compliant by design* processes have some clear advantages: (i) being a preventative methodology, a subsequent compliance verification is not needed, (ii) it is possible to analyse all possible execution paths within the rules, (iii) the generated business process is optimised for execution of the business rules and regulations, as it is specifically designed to exactly represent the behaviour allowed by the rules.

Let us consider which challenges such automated tools need to address. First, we need a formalism able to represent in a coherent, functional, and possibly compact manner the business rules, the organisational objectives, and the normative system. Moreover, the framework should be able to determine whether a particular objective is attainable without violating the relevant norms in a given scenario, and which tasks are involved in this process. Thus, the deliberation effectively generates a plan. A question may arise: why a logical formalism is suitable to represent (business) processes? The *derivation* (or *formal proof*) of a statement is the final phase of a finite sequence of sentences/steps each of which is a fact (a statement that is given as a truth), or follows from the preceding sentences in the sequence by the application of a *rule*. A typical rule consists of a *set of preconditions* (*antecedents*) and some *conclusions* (*postconditions*). Whenever such preconditions are satisfied, the rule is enabled and produces its conclusion; absent the preconditions the action cannot be taken and, if it is taken, the postconditions hold. As such, a derivation has a strong, semantical correspondence with a trace of a process, and we can hence establish a bijection between a process and a logic theory. This is in line with the definition of (business) process: a task is the result of the successful execution of previous tasks (preconditions) and, in turn, may take part in the activation of one or more other tasks. This mechanism fully captures the idea of control flow in terms of satisfiability over a set of formalised constraints: each derivation can be seen a simulation of an *execution trace*. The logical apparatus we take into account is the one proposed in [14,15].

The second challenge lies in the *extraction* of the actual process from the above logical description: we need to "put together" such information to obtain a structured process, i.e., a process where the tasks in the traces are structured in sequential, parallel and alternative patterns. To the extent of our knowledge, two approaches were most successful. The former [28,29] lies within the field of representing business processes through Business Process Model Notation. The latter adopts Petri nets for their intrinsic characteristic of permit a direct formal verification of the net (process) [12].

Our agenda is as follows. We start with Sect. 2, where we give a more detailed description about *capabilities rules* and why they are suitable to represent tasks and control flow. Follows Sect. 3: in there, we introduce the modal, skeptical logics which is able to represent actions, norms and goals. Section 4 describes two different approaches to visualise and operationalise such sets of rules as a verifiable business process. In Sect. 5 we discuss pros and cons of the two proposed methods; the related work follows in Sect. 6. We end the paper with Sect. 7.

2   Rules for Declarative Processes

Governatori *et al.* [14,15] proposed an agent-oriented rule language for the declarative specifications of *norm* and *goal compliant* business processes. The main idea is that the set of rules can be partitioned into three subsets: a set of rules describing the "capabilities" of an organisation, a set of rules corresponding to the norms governing a process, and a set of rules encoding the objectives/goals of an organisation to fulfil in their processes. The intuition behind the *capability rules* is that they model the set of activities/tasks an organisation is able to carry out, the preconditions required for each task, the effects of executing such tasks, and the relationships among them. The language upon which the rules are defined consists of a set of two types of literals: *condition literals* and *task literals*. The condition literals encode the preconditions and effects of tasks or, in general, state variables for a process, while each task literal corresponds to a task that could occur in a process.

Capability rules have the following "*if... then...*" form: $r: l_1, \ldots, l_n \Rightarrow l_{n+1}$, where r is a label that uniquely identifies the rule, and each literal l_i is drawn from the set of literals $\mathsf{Lit} = \mathsf{Prop} \cup \{\neg p | p \in \mathsf{Prop}\}$; Prop is a set of propositional atoms representing conditions c_i and tasks t_j. This form has the clear advantage that it immediately relates preconditions to the corresponding effect of performing the particular action. More specifically, we can identify the following three patterns: (i) $t \Rightarrow c$, where we can look at c as an effect of performing task t (the effect represented by c thus holds after the execution of task t); (ii) the pattern $c_1, \ldots c_n \Rightarrow t$ indicates that $c_1, \ldots c_n$ are preconditions for tasks t, and task t will be executed after the preconditions hold; (iii) $t_1, \ldots, t_n \Rightarrow t$ specifies that the combination of tasks $t_1, \ldots, t_n$ triggers task t, and that task t appears in the process, if $t_1, \ldots, t_n$ appear in the process, before t. (In other words, this pattern describes relationships and dependencies among tasks in a process. In the rule given above, the meaning is that execution of tasks $t_1, \ldots, t_n$ is required to trigger the execution of task t.)

The rules are then used to form (logical) derivations, where a *derivation* D, given a set of facts F represented as literals, is a sequence of literals $D(1), \ldots, D(n)$, such that if $D(m+1) = l$ then either $l \in F$ or there is a rule $r: l_1, \ldots, l_k \Rightarrow l$ such that for all $l_i \in D[1..m]$, $i \leq k$, where $D[1..m]$ is the initial sequence of length m of D.

The rules presented above can be linked to the sequential, parallel, and alternative patterns typical of business process modelling techniques to those that can be found in a logical derivation. Indeed, assume tasks A and B concur to obtain the resources needed for task C to start its execution. This means that C may bring about its effects only when both A and B have finished, and that

A and *B* have no precedence order with respect to one another, that is they can be executed in parallel. From a logical perspective, all this information can simply be represented by a rule where the premises are literals *A* and *B*, and with *S* as conclusion. Accordingly, a derivation (sequence of rules) can encode a possible order in which the tasks are executed to achieve a particular business goal according to the constraints specified by the rules themselves.

Given a set of facts, we can generate a derivation where all applicable rules fire and their conclusions have been added to the derivation. This derivation contains all tasks that are executed given the set of facts (hence facts are the input for a process case). In addition, the derivation contains the literals corresponding to the conditions to trigger the execution of tasks or for activating obligations, the effects of the tasks, the obligations in force, and the expected goals. Notice that obligations and goals are neither actions nor tasks: they only purpose is to determine whether a process execution of the process is compliant and meet the organisation objectives (influencing thus the activities or tasks included in the process). Therefore, rules for goals and norms do not directly contribute to the structure of the process. Goals and obligations can thus be considered as *special kinds* of conditions. Consequently, if we "ignore" obligations, goals and condition literals from a derivation, then a derivation is a sequence of *only* those tasks satisfying the constraints defined by the rules. This is equivalent to a plan as defined in classical planning [11]. For these reasons, in the present paper, we concentrate only on the capability rules.

Notice that, while the set of tasks triggered by a case (set of facts) is unique, multiple derivations are possible. For instance, given the rule '$t_1, t_2 \Rightarrow t_3$', the order in which t_1 and t_2 are executed does not matter. Accordingly, both 't_1, t_2, t_3' and 't_2, t_1, t_3' are valid derivations (and, consequently, plans conforming to the specification given by the rule). This means that, given a case, we can generate a set of plans corresponding to it, which can be understood as alternative ways in which the process can be executed. Using the idea that a business process can be understood as a set of traces (where a trace is a sequence of tasks), we can establish a connection between a set of plans and a business process, where a process provides a concise (formal and graphical) representation of a set of plans, which are obtained from a single case and are combined by using constructions modelling AND-joins and AND-splits. Moreover, given a set of rules, it is possible to give as input different sets of facts, where each set of facts corresponds to a common set of instances for the process. For each case, a corresponding set of plans is created, where the mutually exclusive cases are subsequently merged, adopting XOR-split and XOR-join patterns.

3   Modal Defeasible Logic

The logic Governatori *et al.* [14,15] proposed to implement the intuition presented in Sect. 2 is a modal extension of the well-known skeptical formalism of Defeasible Logic (DL), first introduced in a seminal work by Nute [27]. Specifically, the logic deploys the non-monotonic mechanism of DL to capture:

(i) which actions an agent (enterprise) is capable to perform in a given organisational environment by using a *belief* modality (in other terms, *beliefs* describe both what holds true in the environment as well as which actions the agent is able to perform), (ii) which norms the agent is subject to (by using the *obligation* modality), and (iii) which goals the agent might commit to and which are actually attainable (by using the *outcome* modality).

A modal defeasible theory consists of five different kinds of knowledge: facts, strict rules, defeasible rules, defeaters, and a superiority relation. The set of facts denotes simple pieces of information that are considered always to be true. Rules are distinguished both on their *type* (strict, defeasible and defeaters) and on their *modality*. Such a modality represents which kind of conclusion the rule may lead to. Rules are of three modalities: belief rules, obligation rules, and outcome rules. Belief rules are meant to relate the factual knowledge of an enterprise, and are composed by: a set of actions an organisation can do, the *preconditions* under which tasks can be executed, and the effects derived by the execution of such tasks (also called *postconditions*). Specifically, *belief rules* describe the logical relationship between preconditions and tasks, tasks and their effects, relationships between tasks, relationships between states. *Obligation rules* determine when and which obligations are in force, while outcome rules establish the objectives of an organisation depending on the particular context. *Outcome rules* take inspiration by the main stream of the BDI (Belief-Desire-Intention) literature describing an agent's mental attitudes. Notions of desire, goal, intention, and social intention are taken into account in order to describe various degrees of the agent's commitment towards its objectives.

A *rule* is an expression $r : A(r) \hookrightarrow_\square C(r)$ and consists of: (i) a unique name r, (ii) the *antecedent* $A(r)$ that which is a finite set of (modal) literals, (iii) an arrow $\hookrightarrow \in \{\rightarrow, \Rightarrow, \rightsquigarrow\}$ denoting, respectively, a strict rule, a defeasible rule and a defeater, (iv) a modality $\square \in \{BEL, OBL, OUT\}$ that which denotes the mode the consequent literal shall take, i.e. *BEL* for beliefs, *OBL* for obligations and *OUT* for outcomes (outcomes are themselves distinguished among desires, goals, intentions, and social intentions, those being intentions compliant with the norms (it is out of the scope of the present synopsis to go in further details by describing differences among such mental attitudes), (v) its *consequent* (or *head*) $C(r)$ that which is a single literal, and (vi) the superiority relation $>$ that which is a binary relation indicating the relative strength of two (conflicting) rules. A *strict rule* is a rule in which whenever the premises hold (e.g., facts), so does the conclusion. On the other hand, a *defeasible rule* is a rule that can be defeated by contrary evidence (typically bird fly, but it is not the case for penguins). *Defeaters* are rules that cannot be used to draw any conclusion. Their only use is to prevent some conclusions, i.e., to defeat defeasible rules by producing evidence for the contrary. Lastly, the superiority relation $>$ among rules is used to define when one rule overrides the (opposite) conclusion of another one. The infix notation $r > s$ means that $(r, s) \in >$.

At the heart of the reasoning mechanism of the logic is the notion of derivation. Intuitively a *derivation* (or *proof*) is a sequence of literals where every element (a conclusion) is either one of the facts, or it has been obtained by previous steps by applying some rules. A *conclusion* of a defeasible theory D is a tagged literal and can have one of the following forms:

- $+\Delta_\Box q$, which means that q is definitely provable in D with mode $\Box$, i.e., there is a definite proof for q, that is a proof using facts and strict rules only;
- $-\Delta_\Box q$, which means that q is definitely not provable in D with mode $\Box$ (i.e., a definite proof for q does not exist);
- $+\partial_\Box q$, which means that q is defeasibly provable in D with mode $\Box$;
- $-\partial_\Box q$, which means that q is not defeasibly provable, or refuted in D with mode $\Box$.

Formally, given a defeasible theory D, a proof P of length n in D is a finite sequence $P(1),\ldots,P(n)$ of tagged formulas of the type $+\Delta_\Box q$, $-\Delta_\Box q$, $+\partial_\Box q$ and $-\partial_\Box q$.

The definition of Δ describes just forward chaining of strict rules. Literal q is definitely provable if either is a fact, or there is a strict rule for q, whose antecedents have all been previously, definitely proved. On the other hand, literal q is defeasibly provable $(+\partial_\Box q)$ if q is already definitely provable, or we argue using the defeasible part of the theory. In this last case, there must exist an applicable strict or defeasible rule for q, while every attack is either discarded, or defeated by a stronger rule through $>$. (A rule is merely *applicable* whenever each literal in the set of antecedents has already been proved, while a rule is *discarded* when at least one of the premises has been previously disproved.)

The sets of positive and negative conclusions form, respectively, the *positive* and *negative extensions*. For reasons we are going to explain in the rest of the paper, we shall restrict our attention to the positive extension only.

Let us explain how the derivation mechanism works by considering the following two examples. The first one proposes a rather simple theory; aim is to link derivations to traces. We use second example to show how strict and defeasible proof tags are obtained, as well as the mechanism underlying the team defeat.

Let $D = (\{a, b\}, R, \emptyset)$ be a defeasible theory such that

$$R = \{r_0 : a \Rightarrow_{BEL} c$$
$$r_1 : b \Rightarrow_{BEL} d$$
$$r_2 : c, d \Rightarrow_{BEL} e\}.$$

It is trivial to notice that all the rules are applicable and actually fire producing the following positive extension $E^+(D) = \{+\Delta_{BEL}a, +\Delta_{BEL}b, +\partial_{BEL}a, +\partial_{BEL}b, +\partial_{BEL}c, +\partial_{BEL}d, +\partial_{BEL}e\}$ – recall that $+\Delta a$ implies $+\partial a$. Here, we have six derivations:

$$(1) + \Delta_{BEL}a, +\Delta_{BEL}b, +\partial_{BEL}c, +\partial_{BEL}d, +\partial_{BEL}e$$
$$(2) + \Delta_{BEL}a, +\Delta_{BEL}b, +\partial_{BEL}d, +\partial_{BEL}c, +\partial_{BEL}e$$

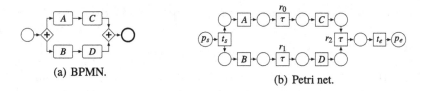

(a) BPMN.

(b) Petri net.

Fig. 1. Two processes representing the traces of theory D.

$$(3) + \Delta_{BEL}a, +\partial_{BEL}c, +\Delta_{BEL}b, +\partial_{BEL}d, +\partial_{BEL}e$$
$$(4) + \Delta_{BEL}b, +\Delta_{BEL}a, +\partial_{BEL}c, +\partial_{BEL}d, +\partial_{BEL}e$$
$$(5) + \Delta_{BEL}b, +\Delta_{BEL}a, +\partial_{BEL}d, +\partial_{BEL}c, +\partial_{BEL}e$$
$$(6) + \Delta_{BEL}b, +\partial_{BEL}d, +\Delta_{BEL}a, +\partial_{BEL}c, +\partial_{BEL}e.$$

Some considerations. a and b have no precedence order between each other. The same happens for the tuples: (c, d), (a, d), and (b, c). On the contrary, a always precedes c, b always precedes d, and so do c and d for e. It is straightforward to see that such derivations can be visualised as proposed in Fig. 1, where Fig. 1(a) shows a BPM notation whilst Fig. 1(b) shows a Petri net.

Now consider the next example and let $D = (F = \{c_1, c_2, c_3, c_4, c_5, c_7, c_8\}, R, >= \{(r_6, r_9), (r_7, r_8)\})$ be a defeasible theory such that

$$R = \{r_0 : c_1, c_2 \rightarrow_{BEL} t_1; \quad r_1 : c_3 \Rightarrow_{BEL} t_2;$$
$$r_2 : t_1, t_2 \Rightarrow_{BEL} c_6; \quad r_3 : t_2 \Rightarrow_{OBL} o;$$
$$r_4 : c_6 \Rightarrow_{BEL} t_4; \quad r_5 : t_4 \Rightarrow_{BEL} o;$$
$$r_6 : c_4 \Rightarrow_{BEL} t_3; \quad r_7 : c_5, OBLo \Rightarrow_{BEL} t_3;$$
$$r_8 : c_7 \Rightarrow_{BEL} {\sim}t_3; \quad r_9 : c_8 \Rightarrow_{BEL} {\sim}t_3;$$
$$r_{10} :\Rightarrow_{OUT} out; \quad r_{11} : t_3 \Rightarrow_{BEL} out\}.$$

We denoted tasks with t_i, conditions with c_j, the only obligation with o, and the final outcome with out. In detail, r_0 strictly proves $+\Delta_{BEL}t_1$, while r_1 defeasibly proves $+\partial_{BEL}t_2$. The combination of these two tasks gives (defeasibly proves) condition c_6, but the execution of t_2 also triggers obligation o (by proving $+\partial_{OBL}o$). Such an obligation is complied with by the execution of task t_4 through the sequential derivation of $+\partial_{BEL}t_4$ by r_4 and $+\partial_{BEL}o$ by r_5. Now, rules r_6 and r_7 form a (winning) team defeater to prove t_3: the superiorities among $r_6 > r_9$ and $r_7 > r_8$, let r_8 and r_9 to be defeated. We hence have two ways to obtain t_3. The only outcome is derived by r_{10}, which is obtained through r_{11}. The positive extension is $E^+(D) = \{+\Delta_{BEL}c_1, \ldots, +\Delta_{BEL}c_6, +\partial_{BEL}c_1, \ldots, +\partial_{BEL}c_6, +\Delta_{BEL}t_1, +\partial_{BEL}t_1, +\partial_{BEL}t_2, +\partial_{OBL}o, +\partial_{BEL}c_7, +\partial_{BEL}t_3, +\partial_{BEL}t_4, +\partial_{BEL}o, +\partial_{OUT}out, +\partial_{BEL}out\}$.

4   Visualisation Methods for Compliant Processes

We introduced a modal logic describing (1) what are the sequences of actions (in terms of literals derivations) an organisation is able/allowed to perform in a given setting/situation (2) to achieve a set of goals (3) while remaining norm compliant with a regulative system. The next step is to define the methods to represent/visualise such derivations (traces) in a compact, explicative manner. We shall report two different approaches. The former, proposed by Olivieri *et al.* in [28,29], adopts a backwards approach and ends up in visualising the process through the BPM Notation. The latter, recently proposed by Ghanbari *et al.* in [12], is otherwise based on the Petri net modelling language.

The algorithms proposed in [14,15] take as inputs (i) a modal logics and (ii) (factual) literals describing a specific situation. The output is the *positive extension* expressing which literals actually hold in that particular setting. This reflects which norms are active and which tasks can be performed by the organisation. Such literals and the rules where such literals appear in as antecedents or as conclusions are used by both methods to visualise the final norm and goal compliant business processes.

4.1   BPMN and the Backwards Approach

We hereafter analyse the approach proposed by Olivieri *et al.* [14,15]. The logic described in Sect. 3 is expressive enough to be able to describe most-preferred to least-preferred objectives. (Such objectives lie within the agent BDI paradigm and are represented as reparative chains, where an *outcome chain* like '$a \odot b$' characterises the idea that a is the most preferred outcome, but when a is not attainable, then b becomes the new outcome the agent strives for. (It is out of the scope of the present paper to go further in detail on outcome chains and their implications on the various degrees of the agent's commitment towards its goals.)

The algorithms of [14,15] work in a backwards manner. They start by considering the *end literals* of the theory in the positive extension (the proved ones), those representing the attainable outcomes. Exclusive choice patterns are created among the outcomes from the same chain. The algorithms then navigate backwards the derivation tree, rule by rule, until the facts of the theory are met. Accordingly, only those rules with both conclusion and set of antecedents in the positive extension are considered. Every time the algorithm considers a (non-already visited) literal, a new node is created in the graph. Given a rule, an edge is created between the antecedent of such a rule and its conclusion. If more than one literal is present in the set of antecedents, an AND-join node is created in between each literal in the set of antecedents and the conclusion. Finally, if more than one rule contributes in proving a given literal, an OR-join structure is made. The final steps of the algorithms consist in giving "more structure" to the graph: (i) nodes representing condition and obligation literals are removed and substituted by labels on edges, (ii) literals *co-occurrences* are identified, and lastly (iii) complex synthesis operations on the graph are performed to create OR-split and AND-join patterns. The algorithms are proved to be sound, complete, and to work in polynomial time.

4.2   The Petri Net Approach

In [12], a formal method to visualise and operationalise business rules in the form of a Petri net is presented. (The reader in need is referred to Appendix A for a brief excerpt on the Petri net formalism.) Figure 2 provides an overview of the steps required in [12] to transform a set of rules into a Petri net, representing the allowed behaviour of the business process according to those rules.

The process to be obtained is imperative and exclusively contains possible execution paths. That is, it defines what *can* or *should* be executed, instead of what *must not* be executed (as is normally the case for declarative process specifications). Consequently, the rules are first pre-processed to remove those rules that do not directly define possible executions of the process. As such, all rules with literals that have not been proved can be removed, as these rules cannot fire and have, therefore, no effect on the resulting process. Additionally, negative tasks represent the absence of a task and can thus be removed from the remaining rules (e.g., $A, \neg B \Rightarrow C$ would be $A \Rightarrow C$).

The rules are generally grouped in different input cases, each representing a specific "scenario" or process instance. For each case, a partial Petri net is obtained, representing the process according to the rules activated (i.e., rules with antecedents and conclusion proved) for that case. That is, the traces of each partial Petri net contain exactly all possible derivations from the rules of its corresponding case. Each literal is represented by a transition in the Petri net, whereas each rule is represented by a τ transition. As a result, each partial Petri net essentially contains a sequence of transitions representing subsequent activities and rules. Multiple rules with an identical antecedent and different consequence result in concurrent branches in the partial Petri net. For instance, rules $A \Rightarrow B$ and $A \Rightarrow C$, would introduce two concurrent paths (with B and C, respectively) after A, whereas $B, C \Rightarrow D$ would merge both branches into a single path with D. Each partial Petri net consists of sequences and/or concurrent branches, as choices are represented by the different cases.

Subsequently, the partial Petri nets are merged into a consolidated Petri net, representing the full process such that it does not contain any duplicate transition labels (i.e., each activity is represented only once). Different paths following a

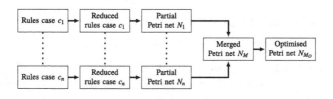

Fig. 2. Method overview (derived from [12]).

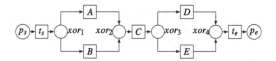

Fig. 3. Consecutive XORs without dependencies.

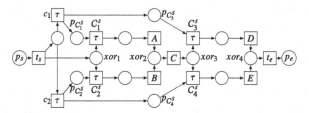

Fig. 4. Consecutive XORs preserving dependencies.

mutual transition between different partial Petri nets result in exclusive paths in the merged Petri net.

However, subsequent exclusive choices may not necessarily be independent. That is, the allowed path at a certain XOR-split may be determined by the preceding path from the previous XOR-split. Consider, for instance, two cases: *Case 1* = $\{r_1 :\Rightarrow A, r_2 : A \Rightarrow C, r_3 : C \Rightarrow D\}$ and *Case 2* = $\{r_4 :\Rightarrow B, r_5 : B \Rightarrow C, r_6 : C \Rightarrow E\}$. The (simplified) resulting merged Petri net would then look as shown in Fig. 3. It is easy to see that the merged Petri net would allow two more traces that are not allowed in the original derivations as specified by Cases 1 and 2 (i.e., $\langle A, C, E \rangle$ and $\langle B, C, D \rangle$ are not allowed).

This is resolved by adding τ transitions representing the underlying cases that preserve dependencies of subsequent exclusive branches, without the necessity of adding conditions. This is shown graphically in Fig. 4, which represents the same process as depicted in Fig. 3 while maintaining consecutive dependencies as specified in the rules. As such, after A, E is not possible, while D is not possible in a trace with B.

Finally, unnecessary τ transitions (i.e., transitions whose removal does not alter the possible visible traces of the net) can be removed by using the reduction techniques as described in [26]. The resulting Petri net is an exact imperative representation of the behaviour as allowed by the input rules.

5   A Brief Analysis of the Two Approaches

5.1   Pros and Cons of the BPMN Approach

Pros:

The modal logics presented before is rich of information regarding all the possible actions and norms; moreover, the calculus of the extension is not only computationally efficient but also gives precise information concerning what is *actually* attainable in every specific situation, and which norms are actually in force.

- Methodologies of [28,29] fully exploit such information: the backwards approach guarantees that no information is lost during the computation. Therefore, the final graph shows which *condition literals are used* and where, as well as which norms impact on the process and, again, exactly where (i.e., which tasks are influenced).
- We recall that the starting point of the synthesis algorithms was to consider which the attainable outcomes were: those were embedded in exclusive choice structures. This gives an immediate feedback to the front-end user about which the alternative (the most to the least preferred) outcomes are in a given setting.
- The merging process of different graphs (each of which representing different initial settings) gives as input a single structured process graph where the various alternatives are represented through XOR structures. Many XOR variants were considered, depending on whether (i) there exists a preferred XOR branch to be executed, (ii) none of the branches involved are to be preferred to the others, and (iii) a branch that does not actually involve the execution of any task and it is used to skip the run to the end of the XOR-join (which is typically considered as the standard course of action).

Cons:

- The merging procedure is not fully operational: the algorithms can only handle the creation of the XOR structures but is not even close to the deepness reached by methods proposed in [12].
- A proper proof of completeness is missing.
- The OR-join gates created when more rules concur in achieving a node cannot properly handle the *resource consumption*.

5.2   Pros and Cons of the Petri Net Approach

Pros:

- This approach has proven to be fast and has shown to outperform state-of-the-art approaches.
- The resulting Petri net only allows behaviour that is allowed by the rules and is, as such, guaranteed to be compliant to those rules. More specifically, a condition-free representation of subsequent exclusive branches is created to maintain their dependencies without duplicating activities. When required, these dependencies can be removed automatically to generalise the behaviour of the Petri net. Existing approaches, however, can only obtain a generalised Petri net and are, therefore, in many cases not fully compliant with the input rules.
- Full proofs of soundness and completeness were given.

Cons:

- The approach does not consider processes with loops (for the same reasons of the other approach).

– Subsequent dependencies are ensured and enforced by creating a specific coordinating transition for each input case. Naturally, this may complicate the resulting Petri net in scenarios with many input cases. However, the number of cases can be significantly reduced by merging, as together they may represent full behaviour. Merging such cases is a direction for future work.

6   Related Work

Some other approaches attempted to create compliant business process by design.

The defeasible modal logic we presented departs from the standard BDI architecture and agent programming languages implementing it (e.g., 3APL-2APL [6,7], JASON [3]), and extensions with norms in several respects (e.g., BOID by [4], while we refer the reader to [1] for an overview). While in the above mentioned approaches the agent has to select (partially) predefined plans from a plan library, we propose that the agent generates a business process on the fly (corresponding to a set of plans) to meet the objectives without violating the norms it is subject to.

Alechina et al. [2] present a BDI-based agent programming language based on 2APL for *norm-aware agents*; a norm-aware agent can deliberate on its goals, norms, and sanctions before deciding which plan to select and execute. A major issue of this work is that if a goal triggers two (or more) sanctions, each of which is lower in rank than the achievement of that goal, the agent will try to achieve that particular goal even if the sum of the two sanctions is higher in rank.

Automated planning is a technique to organise actions with the aim of achieving some pre-specified goal starting from the current state of the system [11]. Each action features a set of preconditions, that must be satisfied prior to its execution, and a set of effects, that specify the state change resulting from its execution. There are frameworks to generate plans (e.g., KPG [22] and Golog [10]), but these are typically based on classical AI planning and do not consider norms. In addition, many automated planning approaches in the business process domain focus on runtime adaptation of pre-specified processes, concerning runtime repair instead of design time process generation based on rules (see [23,36]). Automated planning techniques require a goal to be specified along with an initial state. However, in case of multiple initial states, multiple possible plans need to be generated, that must be merged in order to represent a full business process [21]. As such, providing a business process model that supports *all* possible traces as specified by the rules remains a challenge.

DECLARE provides an approach for declarative specifications of business processes by means of constraints [30] and graphical representations to visualise the constraints and the activities in the model [40]. However, the graphical representation shows the exact constraints and does not provide an actual process model imposed by the rules. In [32], Prescher et al. convert a DECLARE model to a behaviourally equivalent Petri net. However, this approach leads to multiple transitions representing the same activity and, therefore, an highly complicated model. Our approach, on the other hand, provides a model without additional duplication of transitions. In [8], Giacomo *et al.* developed an extension on top of BPMN, BPMN-D, which supports declarative process modelling. It allows to transform DECLARE models into readable BPMN-D models. This approach, however, does not support concurrency. Additionally, DECLARE is based on Linear Temporal Logic, which is not able to represent certain complex norms [13] and cannot, as such, be used for this purpose.

Sardina *et al.* [35] provide an account of goals in the view of declarative aspects by integrating BDI failure mechanisms with Hierarchical Task Network (HTN) planning techniques. HTN planning is notoriously undecidable even if no variables are allowed, or PSPACE-hard if restrictions are given. The main feature of their $CAN^{\mathcal{A}}$ is its detailed operational semantics where, if a plan fails, alternative plans for achieving the goal are tried. Compared to theirs, the two approaches presented in this paper have the advantage that they generate all possible plans at design time.

7   Future Work

Business Process Compliance is an important field of study given the importance for enterprises to have business processes which have to be, at the same time, efficient and compliant with the normative system. Scholars of the fiels have studied, and proposed, different formalisms to describe workflows, business processes, and norms. In the present work, we described two promising approaches which lie in the school of modelling business processes by declarative specifications. This school of thoughts differs from the "more stiffed" family of imperative approaches since it gives knowledge about the relationships among tasks, but most of all because it allows us to represent in the same framework business and normative specifications.

The modal logics [14,15] described in Sect. 3 is a powerful tool exactly for this reason. Still, some drawbacks need to be addressed in future lines of research: (i) loops are not considered, and (ii) resources consumption.

A   Petri Nets

Petri nets (PN) are a popular modelling language used to formalise business processes [37]. Petri nets are mathematical models for the description of distributed systems [31]. Petri nets are directed bi-graphs with nodes consisting of *places* and *transitions*. Transitions within Petri nets represent events, while places represent conditions. *Arcs* form directed edges between place-transition pairs. Places may contain *tokens*. A distribution of tokens over the places is called a *marking*. A transition is enabled and can "fire" when all its input places contain at least one token. When a transition fires, one token is removed from each input place and one token is put into each output place. A Petri net is defined formally as follows [31]:

Definition 1 (Petri net). *A tuple* (P, T, A, λ) *is a* labeled Petri net, *where:*

- *P is a set of* places
- *T is a set of* transitions, *such that* $P \cap T = \emptyset$
- *$A \subseteq (P \times T) \cup (T \times P)$ is a set of arcs*
- *$\lambda : P \cup T \to \mathcal{L}$ is a labelling function.*

The Petri net state, often referred to as the net marking, *$M : P \to \mathbb{N}_0$ is a function that associates a place $p \in P$ with a natural number (viz., place tokens). A marked net $N = (P, T, A, \lambda, M_0)$ is a Petri net (P, T, A, λ) together with an* initial *marking M_0.*

Places and transitions are referred to as *nodes*. The *preset* of a node is denoted by $\bullet y = \{x \in P \cup T \mid (x, y) \in A\}$, and the *postset* of a node is denoted by $y\bullet = \{z \in P \cup T \mid (y, z) \in A\}$.

If $\forall p \in \bullet t : M(p) > 0$, t is said to be *enabled*. The *firing* of t, denoted by $M \xrightarrow{t} M'$, leads to a new marking M', with $M'(p) = M(p) - 1$ if $p \in \bullet t \setminus t\bullet$, $M'(p) = M(p) + 1$ if $p \in t \bullet \setminus \bullet t$, and $M'(p) = M(p)$ otherwise. The marking M_n is said to be reachable from M if there exists a sequence of transition firings $\sigma = t_1 t_2 \ldots t_n$ such that $M \xrightarrow{t_1} M_1 \xrightarrow{t_2} \ldots \xrightarrow{t_n} M_n$.

A *trace* is a sequence $\lambda(t_1), \lambda(t_2), \ldots$ such that $\sigma = t_1, t_2, \ldots$ is a sequence of firing transitions. However, certain control-flow behaviour (like exclusive parallel branches) requires additional transitions that do not correspond to a task literal. These transitions are commonly referred to as silent or τ transitions [9]. For understandability purposes, we will add a label for each τ transition as well throughout the paper. As such, the set of transition labels $\mathcal{L}$ comprises both labels corresponding to task literals and labels corresponding to τ transitions. A *visible trace* is a trace where all τ transitions have been removed (maintaining the order of the transitions representing task literals). For the remainder of this work, we shall refer to visible traces as traces.

References

1. Alechina, N., Bassiliades, N., Dastani, M., Vos, M.D., Logan, B., Mera, S., Morris-Martin, A., Schapachnik, F.: Computational models for normative multi-agent systems, pp. 71–92
2. Alechina, N., Dastani, M., Logan, B.: Programming norm-aware agents, pp. 1057–1064
3. Bordini, R.H., Hübner, J.F.: BDI agent programming in agentspeak using *Jason*. In: Toni, F., Torroni, P. (eds.) CLIMA 2005. LNCS (LNAI), vol. 3900, pp. 143–164. Springer, Heidelberg (2006). https://doi.org/10.1007/11750734_9. (tutorial paper)
4. Broersen, J., Dastani, M., Hulstijn, J., van der Torre, L.W.N.: Goal generation in the BOID architecture. Cogn. Sci. Q. **2**(3–4), 428–447 (2002)
5. Chesani, F., Mello, P., Montali, M., Riguzzi, F., Sebastianis, M., Storari, S.: Checking compliance of execution traces to business rules. In: Ardagna, D., Mecella, M., Yang, J. (eds.) BPM 2008. LNBIP, vol. 17, pp. 134–145. Springer, Heidelberg (2009). https://doi.org/10.1007/978-3-642-00328-8_13

6. Dastani, M.: 2APL: a practical agent programming language. Auton. Agent. Multi-Agent Syst. **16**(3), 214–248 (2008)

7. Dastani, M., van Riemsdijk, M.B., Meyer, J.J.C.: Programming multi-agent systems in 3APL. In: Bordini, R.H., Dastani, M., Dix, J., El Fallah, S.A. (eds.) Multi-Agent Programming. Multiagent Systems, Artificial Societies, and Simulated Organizations (International Book Series), vol. 15, pp. 39–67. Springer, Boston (2005). https://doi.org/10.1007/0-387-26350-0_2

8. De Giacomo, G., Dumas, M., Maggi, F.M., Montali, M.: Declarative process modeling in BPMN. In: Zdravkovic, J., Kirikova, M., Johannesson, P. (eds.) CAiSE 2015. LNCS, vol. 9097, pp. 84–100. Springer, Cham (2015). https://doi.org/10.1007/978-3-319-19069-3_6

9. Dijkman, R., Dumas, M., Ouyang, C.: Semantics and analysis of business process models in BPMN. Inf. Softw. Technol. **50**(12), 1281–1294 (2008)

10. Gabaldon, A.: Making golog norm compliant. In: Leite, J., Torroni, P., Ågotnes, T., Boella, G., van der Torre, L. (eds.) CLIMA 2011. LNCS (LNAI), vol. 6814, pp. 275–292. Springer, Heidelberg (2011). https://doi.org/10.1007/978-3-642-22359-4_19

11. Ghallab, M., Nau, D., Traverso, P.: Automated Planning: Theory and Practice. Morgan Kaufmann, Burlington (2004)

12. Ghooshchi, N.G., van Beest, N.R.T.P., Governatori, G., Olivieri, F., Sattar, A.: Visualisation of compliant declarative business processes. In: Proceedings of EDOC. IEEE (2017, forthcoming)

13. Governatori, G., Hashmi, M.: No time for compliance. In: Proceedings of the International Conference on Enterprise Distibuted Object Computing, pp. 9–18. IEEE (2015)

14. Governatori, G., Olivieri, F., Rotolo, A., Scannapieco, S., Cristani, M.: Picking up the best goal: an analytical study in defeasible logic. In: Morgenstern, L., Stefaneas, P., Lévy, F., Wyner, A., Paschke, A. (eds.) RuleML 2013. LNCS, vol. 8035, pp. 99–113. Springer, Heidelberg (2013). https://doi.org/10.1007/978-3-642-39617-5_12

15. Governatori, G., Olivieri, F., Scannapieco, S., Rotolo, A., Cristani, M.: The rationale behind the concept of goal. TPLP **16**(3), 296–324 (2016)

16. Governatori, G., Padmanabhan, V., Rotolo, A., Sattar, A.: A defeasible logic for modelling policy-based intentions and motivational attitudes. Log. J. IGPL **17**(3), 227–265 (2009)

17. Governatori, G., Rotolo, A.: A conceptually rich model of business process compliance. In: Link, S., Ghose, A. (eds.) APCCM. CRPIT, vol. 110, pp. 3–12. Australian Computer Society (2010)

18. Governatori, G., Rotolo, A.: Norm compliance in business process modeling. In: Dean, M., Hall, J., Rotolo, A., Tabet, S. (eds.) RuleML 2010. LNCS, vol. 6403, pp. 194–209. Springer, Heidelberg (2010). https://doi.org/10.1007/978-3-642-16289-3_17

19. Governatori, G., Sadiq, S.: The journey to business process compliance. In: Handbook of Research on BPM, pp. 426–454 (2008)

20. Hagerty, J., Hackbush, J., Gaughan, D., Jacobson, S.: The governance, risk management, and compliance spending report, 2008–2009: inside the $32B GRC market. AMR Research (2008)

21. Heinrich, B., Schön, D.: Automated planning of process models: the construction of simple merges. In: 24th European Conference on Information Systems (ECIS) (2016)

22. Kakas, A.C., Mancarella, P., Sadri, F., Stathis, K., Toni, F.: The KGP model of agency. In: ECAI, pp. 33–37. IOS Press (2004)

23. Marrella, A., Mecella, M.: Continuous planning for solving business process adaptivity. In: Halpin, T., Nurcan, S., Krogstie, J., Soffer, P., Proper, E., Schmidt, R., Bider, I. (eds.) BPMDS/EMMSAD -2011. LNBIP, vol. 81, pp. 118–132. Springer, Heidelberg (2011). https://doi.org/10.1007/978-3-642-21759-3_9

24. Milner, R., Parrow, J., Walker, D.: A calculus of mobile processes, i. Inf. Comput. **100**(1), 1–40 (1992)

25. Morgan, T.: Business Rules And Information Systems: Aligning IT With Business Goals. Addison-Wesley Professional, Reading (2002)

26. Murata, T.: Petri nets: properties, analysis and applications. Proc. IEEE **77**(4), 541–580 (1989)

27. Nute, D.: Defeasible logic. In: Handbook of Logic in Artificial Intelligence and Logic Programming, vol. 3. Oxford University Press (1987)

28. Olivieri, F., Cristani, M., Governatori, G.: Compliant business processes with exclusive choices from agent specification. In: Chen, Q., Torroni, P., Villata, S., Hsu, J., Omicini, A. (eds.) PRIMA 2015. LNCS (LNAI), vol. 9387, pp. 603–612. Springer, Cham (2015). https://doi.org/10.1007/978-3-319-25524-8_43

29. Olivieri, F., Governatori, G., Scannapieco, S., Cristani, M.: Compliant business process design by declarative specifications. In: Boella, G., Elkind, E., Savarimuthu, B.T.R., Dignum, F., Purvis, M.K. (eds.) PRIMA 2013. LNCS (LNAI), vol. 8291, pp. 213–228. Springer, Heidelberg (2013). https://doi.org/10.1007/978-3-642-44927-7_15

30. Pesic, M., Schonenberg, H., Van der Aalst, W.M.: Declare: full support for loosely-structured processes. In: 11th IEEE International Enterprise Distributed Object Computing Conference, EDOC 2007, pp. 287–300. IEEE Computer Society (2007)

31. Petri, C.A.: Communication with automata, Ph.D. thesis. Universität Hamburg (1966)

32. Prescher, J., Di Ciccio, C., Mendling, J.: From declarative processes to imperative models. SIMPDA **14**, 162–173 (2014)

33. Russell, N.C., van der Aalst, W.M.P., ter Hofstede, A.H.M.: Designing a workflow system using coloured petri nets. In: Jensen, K., Billington, J., Koutny, M. (eds.) Transactions on Petri Nets and Other Models of Concurrency III. LNCS, vol. 5800, pp. 1–24. Springer, Heidelberg (2009). https://doi.org/10.1007/978-3-642-04856-2_1

34. Sadiq, S., Governatori, G.: Managing regulatory compliance in business processes. In: vom Brocke, J., Rosemann, M. (eds.) Handbook on Business Process Management 2. IHIS, pp. 265–288. Springer, Heidelberg (2015). https://doi.org/10.1007/978-3-642-45103-4_11

35. Sardiña, S., Padgham, L.: A BDI agent programming language with failure handling, declarative goals, and planning. Auton. Agent. Multi-Agent Syst. **23**(1), 18–70 (2011)

36. van Beest, N.R.T.P., Kaldeli, E., Bulanov, P., Wortmann, J.C., Lazovik, A.: Automated runtime repair of business processes. Inf. Syst. **39**, 45–79 (2014)

37. van der Aalst, W.M.P.: The application of petri nets to workflow management. J. Circuits Syst. Comput. **8**(1), 21–66 (1998)

38. van der Aalst, W.M.P.: Formalization and verification of event-driven process chains. Inf. Softw. Technol. **41**(10), 639–650 (1999)

39. van der Aalst, W.M.P., Pesic, M.: Decserflow: towards a truly declarative service flow language. In: Leymann, F., Reisig, W., Thatte, S.R., van der Aalst, W.M.P. (eds.) The Role of Business Processes in Service Oriented Architectures, Dagstuhl Seminar Proceedings, vol. 06291. Schloss Dagstuhl, Germany (2006)
40. Westergaard, M., Maggi, F.M.: Declare: a tool suite for declarative workflow modeling and enactment. BPM (Demos) **820**, 1–5 (2011)

Quality

Auction-Based Models for Composite Service Selection: A Design Framework

Mahboobeh Moghaddam[1(✉)] 🆔 and Joseph G. Davis[2]

[1] School of Economics, The University of Queensland, St Lucia, QLD 4072, Australia
m.moghaddam@uq.edu.au
[2] School of Information Technologies, The University of Sydney,
Camperdown, NSW 2006, Australia
joseph.davis@sydney.edu.au

Abstract. Composite service selection refers to the process of selecting an optimal set of web services out of a pool of available candidates based on their quality of service and price. The goal is to logically compose these atomic web services and create value-added composite services which in turn can be used to develop service-based systems. Existing approaches to composite service selection are mostly based on optimization and negotiation techniques. In this paper, we study an emerging trend of composite service selection approaches based on auction models. These techniques benefit from the dynamic pricing of auction models compared to a fixed pricing approach and have the potential to incorporate the dependencies that exist between services constituting a composition. We propose a design framework that introduces two components which need to be addressed when developing an auction-based model for composite service selection: the elements in an auction-based model and a set of design decisions associated with those elements.

Keywords: Composite service selection · QoS-based service selection
Web services · Combinatorial auctions

1 Introduction

Composite web service selection is the process of selecting an "optimal" set of web services that can collectively achieve a specific, complex functionality when logically composed from a pool of available services. Optimality is defined based on the composite service requester's requirements for the composite service QoS profile; i.e. its set of quality attributes. Considering the growing number of available online web services that can perform similar functionalities at different levels of quality and price, composite service selection has been recognized as an important research problem in the context of developing service-based systems (SBS) [1, 2].

The literature on composite service selection can be characterized as a continuum with the following two extremes based on the assumption about the dynamicity of the web service's QoS profile: (1) being pre-determined and not-customizable, or (2) being flexible and negotiable. Corresponding to each of the two extremes are the two important

© Springer International Publishing AG, part of Springer Nature 2018
A. Beheshti et al. (Eds.): ASSRI 2015/2017, LNBIP 234, pp. 101–115, 2018.
https://doi.org/10.1007/978-3-319-76587-7_7

trends in the service selection literature: *Optimization-based approaches* which typically assume a predetermined QoS profiles and, *Negotiation-based approaches* which permit QoS profiles to be flexible and negotiable. However, regardless of the offered QoS profiles being pre-determined or negotiable, the process of deciding the best set of values for the quality and price of web services is far from trivial for either approach.

New proposals based on auction models have recently emerged in order to address this issue. Auction-based approaches draw on theories and models adopted from economics and auction theory. Application of auction models facilitates the price determination for service providers and composite service requesters by providing feedback to the auction participants. Moreover, a specific type of auction model known as combinatorial auction allows the service providers and requesters to express their preferences for combinations of services. This is particularly important for composite service selection as the web services that constitute a composite service typically exhibit dependencies on each other based on a number of factors. These dependencies create complementarity effects among these services, which in turn, affect the service providers' and requesters' preferences for offering *bundles* of services.

In this paper, we present a comprehensive review of the emerging auction-based approaches to composite service selection. In Sect. 2, we identify and elaborate on two important issues in composite service selection problem which have not received adequate attention from the research community. In Sect. 3, we discuss how auction models have the potential to successfully address these issues. In Sect. 4, we propose a design framework for developing auction-based models for composite service selection. The framework has two components that need to be addressed when designing an auction-based model: (1) the elements of an auction-based model and (2) a set of design decisions associated to the elements of model. Section 5 concludes the paper.

2 Challenges in Composite Service Selection

The composite service selection problem is known to offer several challenges. An overview of some of the important challenges and how they have been addressed in the current literature is presented in [3]. However, there are additional issues that need to be considered which can impact the practicality of the proposed approaches to service selection. It is our contention that systematically addressing these issues will not only lead to more realistic assumptions in formulating the service selection problem but it will also enhance their potential application in real world settings.

2.1 Price Determination for Web Services

In the extant literature, there are two alternative assumptions about the pricing models of web services. The first, which is also the more dominant, is that web services are offered at a fixed, predetermined price. The second is that the price of each web service is flexible and is typically determined through a negotiation process between the service requester and service providers. The first assumption is the basis of the optimization-based composite service selection approaches and the second one is the basis for the negotiation-based approaches.

In the first model, the price is fixed for all consumers and, in the best-case scenario, we can imagine that when providers realize the need to change the price of their offers, they have to determine a new price and update the web service specification accordingly. This is a pricing strategy known as posted-price or fixed pricing [4]. This means that the complexity of determining the price of a web service is completely left to the service providers.

Such a pricing strategy can cause serious difficulties for web service providers and requesters. From the pricing theory perspective, web services are considered to be products with low specificity, meaning that it is possible to sell them over and over with a very low marginal cost. This is due to the open, Internet-oriented and standards-based interfaces of web services. As a result, service providers face the problem of pricing their web services based on the supply and demand from the requesters and providers' sides, rather than the cost of production.

However, such information about supply and demand is neither readily available, nor easy to obtain. There is constant fluctuation in the supply and demand of web services offered over the Internet due to its open and changing nature. This means that the service providers need to constantly monitor the market to be able to set the prices at the most profitable level. Clearly, such a continuous monitoring of the market can be costly and time consuming. Considering the nature of web services in typically offering limited functionality at a relatively low price, such a pricing strategy that requires continuous monitoring of the market is unlikely to be profitable for service providers.

In the second pricing model, the price is completely flexible and determined through (automated) negotiation process between the service providers' and requester's software agents. This pricing model still has not found practical applications due to the complexity associated with the automated negotiation process. The more recent proposals with the negotiation-based pricing model have tried to reduce the complexity by creating a simplified model of the negotiation process by imposing restrictive assumptions on the strategies, tactics and utility functions of the negotiators. As a result, it is unlikely that these approaches will find practical applications in the web services domain in near future. Furthermore, the complexity underlying this model makes it very hard for the service selection approaches to find globally optimum solutions.

2.2 Dependencies Between Constituent Web Services of a Composite Service

The dominant assumption in the existing service selection literature is that web services are offered as independent entities. Even if a provider offers more than one service, the offers are assumed to be independent of each other. In other words, providers cannot offer combinations or bundles of web services. We argue that this assumption does not exploit the dependencies that exist between the individual web services participating in a composition.

Atomic web services that constitute the composite service are dependent on each other based on factors such as:

1. Execution time dependency: Participant services in a composition need to be executed in a specific sequence to achieve the high-level goal of the composite service.
2. Data dependency: This dependency exists when (part of) the output of one service is consumed as (part of) the input of another service [5]. This dependency is also known as input/output dependency [6] or message dependency [7].
3. Dependencies driven by different types of constraints: such as technical constraints [8], technological constraints [9], business constraints [9], domain related dependencies [10], and user constraints [6].

The identification, automatic discovery, and modelling of the inter-service dependencies have been important research problems for the composite web service community due to their applications in areas such as: (a) dynamic selection of a web service for a process, mostly considering the message dependency among partner services [9, 11], (b) monitoring the composite service for failure diagnosis and recovery [12], and (c) SLA management including the creation, negotiation and handling of the SLA violations [13].

While these applications mostly incorporate the point of view of composite service requesters (or end-users) and their satisfaction from the composite service execution, the inter-service dependencies can also affect the providers' preferences about offering web services. These dependencies can lead to complementarity effects among web services which create strong motivation for service providers to offer their services in bundles. For example, a provider who can offer a set of sequential services in the composition might be able to offer a discount if the service requester buys these services as a bundle. Bundling can help the service provider internalize some of the costs related to interface compatibility required for data exchange between the offered web services, which leads to the possibility of cost reduction in service provisioning. Bundling may also allow service providers to improve the quality of bundled services with competitive prices [1]. For instance, when bundled services are executed on the same machine, the provider can guarantee a lower execution time for the set of offered services. The competitive price offers for bundles, in turn, can improve the provider's competitive power in the web services market. Increasing the consumer loyalty is another possible advantage of bundling for the providers [14].

3   Auction-Based Approaches: Addressing Pricing and Bundling

3.1   Dynamic Pricing: Reducing the Complexity of Price Determination

Pricing has been a difficult business problem especially when it comes to pricing an item which does not have a standard value. More formally, the price determination problem is to price a finished product or service so as to maximize the total expected revenue over the finite time horizon [15]. Setting the right price for a product or service goes beyond the estimation of the cost and a minimum profit: rather, it is governed by a complex set of variables which, among others, include supply and demand, competitor pricing and the product or service lifecycle.

Pricing can be divided into two categories: static (fixed) and dynamic. In a fixed pricing approach, the prices are fixed by the sellers and might be changed in long term based on market fluctuations [16, p. 30]. For many products and services, it is costly for producers to frequently adjust the prices based on the fluctuations due to their high frequency. In dynamic pricing, the price of a good or service is determined by the market. There are four major configurations of dynamic pricing, depending on the number of buyers and sellers involved (Fig. 1).

Buyers	Many	(Direct) Auction	Exchange
	One	Haggle (Negotiation)	Reverse Auction
		One	Many
		Sellers	

Fig. 1. Categorization of dynamic pricing, adopted from Stein et al. [17]

In the context of composite service selection, negotiation has been employed by some researchers to solve the composite service selection problem. The idea of nego-tiation-based service selection approaches is to have automated agents performing negotiation on behalf of a service requester and the service providers in order to reach an agreement on the price and quality of the offered services. However, to address the inherent complexity of the negotiation process, these approaches need to: (1) rely on simplifying assumptions and straightforward techniques to develop automated negotia-tors, and (2) address the composite service selection problem at a local level for a single web service, rather than for a composite service. The fact that only simplified models have been actualized means that the application of realistic automated negotiation tech-niques for the web service selection problem appears to be unfeasible, at least for the near future.

Auctions are known to be the most widely used mechanism for dynamic pricing [18]. They have been proven to be a success in achieving dynamic pricing and also in solving complex problems with the help of well-established theories from economics and mech-anism design. As a result, auction-based approaches to service selection have emerged as a response to the price determination issue for single and composite services.

3.2 Combinatorial Auctions: Addressing the Dependencies

In traditional auctions, as we know them, one item is auctioned at a time. However, in many auctions, bidders care about a combination of items that they want to win. Imagine a buyer who wants to purchase an airline ticket to a destination and also hire a car at the destination airport through an online auction site that sells different services to travelers. In the traditional way of auctioning, she must attend two separate auctions for the two items. However, if she wins only in the auction for the car rental, she will end up with a car which is of no value to her. Such a bidder strongly prefers an auction model that allows her to bid for the two items together as a bundle. In other words, the satisfaction of such a bidder is determined by the simultaneous allocation of the items.

In combinatorial auctions, multiple distinct items are simultaneously auctioned and the bidders can bid for combination of items, or *bundles*. Bundling is particularly important when bidders have preferences not just for specific items but for bundles due to the complementarity or substitutability effects that exist among the items [19].

Two items are said to be substitutes (have substitutability effect) if their combined value is less than the sum of their individual values [20, p. 362]. An example of items being substitutes is two tickets to two movies which are shown at the same time. Complementarity is the opposite effect of substitutability: two items are said to be complementary if their joint value exceeds the sum of their individual values [20, p. 362]. As an example, consider a left shoe and a right shoe.

Bundling of complementary or substitute items allows the bidders to more fully express their preferences which often leads to greater economic efficiency (allocating items to those who value them most) [19] and greater auction revenue [21, p. 8].

Combinatorial auctions have been proposed and/or applied for practical applications in various industries. Examples include: allocating airport arrival and departure slots to competing airlines [22]; supply chain management (industrial procurement) [23]; procurement of school meals [24]; and resource allocation in the cloud [25].

Combinatorial auctions can be either direct or procurement auctions. In the direct combinatorial auction, there are multiple items or services for sale. While in the combinatorial procurement auction, there is a buyer who is interested in a combination of products or services and the sellers bid to provision these products or services. In practice, combinatorial procurement auctions have been successfully applied by online platforms for industrial procurement. Examples of sourcing companies who have implemented combinatorial procurement auctions for strategic sourcing and supply chain include Logistics.com[1], CombineNet now part of SciQuest[2], and TradeExtensions[3].

4   Design Framework for Developing Auction-Based Models

The design of an auction-based mechanism for the composite service selection problem requires answering the following two questions (Fig. 2):

1. What does an auction-based approach mean? What are the elements that build up an auction model?
2. There are already a variety of auction models, standard and arbitrary, that have been applied in other domains such as transportation, communication networks, resource scheduling. How an auction-based mechanism in composite service selection is different to other existing auction-based mechanisms?

---

[1] <http://www.logistics.com/>.
[2] <http://www.sciquest.com/>.
[3] <http://www.tradeextensions.com/>.

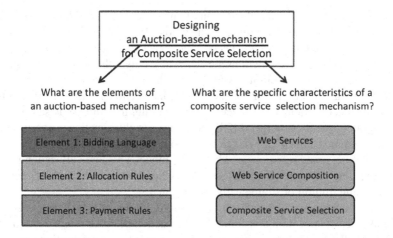

Fig. 2. Designing an auction-based mechanism for composite service selection

To answer the first question, we studied a variety of auction models designed for different domains, in addition to the auction theory literature, to identify the auction design elements. The second question needs to be answered based on the specific characteristics and technologies associated with web services and the current approaches for the web service composition (WSC) and the composite service selection problems. These specific characteristics differentiate an auction model for composite service selection from other existing models. These characteristics lead to a set of design decisions that need to be addressed when designing the elements of the auction-based model.

4.1 Auction Design Elements

Any auction designer needs to make decisions regarding three aspects of an auction, which we have called auction design elements. Many researchers, such as Wurman et al. [26] and Bichler et al. [27], have recognized these aspects, although under different names. These elements are:

1. *The auction protocol (the bidding language)*

The auction protocol determines the structure of the messages sent from the bidders to the auctioneer (the bid), the structure of the information feedback sent from the auctioneer to the bidders, and the sequence of the message exchange between the auction's participants.

2. *Allocation rules (the winner determination problem)*

The set of allocation rules, more famously known as the winner determination problem (WDP), determines which bidders have won and how the items are allocated to them. The auction designer needs to consider two main components here: the auction objective and the set of allocation constraints.

In general, in auction theory, the design of an auction aims to achieve either of the two objectives: efficiency or revenue maximization [28]. These two objectives are not mutually exclusive, yet, it is not always possible to achieve them simultaneously.

However, these objective functions are achievable only if the auction is *truthful* (aka *incentive compatible*). An auction is said to be truthful if, for each participant, truthful reporting of their valuations for the item(s) under auction maximizes their utility, regardless of other participants' choices. In this setting, truthfulness is said to be the dominant strategy for all participants [29]. Designing a truthful auction is a very complex process and requires a deep knowledge of economics, mechanism design and auction theory. Therefore, many researchers, who aim to model a resource allocation problem as an auction, design the auction model's elements based on the received bids, regardless of the bids being truthful or strategically manipulated.

The second component of the allocation rule is the set of allocation constraints. There are several types of allocation constraint that the auction designer might need to add to the WDP formulation. One well-known constraint concerns the reservation price of the seller (direct auction) or budget constraint of a buyer (reverse auction). There are other allocation constraints which are important in reverse auctions. One such constraint is in relation to the quality of the items to be procured. The quality constraint might be demanded at the level of "a single item" or at the level of "a set of items". For example, the auctioneer might be interested in the delivery time of all items under auction collectively, and not in the individual items' delivery time.

3. *Payment rules (the pricing model/scheme or the incentive implications)*

In the familiar form of auctions, the winners usually have to pay their bid as the price to obtain the item. However, for many auctions, that is not the case. In auction design, the pricing scheme is a strong measure employed by designers to install their desirable properties in the auction. Through the payment rules, they install the appropriate incentives for the mechanism's participants to guide their behavior in a certain way that will lead to the mechanism's desirable properties. The design of this component is very complex, and is based on principles of mechanism design.

4.2   The Design Decisions

In this section, we discuss the design decisions that need to be addressed when designing the elements of an auction model for composite service selection.

1. *Decision regarding the auction model*

Direct or reverse auction: Regarding the auction model, one of the first considerations is to decide whether the auction for composite service selection is a direct auction or a reverse auction. In a direct auction, the buyers bid to buy an item and the seller is the bid-taker who decides the winners. As an example, consider an auction to sell art works. In a reverse auction, the buyers bid to sell their items and the seller decides whom should they procure the items from. Example includes an auction to sell spectrum rights to telecommunication firms set up by governments [30].

In composite service selection, the service requester requires a set of different services to achieve a specific goal and it is very likely that these services need to be procured from different providers. Therefore, if the auction is designed as a direct auction, with service providers as bid-takers and service requesters as bidders, the service requesters may need to attend different auctions to procure all their required web services and, more importantly, win in all these auctions to be able to create the composition. If they win in all the auctions except for one, the composite service cannot be realized and the service requester has to withdraw from all other auctions. In most auction settings, withdrawing from an auction after winning it is not allowed or incurs a withdrawing cost. As a conclusion, if the designer decides to have a direct auction for composite service selection, they should consider additional mechanisms to guarantee the simultaneous allocation of all the services in the composition.

In a design based on procurement models, service requester is the bid-taker (auctioneer) and the service providers bid to offer their services. The auction is considered successful only if there are web services available for all the tasks of the composite service, while satisfying the requesters' preferences and constraints. Consequently, the requester can commit to the result of a successful auction without concern for unwanted costs.

Free disposal: To create the composite service, the service requester needs all the tasks to be successfully auctioned and find service providers to provision them. In auction theory, this is referred to as an auction *without free disposal*: the auctioneer has to sell (procure) all the items and the bidders cannot accept more than what they had bid for [31]. Lack of free disposal makes it difficult to apply approximation methods for reducing the complexity of the problem.

Single item or combinatorial: As already discussed, an important issue in composite service selection is the need to consider the dependencies between services constituent a composition. The combinatorial auction model enables providers to more fully express their preferences by offering the possibility of bidding for a combination of services.

However, combinatorial auctions have limitations in terms of the computational cost of determining the winners. Composite service selection problem is proven to be NP-complete [32]. This means that it is not possible to guarantee to find an optimal solution within polynomial time. Combinatorial auctions are also proven to be NP-complete [33]. This indicates that the complexity of a composite service selection approach based on combinatorial auctions is at least as hard as any of these two problems. Therefore, an approach that aims to find optimal solution for composite service selection where bundling is allowed, may not be scalable.

One possibility to reduce the complexity of the problem is to aim for finding near optimal solutions using heuristic approaches, rather than optimal solutions. Many heuristics have already been proposed to solve composite service selection [32, 34, 35] or for combinatorial auctions [33]. However, it is not possible to apply any of these heuristics directly to a composite service selection problem based on combinatorial auctions. The heuristics in composite service selection do not support bundling of services and the heuristics of combinatorial auctions assume free disposal [31]. As discussed before, free disposal does not exist in composite service selection. Therefore, there is a need to new heuristic approaches considering the properties of both composite service selection and combinatorial auction problems.

One-shot or iterative: A one-shot auction consists of a single round of bidding. While in an iterative auction, there are multiple rounds of bidding and, at the end of each round, there is a flow of information from the auctioneer to the bidders about the current status of the auction, for example, the amount of the current winning bid [36]. This information helps the bidders to adjust their bids for the next round. The outcome of the auction will be determined at the end of the last round.

Having an iterative auction for composite service selection implies that the providers have to submit their bids, wait for the result of the first round of the auction, revise their bids based on the information feedback from the first round and re-submit their bids. They need to continue to do so until the final round of the auction. Therefore, a one-shot auction would be much faster than an iterative auction. However, the bidders in iterative auctions benefit from the information feedback to improve their bids and increase their chance of winning the auction. At the same time, designing of iterative auctions is more complex because of the extra decisions required to be made about the type and the time of the information revealed to the bidders that can have many strategic implications.

Therefore, the decision regarding the auction model being one-shot or iterative needs to be made based on the type of the required composite services and the service requesters and providers preferences regarding the time to determine the set of services to form the composition [37].

For example, in service-based mobile applications, where services are required to response close to real time, a one-shot auction can lead to a less time-consuming service selection process. However, in scientific workflow applications where services are used to process, transform and carry out the data in a distributed environment, service requesters may not be much concerned about a real time approach to find the set of services they require.

Moreover, in our context, the items under auction are web services which mostly offer small, limited, functionality at a relatively low price. Therefore, if the composite service under auction is simple, with not many services involved, such as in the mobile application scenario, it is likely that service providers would prefer to attend more auctions for different composite services rather than spending more time in a multi-round auction for the same composite service. However, in the context of scientific workflow applications, the required composite services can be very complex, with hundreds of services, resulting in more expensive compositions [37]. This can encourage service providers to attend iterative auctions and improve their offers to win the auction.

Single-dimensional or multi-dimensional: In conventional auctions, the bidders only express the price of what they are willing to buy or sell. This is known as a single-dimensional auction where the only important aspect of a bid is the price. In a multi-dimensional auction, other aspects of the item are also part of the bid, such as the quality.

An important aspect of web services is the non-functional properties or quality of service attributes (QoS). Two providers that offer the same service functionality may have different values for the QoS attributes of their services. These attributes model the competitive advantage that providers may have over each other [38]. Therefore, it is important for the auction designer to consider the quality attribute when receiving the bids and determining the winners of the auction.

2. *Decisions regarding the bidding language*

Based on the decisions regarding the auction model, the design of the bidding language needs to support the auction model. For example, if the auction model is combinatorial, the bidding language must support multi-item bidding. If the auction is multi-dimensional, the bidding language needs to support more than the traditional price-only bids. In addition to the price, bids need to specify the values offered for other quality attributes such as response time, availability and reputation. Moreover, the auction designer needs to decide on other aspects such as any restrictions on the number of winning bids of a provider.

3. *Decisions regarding the allocation rules*

Objective function: If the auction is single dimensional, the objective function will be based on price only. However, if the auction is multi-attribute, then the allocation rule can be formulated either based on price or all the attributes. The first approach leads to a priced-based formulation, such [39, 40], and the second approach results in a utility-based formulation, such as [1, 41].

In the price-based approach, the objective function is formulated only based on the price; either trying to minimize the cost for service requester or maximize the willingness-to-pay of requesters. In the utility-based approach, the aim of the auction is to maximize the utility of the composite service requester from the execution of the composite service based on all the quality of service attributes and price of the composite service. In this approach, the objective function is similar to the ILP-based optimization-based approaches: maximizing the sum of the utilities of the end-to-end quality attributes (including the price) while taking into account the importance of each quality attribute for the requester through assigning a weight to the attributes.

The main challenge for the utility-based formulation is elicitation of the weights for different quality attributes from the service requester [3]. A utility maximizing objective function usually forces the researchers to include unrealistic assumptions on the model; such as the weights being known for the requesters and the quality attributes not being correlated.

The price-based formulation excludes the need to specify the weights for quality attributes, and at the same time, provides enough support for service requester to specify their end-to-end quality requirements through adding extra constraints to the allocation rule. Such a formulation assumes that service requesters are mainly concerned about quality attributes meeting some criteria. In other words, they generally have a clear understanding of what level of quality is acceptable for them, for example, what should be the maximum response time of the composite service or its minimum availability. This assumption is less restrictive than the assumption of having a clear and perfect utility function that specifies the weight of different quality attributes toward each other, especially when more than two or three quality attributes are involved.

Allocation constraints: Service requesters may need to define different constraints over the combination or configuration of the winning bids. One essential constraint is to define the success of the auction being limited to the situation when the set of winning bids can cover the provisioning of all the required services for composition. Without any of the required services, the auction should not be declared successful.

Other constraints can be defined based on preferences and constraints of service requesters or providers; such as constraints over the end-to-end quality of the composite service, budget, interface compatibility among services, or configuration of winning service providers.

4. *Decisions regarding the payment rule*

Auction designers use the pricing scheme to install properties such as incentive compatibility in the mechanism. The well-known incentive compatible mechanism for multiple items is called the Vickrey Clark Grove (VCG) mechanism [19]. The payment rule in a VCG mechanism is so that any winner's payment is independent from their own valuations for the items (their bids). Therefore, bidders have no incentive for strategically manipulating their declared valuations, as the manipulation will not increase their gained utility [42, p. 219].

However, the VCG mechanism has serious drawbacks that make its application rather impractical, including making bidding very complex for bidders, needs the bidders to reveal many information about their valuations, possibility of very low revenue outcome, highly susceptible to collusion, and most importantly, not being budget-balanced which means that the mechanism need to be subsidized from outside [43, 44]. Therefore, although in theory it is possible to adopt the VCG payment to achieve an incentive-compatible mechanism, it does not suit practical applications.

Therefore, a popular alternative is to follow the first price auction model for the payment where the winning bidders will pay or be paid (depending on the auction being direct or reverse) the amount that they have bid for, and zero otherwise.

An auction based on such pricing rule may or may not be truthful. Therefore, the price-based formulation of the objective function can minimize the cost for service requester (reverse auction) or maximize the willingness-to-pay of requesters (in a direct auction), which does not necessarily maximize the profit of providers nor is economically efficient. Similarly, the utility maximizing formulation requires a pricing function that makes the bidder truthful in all aspects of their bids, and not just the price. Therefore, a payment rule based on the pay-your-bid model does not lead to profit maximizing nor economically efficient auctions in this formulation either.

5   Conclusion

In this paper, we have addressed two important issues that have not received sufficient research attention: the complexity of price determination for web services and the dependencies between web services forming a composite service. Dealing with these issues has the potential to improve the practicality of service selection approaches by rendering the models of web service offers and composite services to be more realistic.

We also discussed auction models with dynamic pricing and how they can facilitate the price determination for single and composite services. Moreover, a specific type of auction, known as combinatorial auctions, was introduced, that enables service providers and requesters to explore the dependencies between web services of a composition and utilize the dependencies to improve their offers.

Finally, we proposed a design framework that has two components which need to be considered when developing an auction-based model for composite service selection: (1) the elements of an auction-based model and (2) the design decisions that need to be discussed with regard to the specific characteristics of web services and the service providers' and requesters' preferences. This framework can improve the design and development of new auction-based approaches and provide a basis for comparing different auction-based approaches to composite service selection.

References

1. He, Q., Yan, J., Jin, H., Yang, Y.: Quality-aware service selection for service-based systems based on iterative multi-attribute combinatorial auction. IEEE Trans. Softw. Eng. **40**(2), 192–215 (2014)
2. Calinescu, R., Grunske, L., Kwiatkowska, M., Mirandola, R., Tamburrelli, G.: Dynamic QoS management and optimization in service-based systems. IEEE Trans. Softw. Eng. **37**(3), 387–409 (2011)
3. Moghaddam, M., Davis, J.: Service selection in web service composition: a comparative review of existing approaches. In: Bouguettaya, A., Sheng, Q.Z., Daniel, F. (eds.) Web Services Foundations, vol. 1, pp. 321–346. Springer, New York (2014). https://doi.org/10.1007/978-1-4614-7518-7_13
4. Wang, R.: Auctions versus posted-price selling. Am. Econ. Rev. **83**(4), 838–851 (1993)
5. Milanovic, N., Malek, M.: Current solutions for web service composition. IEEE Internet Comput. **8**(6), 51–59 (2004)
6. Omer, A.M., Schill, A.: Web service composition using input/output dependency matrix. In: Proceedings of the 3rd workshop on Agent-Oriented Software Engineering Challenges for Ubiquitous and Pervasive Computing, pp. 21–26 (2009)
7. Yang, J., Papazoglou, M.P.: Web component: a substrate for web service reuse and composition. In: Pidduck, A.B., Ozsu, M.T., Mylopoulos, J., Woo, C.C. (eds.) CAiSE 2002. LNCS, vol. 2348, pp. 21–36. Springer, Heidelberg (2002). https://doi.org/10.1007/3-540-47961-9_5
8. Ai, L., Tang, M.: QoS-based web service composition accommodating inter-service dependencies using minimal-conflict hill-climbing repair genetic algorithm. In: IEEE Fourth International Conference on eScience (eScience 2008), pp. 119–126 (2008)
9. Aggarwal, R., Kunal, V., Miller, J., Milnor, W.: Constraint driven web service composition in METEOR-S. In: Proceedings 2004 IEEE International Conference on Services Computing, (SCC 2004), pp. 23–30 (2004)
10. Verma, K., Akkiraju, R., Goodwin, R., Doshi, P., Lee, J.: On accommodating inter service dependencies in web process flow composition. In: AAAI Spring Symposium (on Semantic Web Services), pp. 37–43 (2004)
11. Verma, K., Gomadam, K., Sheth, A., Miller, J., Wu, Z.: The METEOR-S Approach for Configuring and Executing Dynamic Web Processes. Technical Report (TR6-24-05) (2005)

12. Wassermann, B., Emmerich, W.: Monere: monitoring of service compositions for failure diagnosis. In: Kappel, G., Maamar, Z., Motahari-Nezhad, Hamid R. (eds.) ICSOC 2011. LNCS, vol. 7084, pp. 344–358. Springer, Heidelberg (2011). https://doi.org/10.1007/978-3-642-25535-9_23

13. Winkler, M., Springer, T., Schill, A.: Automating composite SLA management tasks by exploiting service dependency information. In: Proceedings of the 2010 Eighth IEEE European Conference on Web Services, pp. 59–66 (2010)

14. Herrmann, A., Huber, F., Coulter, R.H.: Product and service bundling decisions and their effects on purchase intention. Pricing Strategy Pract. **5**(3), 99–107 (1997)

15. Gallego, G., van Ryzin, G.: A multiproduct dynamic pricing problem and its applications to network yield management. Oper. Res. **45**(1), 24–41 (1997)

16. Schwind, M.: Dynamic Pricing and Automated Resource Allocation for Complex Information Services. Springer, Heidelberg (2007)

17. Stein, A., Hawking, P., Wyld, D.C.: The 20% solution?: a case study on the efficacy of reverse auctions. Manage. Res. News **26**(5), 1–20 (2003)

18. Bichler, M.: Electronic commerce and electronic marketplaces. In: The Future of eMarkets: Multi-Dimensional Market Mechanisms. Cambridge University Press (2001)

19. de Vries, S., Vohra, R.V.: Combinatorial auctions: a survey. INFORMS J. Comput. **15**(3), 284 (2003)

20. Shoham, Y., Leyton-Brown, K.: Multiagent Systems: Algorithmic, Game-Theoretic, and Logical Foundations, vol. 54, no. 1–4. Cambridge University Press, New York (2009)

21. Cramton, P.C., Shoham, Y., Steinberg, R.: Combinatorial Auctions. MIT Press, Cambridge (2006)

22. Rassenti, S.J., Smith, V.L., Bulfin, R.L.: A combinatorial auction mechanism for airport time slot allocation. Bell J. Econ. **13**(2), 402–417 (1982)

23. Chen, J., Huang, H., Kauffman, R.J.: A public procurement combinatorial auction mechanism with quality assignment. Decis. Support Syst. **51**(3), 480–492 (2011)

24. Olivares, M., Weintraub, G.Y., Epstein, R., Yung, D.: Combinatorial auctions for procurement: an empirical study of the chilean school meals auction. Manage. Sci. **58**(8), 1458–1481 (2012)

25. Zaman, S., Grosu, D.: Combinatorial auction-based allocation of virtual machine instances in clouds. J. Parallel Distrib. Comput. **73**(4), 495–508 (2013)

26. Wurman, P.R., Walsh, W.E., Wellman, M.P.: Flexible double auctions for electronic commerce: theory and implementation. Decis. Support Syst. **24**(1), 17–27 (1998)

27. Bichler, M., Davenport, A., Hohner, G., Kalagnanam, J.: Industrial procurement auctions. In: Cramton, P.C., Shoham, Y., Steinberg, R. (eds.) Combinatorial Auctions, pp. 593–612. MIT Press, Cambridge (2006)

28. Ausubel, L.M.: Auction theory for the new economy. In: Jones, D.C. (ed.) New Economy Handbook, San Diego, pp. 123–162 (2003)

29. Jackson, M.O.: Mechanism theory. In: Derigs, U. (ed.) Optimization and Operations Research. The Encyclopedia of Life Support Systems, Oxford, p. 274 (2003)

30. McMillan, J.: Selling spectrum rights. J. Econ. Perspect. **8**(3), 145–162 (1994)

31. Sandholm, T., Suri, S., Gilpin, A., Levine, D.: Winner determination in combinatorial auction generalizations. In: Proceedings of the First International Joint Conference on Autonomous Agents and Multiagent Systems: Part 1, pp. 69–76 (2002)

32. Yu, T., Zhang, Y., Lin, K.J.: Efficient algorithms for Web services selection with end-to-end QoS constraints. ACM Trans. Web (TWEB) **1**(1), 6:1–6:26 (2007)

33. Sandholm, T.: Algorithm for optimal winner determination in combinatorial auctions. Artif. Intell. **135**(1), 1–54 (2002)

34. Berbner, R., Spahn, M., Repp, N., Heckmann, O., Steinmetz, R.: Heuristics for QoS-aware web service composition. In: International Conference on Web Services (ICWS 2006), pp. 72–82 (2006)

35. Menascé, D.A., Casalicchio, E., Dubey, V.: On optimal service selection in service oriented architectures. Perform. Eval. **67**(8), 659–675 (2010)

36. Parkes, D.: Iterative combinatorial auctions. In: Cramton, P.C., Shoham, Y., Steinberg, R. (eds.) Combinatorial Auctions, pp. 41–77. MIT Press, London (2006)

37. Moghaddam, M.: Combinatorial Auction-based Mechanisms for Composite Web Service Selection. University of Sydney, Sydney (2015). http://hdl.handle.net/2123/13512

38. Medjahed, B., Atif, Y.: Context-based matching for web service composition. Distrib. Parallel Databases **21**(1), 5–37 (2007)

39. Prashanth, B., Narahari, Y.: Efficient algorithms for combinatorial auctions with volume discounts arising in web service composition. In: 2008 IEEE International Conference on Automation Science and Engineering, pp. 995–1000 (2008)

40. Moghaddam, M., Davis, J., Viglas, T.: A combinatorial auction model for composite service selection based on preferences and constraints. In: 10th IEEE International Conference on Services Computing (SCC 2013). IEEE, Santa Clara (2013)

41. Blau, B., Conte, T., van Dinther, C.: A multidimensional procurement auction for trading composite services. Electron. Commer. Res. Appl. **9**(5), 460–472 (2010)

42. Nisan, N., Roughgarden, T., Tardos, E., Vazirani, V.V.: Algorithmic Game Theory. Cambridge University Press, Cambridge (2007)

43. Ausubel, L.M., Milgrom, P.: The lovely but lonely vickrey auction. In: Cramton, P.C., Shoham, Y., Steinberg, R. (eds.) Combinatorial Auctions. MIT Press, London (2006)

44. Rothkopf, M.H.: Thirteen reasons why the vickrey-clarke-groves process is not practical. Oper. Res. **55**(2), 191–197 (2007)

A Game-Theoretic Approach to Quality Improvement in Crowdsourcing Tasks

Mohammad Allahbakhsh[1,3]($\boxtimes$) (iD), Haleh Amintoosi[2,3], and Salil S. Kanhere[3]

[1] University of Zabol, Zabol, Iran
allahbakhsh@uoz.ac.ir
[2] Ferdowsi University of Mashhad, Mashhad, Iran
amintoosi@um.ac.ir
[3] The University of New South Wales, Sydney, Australia
{mallahbakhsh,haleha,salilk}@cse.unsw.edu.au

Abstract. Together with the rise of social media and mobile computing, crowdsourcing increasingly is being relied on as a popular source of information. Crowdsourcing techniques can be employed to solve a wide range of problems, mainly Human Intelligence Tasks (HITs) which are easy to do for human, but difficult or even impossible for computers. However, the quality of crowdsourced information always has been an issue. Several methods have been proposed in order to increase the chance of receiving high quality contributions from the crowd. In this paper, we propose a novel approach to improve the quality of contributions in crowdsourcing tasks. We employ the game theory to motivate people towards providing information of higher quality levels. We also take into account players' quality factors such as reputation score, expertise and the level of agreement between players of the game to ensure that the problem owner receives an outcome of an accepted quality level. Simulation results demonstrate the efficacy of our proposed approach in terms of improving quality of the contributions as well as the chance of successful completion of the games, in comparison with state-of-the-art similar methods.

1 Introduction

User-contributed or crowdsourced information is increasingly becoming common. Together with the rise of social media, it is progressively being relied on as an alternate source of information that supplements, or in some instances even replaces traditional information channels. An illustrative example is the extensive use of Twitter (www.twitter.com) in supporting affected individuals during the 2011 tsunami disaster in Japan for a range of relief functions ranging from safety identification to displaced-persons locating, damage information provision, volunteer organization, fund-raising, and moral support systems [1].

Despite the widespread use of crowdsourcing systems [2] and emergence of very useful applications such as Be My Eyes (bemyeyes.org), Uber (www.uber.com),

© Springer International Publishing AG, part of Springer Nature 2018
A. Beheshti et al. (Eds.): ASSRI 2015/2017, LNBIP 234, pp. 116–130, 2018.
https://doi.org/10.1007/978-3-319-76587-7_8

MiFlight (miflightsapp.com/) and many more similar examples, obtaining high-quality contribution is still an important issue in the success of a crowdsourcing campaign. Although the volume, variety, velocity and veracity of human generated data can raise serious challenges for which several techniques and solutions has been proposed [3,4], the quality of the received contributions is still one of the major concerns of the requesters. Several methods have been proposed to provide the task owner (i.e., the requester) with high quality contributions [5–8].

Gamification (i.e., the application of game design techniques to solve non-game problems) is one of the common techniques in which workers are motivated to participate in online tasks, in the form of playing a game. In the ESP game [9, 10], for instance, online players contribute to image annotation tasks; in this way, the images indexed by Google in 2004 (425,000,000 images could be annotated in just 31 days).

In this paper, assuming that the tasks are defined in the form of multiple-choices, we propose a novel game-theoretic approach to improve quality of received contributions. The proposed approach is inspired by the Nash theory [11], collaborative games [9] and online shepherding [12] ideas. We propose a collaborative game in which two players collaboratively solve a problem. In the proposed game, the maximum benefit is gained only when players agree on one choice. On the other hand, since players are chosen anonymously, they cannot collude on one choice. So, the only possible way for players to maximize their benefit is to behave honestly, hoping that the other player also does the same. Unlike the standard Nash game, our proposed approach encourages players to revise their choices, if the quality of provided contributions does not seem good enough. In summary the contributions of the paper are as follow:

- We have proposed a data model for representation and better understanding of the multi-choice crowdsourcing tasks in the form of online games.
- We have proposed a new game-theoretic technique, inspired from Nash equilibrium and online shepherding ideas, which improves the quality of contributions received from the crowd by providing players with online feedback as well as motivating them to change mind towards the higher qualities using rewards. In a two stage process, we take into account several quality metrics such as reputation score, expertise and the players' agreement level in order to improve the quality of the game outcome, as well as, to increase the successful completion chance of the game.
- We have implemented and evaluated our proposed game and the results show a significant improvement in the quality of tasks, in comparison with other related approaches.

The rest of the paper is organized as follows: In Sect. 2 we introduce the proposed data model and notations. In Sect. 3 our game is proposed. Section 4 represents the experimentation details and evaluation results. We study related work in Sect. 5, and finally, we conclude in Sect. 6.

2   Definitions and Basic Notations

Assume that in a crowdsourcing system, a set of N_R *requesters*, denoted by $R = \{r_i | 1 \leq i \leq N_R\}$, submit their tasks expecting to hire workers to respond to their requests. A set of N_W *workers*, denoted by $W = \{w_i | 2 \leq i \leq N_W\}$ select such tasks and contribute to the submitted problems. Each worker has a set of expertise and a reputation score. We denote the reputation score of the worker w by w_ρ and the set of worker's expertise by w_E. Furthermore, we assume that each worker has a level of confidence, that we denote with the w_κ. Degree of confidence of a worker is the extent to which a worker is confident that she has enough expertise to accomplish the task and her submitted answer is right. Degree of confidence is well-known in academia when reviewers submit their review on a research and the system asks them about their confidence of their judgment. The w_κ is a number in the range of $[0, 1]$. The higher the value of w_κ, the more confident the worker is about her choice.

Tasks are assumed to be simple multi-choice tasks. For complex task, however, the requester may decompose it to simple tasks and then submit them eliciting for contributions [13,14]. As we refer to the Nash game-theoretic approach when solving each simple task, we follow the notation of game theory and call each generated simple task a *game* and denote it by g.

A game g consists of one question along with a set of choices. Let's use $\Upsilon = \{v_l | 2 \leq l \leq L\}$ to represent the set of choices available for a game. Moreover, each game has a specific predefined set of requirements. The game may need specific expertise (e,g,. knowing a specific language in a crowdsourced translation task) to be accomplished. It may also require workers who are reputable enough to provide trustable contributions. These requirements are defined and assigned by the requester upon the task definition. We denote the set of required expertise of a given game g by g_E and the minimum level of accepted reputation score by g_ρ.

3   The Proposed Game

In this section, inspired from the Nash theory, we propose a novel game theoretic approach to solve multi-choice tasks, based on human intelligence and online shepherding. Assume that two players w_1 ad w_2 have chosen the game g to play. The steps of a typical HI game are represented in the Fig. 1 and are described in the followings.

3.1   Contribution Collection

In the first step of the game, the contribution of the players to the given game are collected. In order to collect such contributions, the game is prepared, submitted to the crowdsourcing platform and the players are selected. In the player selection step, two players, say p_1 and p_2, are selected. There are several recruitment scenarios which can be employed. However, to motivate more people to

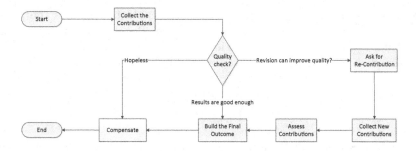

Fig. 1. Steps of a typical HI game.

contribute to the games, and also to increase the chance of faster recruitment, our proposed game follows an open-to-all player selection scenario [6]. It simply means that, the first two players who apply for the game are recruited. It is worth mentioning that, the players are selected anonymously and do not know the identity of each other. Each selected player is given a short time to read the question, see the choices, think, and make their decision. The selected choice is submitted and collected as the contribution of the player. Players also express their level of confidence along with their contributions. We denote the contribution of the player p to the game g with c_p^g and the level of confidence corresponding to this contribution by κ_p^g.

3.2   Quality Check

In this step, the quality of the submitted contribution is assessed. The quality of a contribution depends on two parameters: (i) suitability of the player to participate in the game, and (ii) the level of agreement between the players. In the followings, we describe these parameters in more details.

Player Suitability Check. Quality of the contribution of a player to a game is directly impacted by the suitability of the player to participate [5,6]. When a player takes part in a game, we assign her a suitability score to reflect how suitable she is to participate in such a game. In other words, the suitability score reflects the conformance between the game requirements and the worker's profile. We denote the suitability score of the player p to contribute to the game g by σ_p^g. We employ four parameters in the suitability score computations: *reputation match, expertise match, profile match* and *the level of confidence.*

Table 1. Fuzzy rule base for defining F_p^g according to ρ_p^g and E_p^g

Rule no.	if ρ_p^g	and E_p^g	Then F_p^g
1	Low	Low	VL
2	Low	Med	L
3	Low	High	M
4	Med	Low	L
5	Med	Med	M
6	Med	High	H
7	High	Low	M
8	High	Med	H
9	High	High	VH

Reputation match shows to what extent the reputation score of the player matches the reputation requirement of the game. Recall that each game has a minimum level of accepted reputation score denoted by g_ρ. We denote the reputation match of the player p to the game g by ρ_p^g and calculate it as follows:

$$\rho_p^g = \begin{cases} p_\rho & \text{if } p_\rho \geq g_\rho \\ 0 & \text{otherwise} \end{cases} \tag{1}$$

Equation 1 says that the reputation of a player is taken into account, when calculating her suitability score, only if her reputation score is greater than or equal to the minimum level of reputation score required by the game. Otherwise, the reputation score is deemed to be zero in further calculations.

Expertise match shows to what extent a player has the expertise and skills that are required to be eligible to participate in a game. The expertise match of the player p to the requirements of the game g is denoted by E_p^g and is calculated as follows:

$$E_p^g = \frac{|p_E \cap g_E|}{|g_E|} \tag{2}$$

In Eq. 2, p_E is the set of expertise of the player p, and g_E is the set of required expertise of the game g.

Profile match shows the extent to which the profile of p matches requirements of the g. We denote the profile match of the player p to the requirements of the game g by F_p^g. The F_p^g is computed by combining ρ_p^g and E_p^g via a fuzzy inference engine, i.e.,

$$F_p^g = Fuzzy(\rho_p^g, E_p^g) \tag{3}$$

Fuzzy inference system. We employ fuzzy logic to calculate the profile match (F_p^g) of the player p to the requirements of the game g. Leveraging fuzzy logic allows us to achieve a meaningful balance between ρ_p^g and E_p^g and the profile match. We cover all possible combinations of ρ_p^g and E_p^g and address them by using fuzzy logic in mimicking the human decision-making process. The inputs to the fuzzy inference system are the crisp values of ρ_p^g and E_p^g, and the output is F_p^g. Figure 2(a) represents the membership function of ρ_p^g and E_p^g and Fig. 2(b) depicts the F_p^g membership function. Moreover, the fuzzy rule base for defining F_p^g according to ρ_p^g and E_p^g is depicted in Table 1.

Player's Suitability Score. The suitability score of the player p depends on her profile match (F_p^g) and her level of confidence (κ_p^g). We compute the suitability score of the player p to take part in the game g as follows:

$$\sigma_p^g = F_p^g \times \kappa_p^g \tag{4}$$

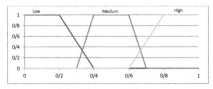
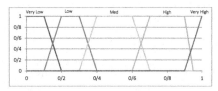

(a) Membership function for ρ_p^g, E_p^g and F_p^g

(b) Membership function for η

Fig. 2. Membership functions of input and output linguistic variables

Players Agreement Check. Mutual agreement between workers is one of the popular methods of quality control in crowdsourcing systems [5,9]. In our proposed approach, the level of agreement between the players depends on the distance between the choices submitted by them. Assume that v_1 is the contribution of the player p_1 and v_2 is the contribution of p_2. We denote the agreement between players with α and compute it as follows:

$$\alpha = \left(1 - \frac{|v_1 - v_2|}{L}\right) \times \frac{\rho_1 + \rho_2}{2} \tag{5}$$

in which, L is the number of options in the multi-choice game and ρ_1 and ρ_2 are the reputation scores of p_1 and p_2, respectively.

Computing Quality Score. Quality of the game outcome is the weight of the outcome computed for the game. In other words, the quality of the game outcome, independent of the outcome value, shows to what extent the requester can trust the outcome received from the players. Outcome quality depends on the players' quality scores. Quality of players is reflected by their corresponding suitability scores. So, the quality of the outcome depends on the suitability scores of both players. Also, the agreement of the players on a choice can be used as a supporting evidence for the outcome quality. Therefore, the quality depends on the suitability scores of players along with their level of agreement. We denote the quality of the game outcome by q_g and calculate it as follows:

$$q_g = \sqrt{\sqrt{\sigma_{p_1}^g \times \sigma_{p_2}^g} \times \alpha} \tag{6}$$

Quality of a player's contribution directly impacts the reward she receives. Higher qualities are compensated with higher rewards, and lower qualities will result in lower income. Assume that g_r is the amount of the reward specified by the requester for the players who contribute to a game. The reward amount each player receives is calculated as follows:

$$r_p^g = \sqrt{\sigma_p^g \times \alpha} \times g_r \tag{7}$$

in which r_p^g is the reward received by player p for her contribution to the game g.

3.3   Changing Mind

Once the outcome quality is computed, it is compared to two predefined thresholds: th_1 and th_2. If the outcome quality is less than th_1, it means that the outcome does not satisfy the minimum requirements and the computed outcome is not only of very low quality, but also there is no hope to improve it by shepherding and providing online support to the players. So, we discard the outcome and directly go to the compensation phase. On the other hand, if the outcome quality is higher than th_2, it means that the outcome quality acceptable and does not require further improvement. Therefore, the outcome is directly accepted without online shepherding.

The third scenario happens when the quality is between th_1 and th_2. This is the setting for which our game is designed. Players receive a reward based on the quality of their contribution in the first round. In this round, we offer players a new chance to increase their income by selecting a new choice. Refer to Eq. 7, the maximum reward a player can receive based on her choice is obtained when she has full agreement with the other player and the $\alpha = 1$. More precisely, the maximum obtainable reward for a player with suitability score of σ_p^g from the contribution to a game g is:

$$Max\left(r_p^g\right) = \sqrt{\sigma_p^g \times \frac{\rho_1 + \rho_2}{2}} \times g_r \tag{8}$$

Since choosing a new option can lead to reduced agreement between players, it may result in decreasing the players' rewards. The minimum reward a player p may gain from contribution to the game g is obtained when the value of α is in its minimum level, i.e., refer to the Eq. 7:

$$Min\left(r_p^g\right) = \sqrt{\sigma_p^g \times \left(1 - \frac{L-1}{L}\right) \times \frac{\rho_1 + \rho_2}{2}} \times g_r \tag{9}$$

In the changing mind step, we reveal $Min\left(r_p^g\right)$ and $Max\left(r_p^g\right)$ values to the players and let them choose to risk what they have for gaining more, or stay on their choices. This will encourage players to do their best to gain the most agreement with the other player. Since players do not know each other, and they have no means to share their thoughts, they have to try their best to find the right answer, knowing that the other party does the same. This can lead to contributions with higher quality levels. Moreover, users who are confident of their decision, will stay with their choice, while the people who are not sure might use the opportunity of changing their mind to try their chance once again to gain more.

After collecting the new possible contributions, they are evaluated again using the methods presented in Eqs. 4 to 6. According to the computed quality level of he contributions, the players are rewarded using the Eq. 7.

3.4   Final Outcome

Once the contributions are collected and players are rewarded, the system builds the final outcome of the game. The final outcome of the game depends on the players' profiles, their choices and their corresponding confidence levels. When a player p selects a choice, say l, with the confidence level of κ in the game g, from the p's point of view, the l is the right answer with he confidence level of κ_p^g. The credibility of the p's opinion depends on her profile match with the game requirements, i.e., F_p^g. So, from the requester's point of view, l is the right answer with the credibility level of $F_p^g \times \kappa_p^g$.

On the other hand, one can say that p believes that with the confidence level of $(1 - \kappa_p^g)$ the right answer is a choice different from the l. In other words, κ_p^g percent of the credibility of the player goes to the choice l and the rest, that is $\left((1 - \kappa_p^g) \times F_p^g\right)$, goes to the rest of the choices. Moreover, we believe that when a player selects l as her submitted answer, the chance to find the right answer in the choices around the l is more than the further

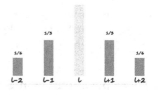

Fig. 3. Distribution of un-confidence.

choices. For example, if a player has selected 5 as her choice out of the list of numbers from 1 to 10, assuming that she has not submitted a random choice, the chance to find the right answer around 5 is higher than others. Having this intuition behind, we distribute the un-confidence of the player $(1 - \kappa_p^g)$ among the choices around the l. As represented in Fig. 3, one third of the un-confidence goes to each of the $(l + 1)$ and $(l - 1)$, and one sixth goes to each of $(l + 2)$ and $(l - 2)$.

Let's call the credibility that each choice $l (l \in 1...L)$ receives from the player p_i, the gain of l from p_i, and denote it by $\gamma_{p_i}^l$. We calculate $\gamma_{p_i}^l$ for each available choice and each player. As a result, there are two gains available for each quality level. For the choices too far (further than two steps), gain might be zero. So, the overall gain of each choice will be:

$$\gamma^l = \gamma_{p_1}^l + \gamma_{p_2}^l , \qquad l \in 1..L \tag{10}$$

There are two ways to build the outcome of a multi-choice task: *competition* and *combination* [15]. In the competition mode, one of the available options is selected out of the list, as the game outcome. For instance, the option with the highest gain is selected as the game outcome. If we denote the outcome of a game with OUT_g, then we can say that the

$$OUT_g = o \quad \text{where} \quad \forall l \in \{1..L\} \mid \gamma^o \geq \gamma^l \tag{11}$$

In the combination mode, the final outcome of a task is the combination of all collected answers. Despite the competition mode, in this method, the outcome might not be one of the levels. The outcome is a real number in the range of $[1, L]$. The weighted averaging method is one of the popular methods which is employed to calculate such outcomes [16]. A simple weighted average is computed as follows:

$$OUT_g = \sum_{1 \leq l \leq L} \frac{i \times (\gamma^l)^2}{\sum_{1 \leq j \leq L} (\gamma^j)^2}. \tag{12}$$

4   Experimentation and Evaluation

In this section, we conduct a simulation-based evaluation to analyse the behaviour of our proposed framework. First, we explain experimentation setup, the metrics we use for performance evaluation and the datasets we used in the experiments in Sect. 4.1. Then, we compare the performance of our proposed framework with other methods in Sect. 4.2.

4.1   Experimentation Setup

To undertake the preliminary evaluations outlined herein, we chose to conduct simulations, since real experiments in social participatory networks are difficult to organize. Simulations afford a controlled environment where we can carefully vary certain parameters and observe the impact on the system performance. Our simulations have been conducted on a PC running Windows 10 professional and having 8 GB of RAM. We used Matlab R2014a for developing the simulator.

We have also set $th1$ and $th2$ to 0.1 and 0.9, respectively. The intuition behind this selection is based on the experience and believes that were reflected in designing the fuzzy rules in Table 1.

Dataset. The dataset that we use for our experiment is the real web of trust of Advogato.org [17]. Advogato.org is a web-based community of open source software developers in which, site members rate each other in terms of their trustworthiness. The result of these ratings among members is a rich web of trust, which comprises of 14,019 users and 47,347 trust ratings. We also pre-processed the dataset in order to remove the isolated users that have no connections. 174 users were identified as isolated and were removed.

To use this graph as a crowdsourcing system, members should have attributes reflecting their social behavioural factors such as the reputation score, number of expertise and the level of confidence. We have computed a reputation score for each member by calculating the average of all pairwise trust scores the member received from his friends. The reputation score is a number in the range of $[0, 1]$.

In order to simulate a real-world scenario, and assign real values to other attributes, we enriched the Advogato dataset using the Stackoverflow dataset[1] created by the Stack Exchange, Inc. In other words, we extracted various statistical parameters from Stackoverflow and used them as a guide to assign values

---

[1] https://archive.org/details/stackexchange.

to nodes' main attributes in Advogato graph. We use the Programmer subset of the Stackoverflow which contains 30060 posts (both questions and answers) created by 12081 users. These users have earned 24863 badges based on their activities in the community. The badges reflect the expertise of the participants. Using the standard statistical estimation tools provided by Matlab® software package, we have determined that in Stackoverflow dataset, number of badges per participant follows a normal distribution $X = \mathcal{N}(5.57, 6.52)$ (where X is a random variable). We used the above knowledge to initialize attributes for participants. Specifically for 'number of expertise', we utilize the random variable X and assign each participant a value k representing their number of expertise. We then uniformly select k numbers from the range of $[1, 20]$ as expertise values. The intuition behind this selection is that based on literature, approximately twenty different types of tasks can be identified in a typical crowdsourcing system[2] [18]. The participant's expertise reflects how good he is in accomplishing tasks of various types.

The other main attribute that should be assigned to each member is her average level of confidence. Later, we use the average level of confidence to assign a level of confidence to each player when participating in a game. Literature shows that, there is a positive correlation, with the correlation coefficient of 0.445, between the quality of a player (reflected in the quality of her contributions) and her average level of confidence [19]. In other words, when the quality of a person increases, her level of confidence should increase as well.

Evaluation Method and Metrics. In order to evaluate the performance of our proposed framework, we run the experiment for 10000 tasks. A simple experimentation round contains the following steps: In the first step, we generate a game. Also, a minimum level of accepted reputation score and a number of required expertise is assigned to each task randomly. Furthermore, we assign each task an answer, randomly selected out of the range of $[1, L]$, and use it as a measure to check the accuracy of the computed outcomes. Then, we choose two players out of the members of Advogato community. This selection is performed uniformly, meaning that all members have the same chance to be chosen as the players.

Once the game is generated and players are recruited, players contribute to the game based on the methods we explained in the Sect. 3. The players' confidence level is generated according to the player's average level of confidence. The confidence level that supports each contribution, as well as the confidence level which is used to decide on a changed decision are uniformly selected out of the range of 0 and 2 ∗ (Average Confidence Level) of each player. If a player decides to change her decision, her contribution is collected again and assessed based on the proposed method.

In order to show the efficiency of our proposed approach, we compare its performance with two other popular similar approaches. The first approach is the *ESP game* [9]. As explain in Sect. 5, this game is the closest related prior work

---

[2] http://gigaom.com/2010/11/19/18-tasks-you-can-crowdsource/.

to our approach. We refer to the ESP game in the comparison charts as ESP. In addition, we also include a profile-based method, a well-known recruitment strategy in crowdsourcing [6], in our comparisons.

The performance comparison between these three approaches is done based on three evaluation metrics. The first metric is *quality*. The quality of the outcome of a game is a desired quality that can give the requester a guide to decide on the credibility of the outcome. Quality is calculated based on the Eq. 6. The second parameter is the *error rate*. When we generate a game, we specify the right answer and use it to determine the accuracy of the outcome provided by the players. The game outcome is computed according to the Eq. 12. The error rate reflects the distance between the game outcome and the answer of the task. The *successful completion* of a game is the third performance comparison metric. In the ESP game, when the players do not agree on an answer, the game remains unsolved, i.e., it has not been completed successfully. Also in our proposed approach, when the quality of an outcome is less than $th1$, we deem that the game was not completed successfully. This metric is not applicable to the profile based approach, so we use it just to compare our approach with the ESP game. All results shown in charts are averaged over 10000 independent rounds of the experiment.

4.2   Performance Comparison

In this section we compare the performance of our proposed method with ESP game and Profile based approaches. Using the evaluation metrics defined in the previous section, first, we compare the quality of outcome received from the three approaches. The quality of outcome is illustrated in Fig. 4(a). The horizontal axis of the chart shows the number of choices available to the players and the vertical axis shows the average quality of the game outcome. As it is expected, for both ESP and our approach, when the number of choices increases the quality of outcomes decreases. The quality of outcome does not decrease for the profile based approach because it only computes the quality based on the profile match of the workers and agreement or disagreement of players is not taken into account. The outcome quality of our approach is higher than the

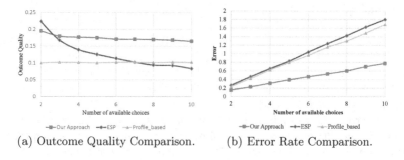

(a) Outcome Quality Comparison.   (b) Error Rate Comparison.

Fig. 4. Performance comparison

others, and decreases with a lower gradient, in comparison with the ESP, when the number of choices increases. The reason for this quality improvement is the fact that our approach leverages players' quality factors along with their level of agreement to compute the quality of contributions. The proposed method also, controls the quality in a two-stage manner, to make sure that they meet a minimum desired level of quality.

The second evaluation metric is the error rate of the three approaches. The results of this comparison is depicted in Fig. 4(b). The horizontal axis of the chart shows the number of available choices. We increase the number of choices from 2 to 10 and measure the error in the task outcome. The vertical axis shows the error rate. As we expected, when the number of available choices increases, the error rate is expected to increase as well. This increment in error rate is observed in all three approaches. But, as shown in Fig. 4(b), the

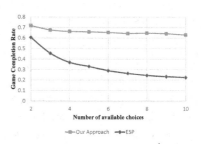

Fig. 5. Successful completion rate comparison.

error rate of our proposed approach is always lower than the other two methods. One can readily observe that the rate of increase in the error rate is lower with our approach as compared to the others. Two-stage quality control mechanism in our approach is responsible for this low error rate. Along with checking suitability of players, our proposed approach makes sure that, if in the first round, a game comes up with a low quality outcome, players are given a new chance to revise their decision and move towards a higher quality decision, that consequently decreases the error rate.

The third performance comparison metric is the successful completion rate of the games. Some of the games can remain incomplete in both ESP and our method. In the former, this is due to disagreement amongst the players. In the latter, this is possible if the outcome is of low quality. Achieving a high rate of successful completions of games is important for the success of the campaigns. In Fig. 5, we illustrate the successful completion rate of the games in ESP and our approach. The vertical axis of the chart shows the completion rate of the games, as the number of choices available to players increase from 2 to 10, shown in the horizontal axis. As one can see in the chart, the completion rate for our approach reduces from 0.72 to 0.6 as the number of choices available increase from 2 to 10. In contrast, for ESP the completion rate drops from 0.6 to 0.22 for the same range of choices. Thus, our game exhibits significantly improved performance in successful completion of games.

In summary, the performance of our proposed approach is better than the other two methods in all compared aspects.

5   Related Work

Quality control is a challenging issue in the success of a crowdsourcing campaign. Addressing this issue has attracted lots of attention. Based on the literature, several parameters might impact the quality of contributions, mainly quality of workers and quality of task [5,8,20–24]. Increasing the motivation of workers is also shown to impact the quality of contributions [21,22,25,26].

In the area of incentive design, one of the most popular developments in recent years has been titled as gamification. Gamification is defined as a process of enhancing services with (motivational) affordances in order to invoke gameful experiences and further behavioral outcomes [27]. Tomnod[3] is an example which uses images taken by Digital Globe satellites to pinpoint objects and places in the aftermath of natural disasters and man-made catastrophes. Genes in Space[4] is a mobile game that uses the collective force of players to analyze real genetic data to help with cancer research. Smorball[5] is another game in which, players are presented with phrases from scanned pages in the Biodiversity Heritage Library and they are asked to type the words they see as quickly and accurately as possible. The result makes historic literature more usable for institutions, scholars, educators, and the public.

More similar to our work, gamification has been used in crowdsourcing [28]. In [29], authors have proposed a game called Wordsmith. Wordsmith is a single player game in which players attend in an image labelling task. Players receive feedback based on their contributions. While Feedbacks in Wordsmith motivate users to improve their behaviour,they do not have the opportunity to change their mind, and this is how our proposed game is different from Wordsmith. In another similar game called Game of Words [30], authors propose a game for collecting relevant keywords about a specific location. Game of Words is a single player game in which players cannot change their mind and do not receive any online support, while our proposed game tries to improve quality by relying on opinion of two players and giving them feedback and the opportunity to change their choice.

6 Conclusion

In this paper, we proposed a game-theoretic approach to improve quality of the crowdsourced information. Inspired from the Nash equilibrium, our approach leverages gamification techniques to motivate people towards providing high quality contributions. The proposed approach also employs people quality metrics such as reputation, expertise and agreement between players to ensure that the collected contribution is of an accepted quality level. Using real world datasets, simulations demonstrated that our method increases the quality of collected contributions as well as the chance of successful completion of games, in comparison with other state-of-the-art similar techniques.

Acknowledgements. The authors would like to acknowledge Professor Boualem Benatallah at The University of New South Wales, Australia, for his invaluable supports and guidance.

---

[3] http://www.tomnod.com/.

[4] http://genesinspace.org/.

[5] http://smorballgame.org/.

References

1. Peary, B.D., Shaw, R., Takeuchi, Y.: Utilization of social media in the east Japan earthquake and tsunami and its effectiveness. J. Nat. Disaster Sci. **34**(1), 3–18 (2012)
2. Doan, A., Ramakrishnan, R., Halevy, A.Y.: Crowdsourcing systems on the world-wide web. Commun. ACM **54**(4), 86–96 (2011)
3. Beheshti, S., et al.: A systematic review and comparative analysis of cross-document coreference resolution methods and tools. Computing **99**(4), 313–349 (2017)
4. Beheshti, S., Nezhad, H.R.M., Benatallah, B.: Temporal provenance model (TPM): model and query language (2012). CoRR vol. abs/1211.5009
5. Allahbakhsh, M., Benatallah, B., Ignjatovic, A., Motahari-Nezhad, H.R., Bertino, E., Dustdar, S.: Quality control in crowdsourcing systems: Issues and directions. IEEE Internet Comput. **17**(2), 76–81 (2013)
6. Amintoosi, H., Kanhere, S.S., Allahbakhsh, M.: Trust-based privacy-aware participant selection in social participatory sensing. J. Inf. Secur. Appl. **20**, 11–25 (2015)
7. Rogstadius, J., et al.: An assessment of intrinsic and extrinsic motivation on task performance in crowdsourcing markets. In: ICWSM (2011)
8. Amintoosi, H., Kanhere, S.: A reputation framework for social participatory sensing systems. Mobile Networks Appl. **19**(1), 88–100 (2014)
9. Von Ahn, L.: Games with a purpose. Computer **39**(6), 92–94 (2006)
10. Welinder, P., Perona, P.: Online crowdsourcing: rating annotators and obtaining cost-effective labels. In: 2010 IEEE Computer Society Conference on Computer Vision and Pattern Recognition Workshops (CVPRW), pp. 25–32. IEEE (2010)
11. Nash, J.F., et al.: Equilibrium points in N-person games. Proc. Nat. Acad. Sci. USA **36**(1), 48–49 (1950)
12. Dow, S., Kulkarni, A., Klemmer, S., Hartmann, B.: Shepherding the crowd yields better work. In: Proceedings of the ACM 2012 Conference on Computer Supported Cooperative Work, pp. 1013–1022. ACM (2012)
13. Kittur, A., Smus, B., Khamkar, S., Kraut, R.E.: Crowdforge: Crowdsourcing complex work. In: Proceedings of the 24th Annual ACM Symposium on User Interface Software and Technology, pp. 43–52. ACM (2011)
14. Kulkarni, A., Can, M., Hartmann, B.: Collaboratively crowdsourcing workflows with turkomatic. In: Proceedings of the ACM 2012 Conference on Computer Supported Cooperative Work, pp. 1003–1012. ACM (2012)
15. Vuković, M.: Crowdsourcing for enterprises. In: 2009 World Conference on Services-I, pp. 686–692. IEEE (2009)
16. Allahbakhsh, M., Ignatovic, A.: An iterative method for calculating robust rating scores. IEEE Trans. Parallel Distrib. Syst. **26**(2), 340–350 (2015)
17. Levien, R., Aiken, A.: Attack-resistant trust metrics for public key certification. In: 7th USENIX Security Symposium, pp. 229–242 (1998)
18. Doan, A., et al.: Crowdsourcing systems on the world-wide web. Commun. ACM **54**(4), 86–96 (2011)
19. Oyama, S., Baba, Y., Sakurai, Y., Kashima, H.: Accurate integration of crowd-sourced labels using workers' self-reported confidence scores. In: Proceedings of the Twenty-Third International Joint Conference on Artificial Intelligence, IJCAI 2013, pp. 2554–2560 (2013)

20. Chen, J.J., et al.: Opportunities for crowdsourcing research on amazon mechanical turk. Interfaces **5**(3) (2011)
21. Zheng, H., Li, D., Hou, W.: Task design, motivation, and participation in crowdsourcing contests. Int. J. Electron. Commer. **15**(4), 57–88 (2011)
22. Zhao, Y.C., Zhu, Q.: Effects of extrinsic and intrinsic motivation on participation in crowdsourcing contest: A perspective of self-determination theory. Online Inf. Rev. **38**(7), 896–917 (2014)
23. Allahbakhsh, M., Ignjatovic, A., Benatallah, B., Beheshti, S., Foo, N., Bertino, E.: Detecting, representing and querying collusion in online rating systems (2012). CoRR, vol. abs/1211.0963. http://arxiv.org/abs/1211.0963
24. Allahbakhsh, M., Ignjatovic, A., Benatallah, B., Beheshti, S., Foo, N., Bertino, E.: An analytic approach to people evaluation in crowdsourcing systems (2012). CoRR abs/1211.3200. http://arxiv.org/abs/1211.3200
25. Kaufmann, N., Schulze, T., Veit, D.: More than fun and money, worker motivation in crowdsourcing-a study on mechanical turk. In: AMCIS 2011, pp. 1–11 (2011)
26. Hamari, J., Koivisto, J., Sarsa, H.: Does gamification work?-a literature review of empirical studies on gamification. In: 2014 47th Hawaii International Conference on System Sciences (HICSS), pp. 3025–3034. IEEE (2014)
27. Huotari, K., Hamari, J.: Defining gamification: a service marketing perspective. In: Proceeding of the 16th International Academic MindTrek Conference, pp. 17–22. ACM (2012)
28. Morschheuser, B., Hamari, J., Koivisto, J.: Gamification in crowdsourcing: a review. In: 2016 49th Hawaii International Conference on System Sciences (HICSS), pp. 4375–4384. IEEE (2016)
29. Feyisetan, O., Simperl, E., Van Kleek, M., Shadbolt, N.: Improving paid microtasks through gamification and adaptive furtherance incentives. In: Proceedings of the 24th International Conference on World Wide Web, pp. 333–343. ACM (2015)
30. Goncalves, J., et al.: Game of words: Tagging places through crowdsourcing on public displays. In: Proceedings of the 2014 Conference on Designing Interactive Systems, DIS 2014, pp. 705–714. ACM, New York (2014)

Investigating Performance Metrics for Evaluation of Content Delivery Networks

Seyed Jalal Jafari[1]($\boxtimes$), HamidReza Naji[2], and Masoumeh Jannatifar[3]

[1] University of Zanjan, Zanjan, Iran
sj.jafari@znu.ac.ir
[2] Kerman Graduate University of Advanced Technology, Kerman, Iran
[3] AmirKabir University of Technology, Tehran, Iran

Abstract. Content Delivery Networks are one of the most common services in order to overcome performance problems caused by massive data requests in popular web applications. CDNs improve clients' perceived quality of service by placing replica servers scattered around the globe and consequently redirecting users to closer servers. While CDNs' ultimate goal is to improve the performance of data delivery, their own efficiency can also be an issue to investigate. Due to the complexity of these services, plenty of factors can impact the performance of CDNs. As a result, the efficiency of CDNs can be measured using various metrics. In this paper we review some of the well-known performance metrics in the literature for evaluating CDNs. We also present some other measures including Fairness and Content Travel. In order to attain an overall insight about a CDN, a Cost Function is also presented which incorporates most of the metrics in a single formula.

Keywords: Content Delivery Networks · Performance
Measurement · Metrics · QoS

1 Introduction

Recently, Internet-based services have turned into an inseparable part of people's everyday life. The rapid growth in the popularity of some services causes them to face performance issues and bottlenecks in terms of latency, bandwidth consumption, etc. In order to avoid performance related concerns as well as improving QoS and QoE for end users, large-scale web applications deliver contents through Content Delivery Networks. CDNs act as a trusted overlay network that offers high-performance delivery of common Web objects, static data, and rich multimedia content by distributing load among servers that are close to the clients [1]. CDNs provide services that improve network performance by maximizing bandwidth, improving accessibility and maintaining correctness through content replication [2]. This is achieved by spreading some surrogate servers across a geographic area. When a user issues a request for some content,

© Springer International Publishing AG, part of Springer Nature 2018
A. Beheshti et al. (Eds.): ASSRI 2015/2017, LNBIP 234, pp. 131–145, 2018.
https://doi.org/10.1007/978-3-319-76587-7_9

the surrogate server, which is more proper than the others, will respond to that request. Figure 1 shows a typical CDN architecture [3].

The very last few years have seen an astonishing development in CDNs' technology, and today's Internet content is largely delivered by major CDNs like Akamai or Google CDN [4]. Facebook contents, for example are mainly hosted by Akamai CDN servers [4]. Despite the commercial stability of CDNs, researches to improve these systems are still ongoing. There are different research aspects in CDNs e.g. Replica Server Placement, Request Routing Mechanisms, Caching Policies, etc. which can in turn lead to improvements in the performance of CDNs. However, due to complexity and intricate structure of CDNs, measuring the performance of them can also be a subject of great interest. There are plenty of factors which impact the performance of CDNs. As a consequence, several performance metrics can be employed to investigate efficiency from different angles. RTT (Round Trip Time), for example, is one of the most considered metrics for evaluating CDNs in the literature. Although RTT can provide an acceptable overview of how well CDNs performs, it does not necessarily reflect all performance subtleties in these systems. In this paper we will discuss the existing performance metrics which are currently used to evaluate CDNs in details. Furthermore, some new performance metrics will be presented.

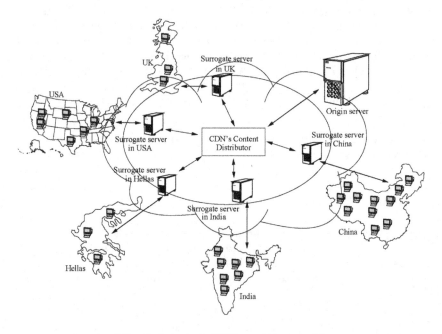

Fig. 1. A typical CDN's architecture [4]

2   Literature Review

From the early ages of CDNs to the time being, clients' perceived latency (AKA: response time, Round Trip Time – RTT) has been the top priority metric for researchers when measuring CDNs' performance [4–6]. Akhtar et al. [7] employ statistical functions operating basically on latency in order to evaluate users' perceived performance in different commercial CDNs. While reducing latency is the ultimate goal of CDNs, the performance of CDNs can also be measured from other points of views.

Looking at some recent works, Hours et al. [8] examine the impact of DNS resolving methods in CDNs on the performance of web browsing in terms of External TTL and also Throughput (Mbps). Although geographical distance can affect the performance of CDNs, few works use this metric for evaluations. However, this metric has been employed in some recent works. In [9], authors take physical distance between clients and servers as a metric to measure the performance of AnyCast DNS resolving. Mapping distance is the term which Chen et al. use to indicate the great circle distance between a client and the server as a metric for evaluating CDNs [10]. They also introduce time to first byte (TTFB) as another parameter which is basically the duration from when the client makes a HTTP request for the base web page to when the first byte of the requested web page was received by the client.

In [2], Pathan et al. mention performance measurement as an issue in CDNs. They consider Cache hit ratio, Reserved bandwidth, Latency, Surrogate server utilization and Reliability (packet loss) as important measures to investigate.

3   Metrics Discussion

In this section we present and discuss a variety of metrics which can be used to evaluate CDNs' performance. In abstract, some of the measures can be seen from the clients' point of view e.g. RTT (latency) and Throughput while others belong to the internal architecture of CDNs like server cache misses, fairness, etc.

Some metrics mentioned in this section have been employed in the literature before, however we discuss them here in order to establish a comprehensive image on the issue. We also introduce some other performance metrics to evaluate CDNs including fairness, Content Travel and CDN Cost.

3.1   Latency (RTT)

As it was mentioned before, latency is the most straightforward metric for evaluating CDNs' performance. In a large number of works, Round Trip Time is considered as an appropriate measure to indicate users' perceived latency. RTT is the amount of time that takes an IP packet to travel from the source machine to the target machine plus the time of receiving an ACK (Acknowledgement) for that packet.

RTT can be seen as a metric in different places and various forms, each of which indicating the performance from a specific angle. Although RTT is usually measured on the client side, it might be interesting if we take it into account on the server side too. RTT on the client side depicts the amount of time users wait for their requests, however this metric on the server side can be interpreted as a ground to measure how fast are the communications of a server with respect to its clients. This can lead to decisions like changing a server's location or strengthening its links.

Investigating RTT can be useful at different levels. As it is stated in [4], RTT to any specific IP address consists of both the propagation delay and the processing delay. Considering a large number of packet exchange, min RTT can be assumed as an approximation for propagation delay. In other words, min RTT can correspond to network distance between clients and servers. Mean RTT can also be another noticeable variation of RTT which can be also a suitable factor to evaluate the response time of clients and servers. In other words, mean RTT indicates the average amount of time that clients or the servers wait for their requests to be fulfilled.

Processing delay is a hidden metric which lies within RTT. We can assume the difference between max RTT and min RTT in every TCP flow to approximate processing delay for a given network element e.g. a replica server. Equation 1 indicates this metric. Mean processing delay of each network element equals to the mean processing delay of all TCP flows toward that element. It can help to evaluate how busy the servers are, for example.

$$\overline{PD}_{element} = \frac{\left(\sum_{i=1}^{n_{flow}} \max RTT_{flow_i} - \min RTT_{flow_i}\right)}{n_{flow}} \quad (1)$$

3.2 Cache Miss

Caching is a key element in CDNs. Improvement in content delivery is achieved by caching web objects on surrogate servers which are located somewhere close to the request source. Whenever a client is redirected to a surrogate server but the requested object does not exist in that server, a cache miss occurs and the surrogate server has to retrieve the object from origin server. Cache misses can affect the performance of content delivery dramatically. There are plenty of factors which influence cache miss ratio in surrogate servers. Cache size, caching policies, prefetching mechanisms [11,12] and server congestion can be considered as some of these factors. Not only does lower cache miss improve the quality of services, it also indicates that server has imposed lower load on the network. Depending on the investigation scenario, cache miss can be a proper metric to measure surrogate servers' performance in CDNs.

3.3 Throughput (Average Bits/Sec)

In computer networks throughput generally indicates the performance of network elements in terms of data transmission rate per a time unit. It is usually expressed as average sent and/or received bits/sec. Interpreting throughput in CDNs may not be as plain as other metrics. In fact, higher throughput can be considered as both a negative or a positive phenomenon depending on the scenario conditions.

When higher throughput in servers results in lower latencies, we can claim that servers have put more effort to deliver better quality services. On the other hand, we can imagine a scenario in which overall throughput in servers is high while no significant change is seen in the latency numbers. In this case we can say that servers may have been uselessly busy because of improper topology or inefficient caching. In [13] authors state that "even though most clients are served by a geographically nearby CDN node, a sizeable fraction of clients' experience latencies several tens of milliseconds higher than other clients in the same region. Second, we find that queueing delays often override the benefits of a client interacting with a nearby server." This indicates higher throughput of servers can lead to lower response time in some cases. Similarly, as it is mentioned in [14], latency can also be affected by throughput bottlenecks along the path between client and server. In this case rethinking path selection mechanisms can be a solution.

3.4 Geographical Distance

Sometimes the distance between clients and servers is approximated with min RTT [4]. Although it can indicate the delay between a server and a client but it may not be stable due to congestion or throughput bottlenecks. Geographical location of clients and servers can be employed as a solid factor to measure the distance between clients and servers. IP geolocation services [15] can be used to provide this data. In a CDN evaluation scenario, if we provide the geographical coordinates of clients and servers, we can eventually extract the average physical distance of surrogate servers from their clients. Average client distances can tell us how efficiently the surrogate servers are scattered in a given area. As this value is higher the effectiveness of CDN drops.

3.5 Fairness

As it was mentioned before, there are multiple surrogate servers in a CDN. It would be ideal to distribute the load among them equally. The worst case scenario occurs when some servers work with their maximum capacity while there are other idle servers available in the CDN. We can say that if the load on servers is distributed approximately equal, the requests will be routed to the surrogate servers fairly. The number of served requests by each server can be used as a basis to calculate the fairness measure. In order to calculate fairness we use Jain's fairness index [16]:

$$J\left(S_1, S_2, ..., S_n\right) = \frac{\left(\sum_{i=1}^{n} S_i\right)^2}{n \times \sum_{i=1}^{n} S_i^{\,2}} \tag{2}$$

In this equation n is the number of servers and S_i is the load amount tolerated by server i (precisely, the number of requests served by server i but normalized to a value between 0 and 1). The result is a number between 0 and 1. As the result of this equation is closer to 1, the load is distributed among the servers more fairly.

3.6 Overall Consumed Bandwidth

CDN topology directly impacts the routes on which packets travel in the network. As the surrogate servers are farther from users, the packets travel a longer distance in the network. Therefore, more equipment (like routers) should be involved in the process of request fulfilling and also more control packets should be generated. Hence overall consumed bandwidth will rise. On the other hand, it is rational to say that perceived response time by final users is directly proportional to overall consumed bandwidth in the network. Under normal conditions, more bandwidth consumption can be interpreted as the fact that the packets have traveled longer routes, so the users must have tolerated more delays. Therefore, the amount of overall bandwidth used in a network can be regarded as another decent measure to evaluate CDNs' performance.

3.7 Content Travel Measure

As it was stated, it is desired that contents travel shorter routes through the CDN network. If the overall delivered contents travel longer paths to reach their destination, there will be some consequences for this incident:

- Obviously there will be an increase in average content delivery latency;
- More network equipment (e.g. routers) must be involved in content delivery process. Therefore, more processing resources will be used;
- More bandwidth will be consumed in the whole network infrastructure.

As a result, we can say that when contents travel longer routes in the network, CDNs performance diminishes in terms of latency, resource usage and bandwidth consumption. If location information for the clients is provided for a CDN scenario, it is possible to define a factor to measure this event. Mean travelled distance by packets multiplied by overall contents size served in the network will give us a measure for evaluating CDN's performance for this phenomenon which we call "Content Travel" measure. In a content delivery process, it gives us an insight about the path length between a surrogate server and its clients and also the content size served by that server, all integrated into a single value. As the Content Travel value is higher, it can be said that the massive contents have traveled longer routes in the network, therefore CDN has been affected in terms of performance measures discussed above. One of the goals can be to minimize this factor. Equation 3 describes this measure. First the mean distance between request sources and each server must be calculated. $\overline{D_s}$ is the mean traveled distance for requests (D_{req_i}) destined to server S in kilometers. n_{req} indicates the number of requests which have been sent to a specific server. C_{earth} is a constant value which is considered to calculate the great circle distance between two points instead of a simple Euclidean distance. This value usually is set to 111 [16]. Then the Content Travel measure can be calculated for all servers in the network. n_S is the number of servers available in CDN and $ServedSize_S$ indicates the size of content served by Server S.

$$\overline{D}_S = \frac{\sum_{i=1}^{n_{req}} D_{req_i}}{n_{req}} \times C_{earth}$$

$$ContentTravel = \frac{\sum_{S=1}^{n_S} \left(\overline{D}_S \times ServedSize_S\right)}{n_S} \tag{3}$$

3.8   CDN Cost

Finally, a cost function can be defined to summarize different parameters (from different aspects). Its value shows how well the CDN has performed in a scenario. Here we have picked some of the important metrics discussed above to build this function. The CDNCost function is defined as follows:

$$CDNCost = w_1 RTT_{Clients} + w_2 RTT_{Servers}$$
$$+ w_3 Throuput + w_4 ContentTravel + w_5 \left(1 - Fairness\right) \tag{4}$$

- $RTT_{Clients}$ and $RTT_{Servers}$ are the mean perceived RTT measure by Clients and Servers.
- Throughput is the mean bits transferred in a second by all the devices working in the network (clients, server and routers).
- Content Travel and Fairness are the parameters which were discussed earlier. The fairness value is subtracted from 1 because we desire lower values for CDN Cost measure while higher fairness values indicate better performance in terms of this measure.

All the parameters in Eq. 4 must be scaled to a value between 0 and 1. CDN Cost value is also a number between 0 and 1. As it is closer to 0, it means that CDN is performing better. Every parameter in this formula has a weight coefficient which reflects the importance of that parameter. Sum of all weights must be equal to 1. For example, if we want to pay equal attention to all parameters we should set all the weights equal to 0.2. By changing the weight values any parameter can be bolded or faded out according to the desires of experimenter.

4   Experiments

In this section we employ some of the important metrics discussed in previous sections for evaluating an example experiment. This experiment aims to investigate Replica Server Placement problem by simulating some approaches from the literature including hotspot [5] and GeoIP clustering [17]. It is assumed that in the CDN topology we have at most three replica servers for which we need to choose a place (besides the one fixed origin server). Three different approaches have been employed in order to determine a place for the replica servers:

1. Random selection: replica server places are selected randomly. This approach is never used in reality but the results can give us an insight about the effectiveness of other approaches.
2. HotSpot [5]: the main idea behind this approach is to put replica servers where higher request rates are observed.
3. GeoIP Subtractive [17]: this approach uses client's geographical coordinates to cluster the users. It employs subtractive clustering for this purpose.

In the following we will execute the aforementioned approaches in a simulation environment (using INET Framework under OMNet++) and then we will evaluate the results. Six-month access log of a Swedish webapp is used to create content and clients' datasets for all scenarios. The dataset is called googlecreeper and represents the search history of Swedish users. In all experiments the origin server is placed in the US.

4.1   Scenario #1: Random Selection

The first scenario chooses two random Routers in the network infrastructure and connects the surrogate servers to them. There is no rationale behind this approach and it is only executed to be compared with other schemes. Suppose that a router in Australia and another router in Iran are chosen as replicas for this scenario. The origin server is connected to a router in the USA. Table 1 indicates the result of simulation using these configurations.

4.2   Scenario #2: HotSpot

HotSpot considers the places where most of the requests come from as a suitable choice for placing the replica servers. With the given dataset and in a classic client-server network, simulation results indicated that the most congested routers are somewhere in Sweden, Canada and Mexico. These are the top three routers which receive the highest number of requests in the first hop. Hence, HotSpot elects those areas to place replica servers. Table 2 shows the result of simulation with this configuration.

Table 1. The result of Random Replica Server Selection

Module name	Mean RTT (ms)	Max RTT (ms)	Min RTT (ms)	Receive throughput (bit/sec)	Send throughput (bit/sec)	Served web objects	Served content size (MB)	Cache misses	Average distances (KM)
originServer	230	870	180	3.25	23.30	353	22.21	-	-
surrogateServer1 (AU)	240	1090	066	46.49	321.28	681	315.19	383	6105
surrogateServer2 (IR)	280	1109	120	210.63	1809.44	5063	1518.76	663	9546
Clients	230	1220	60	34.31	3.7	-	-	-	-
Routers	-	-	-	27.58	27.58	-	-	-	-
Overall average	250	1220	65	28.42	28.42	-	-	-	-

Table 2. The result of HotSpot Replica Server Selection

Module name	Mean RTT (ms)	Max RTT (ms)	Min RTT (ms)	Receive throughput (bit/sec)	Send throughput (bit/sec)	Served web objects	Served content size (MB)	Cache misses	Average distances (KM)
originServer	172	680	90	4.55	34.51	467	33.28	-	-
surrogateServer1 (SE)	242	1320	66	143.10	1189.23	4017	1171.70	812	5106
surrogateServer2 (CA)	187	900	90	59.40	442.30	804	435.87	121	666
surrogateServer3 (MX)	174	1100	85	65.89	500.94	923	493.47	227	3219
Clients	178	1360	65	34.32	3.71	-	-	-	-
Routers	-	-	-	13.32	13.34	-	-	-	-
Overall average	200	1360	65	15.45	15.45	-	-	-	-

4.3   Scenario #3: GeoIP Subtractive

GeoIP Subtractive [17] is another approach that can be employed for replica server placement problem. This scheme clusters clients according to their geographical location and places the servers near the cluster centers. Applying this method on the given dataset gives us some coordinates in Canada, Sweden and China as the best candidates to place replica servers. The results of simulation using this configuration can be seen in Table 3.

Table 3. The result of simulation for GeoIP Subtractive Replica Server Selection

Module name	Mean RTT (ms)	Max RTT (ms)	Min RTT (ms)	Receive throughput (bit/sec)	Send throughput (bit/sec)	Served web objects	Served content size (MB)	Cache misses (KM)	Average distances (KM)
originServer	179	0790	83	4.57	34.52	496	33.29	-	-
surrogateServer1 (SE)	200	860	66	82.26	638.61	2436	628.12	562	888
surrogateServer2 (CA)	172	1100	63	114.02	941.524	1727	929.23	241	2886
surrogateServer3 (CN)	271	1055	65	72.13	552.45	1581	543.68	386	888
Clients	157	1140	65	33.778	3.655	-	-	-	-
Routers	-	-	-	9.073	9.087	-	-	-	-
Overall average	186	1140	63	11.55	11.55	-	-	-	-

5   Discussion

As it was demonstrated in the previous section, we employed some of the discussed metrics in this paper to evaluate three different scenarios for replica server placement problem. In this section we will discuss these scenarios by scrutinizing each of those metrics.

5.1   RTT

Figure 2 indicates the observed RTT in different scenarios. Besides the mean RTT of all modules in the network, RTT measure is also calculated for different network elements which can give us useful information to analyze the network components separately. For example, mean RTT among all clients indicates the average response time tolerated by end users. RTT in replica servers can indicate their distance from the machines they communicate with. In other words, as the replica servers are closer to the clients, the RTT in replica servers will be lower. Lower RTT in replica server tells us that they are placed in proper locations. Beside the distance parameter, higher RTT in servers can also be a sign of longer packet processing time. RTT in origin server shows the communication overhead between the origin server and replica servers. This measure can influence of object fetching when a cache miss occurs. Max and Min RTT exhibit the worst and the best cases in terms of response time. As the simulation results show, scenario #3 performs better in terms of all aspects of RTT measure. The reason is that this approach has placed the replica servers where the average distance between them and clients is minimized. Processing load has been insignificant in these experiments.

5.2   Fairness

As it was mentioned in Sect. 3.5, fairness is another factor which can indicate how the network's load is distributed among replica servers. We can say that it is unfair if a server is congested with massive amount of traffic while other servers are idle. Since the request routing mechanism in these scenarios chooses the nearest server in terms of network distance, placing servers in farther locations

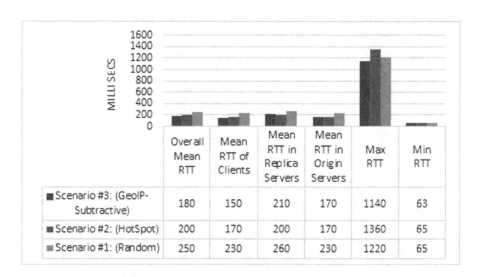

	Overall Mean RTT	Mean RTT of Clients	Mean RTT in Replica Servers	Mean RTT in Origin Servers	Max RTT	Min RTT
■ Scenario #3: (GeoIP-Subtractive)	180	150	210	170	1140	63
■ Scenario #2: (HotSpot)	200	170	200	170	1360	65
■ Scenario #1: (Random)	250	230	260	230	1220	65

Fig. 2. RTT in different scenarios

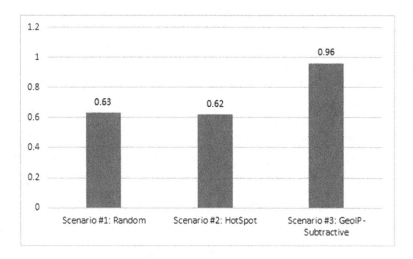

Fig. 3. Jain's fairness index

will result in pressure on some servers while others remain idle. On the other hand, if the servers are scattered around the network appropriately, the load is distributed among them fairly.

Jain's fairness index can give us a good insight here. Fairness measure gives a number between 0 and 1 for each scenario. As this measure is closer to 1, the load is distributed among replica servers more fairly. Figure 3 illustrates Jain's fairness index for the simulated scenarios. As it stands out from the graph, Scenario #3 has operated more fairly than the others in distributing load among servers equivalently.

5.3   Content Travel Measure

In this section we investigate Content Travel measure (explained in Sect. 3.7) for the simulated scenarios. Each row in Table 4 demonstrates Content Travel measure for a surrogate server in one scenario. More specifically it tells us the mean distance of clients from that replica server, Served Content size by that server and finally the calculated Content Travel measure for that server. As it was mentioned before lower values in this measure indicate better performance of a replica server in CDN.

Figure 4a indicates mean distance of clients from replica servers and mean served content size by replica servers in two column groups. Also mean Content Travel measure for each scenario can be seen in Fig. 4b. As the result shows, scenario #3 has performed better in terms of Content Travel. In other words, massive contents have traveled shorter paths in the aforementioned scenario. This means the resources of CDN have been used more efficiently.

Table 4. Content Travel statistics for simulated scenarios

Servers in different scenarios	Mean distance of clients from servers (KM)	Served content size (MB)	Content Travel measure (MB KM)
Scenario #1: (Random) surrogateServer1 (AU)	6105	315.19	1924235
Scenario #1: (Random) surrogateServer2 (IR)	9546	1785.73	17046579
Scenario #2: (HotSpot) surrogateServer1 (SE)	5106	1171.70	5982700
Scenario #2: (HotSpot) surrogateServer2 (CA)	666	435.87	290289.4
Scenario #2: (HotSpot) surrogateServer3 (MX)	3219	493.4	1588255
Scenario #3: (GeIP-FCM) surrogateServer1 (SE)	5106	1171.70	5982700
Scenario #3: (GeIP-FCM) surrogateServer2 (CA)	2886	929.25	2681816
Scenario #4: (GeIP-Subtractive) surrogateServer1 (SE)	888	628.12	557770.6
Scenario #4: (GeIP-Subtractive) surrogateServer2 (CA)	2886	929.23	2681758
Scenario #4: (GeIP-Subtractive) surrogateServer3 (CN)	888	543.68	482787.8

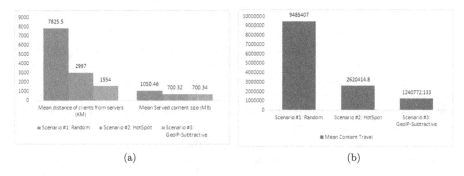

(a)   (b)

Fig. 4. Mean distance of clients from replica servers in different scenarios (a), Mean Content Travel measure for each scenario (b)

5.4 Overall CDN Cost

Using various performance measures, CDN's performance was evaluated from different perspectives. In order to attain an insight about the overall performance of a CDN topology, the CDN Cost measure was proposed above. All the incorporated factors in this formula are normalized to a value between 0 and 1. The impact of each factor can be determined by a weight coefficient. Sum of weights must be equal to 1. As the CDN Cost value is lower in a scenario it means that CDN has performed better under the configurations of that scenario. Figure 5 depicts the normalized values for different metrics in the scenarios we have discussed. The last column group indicates CDN Cost measure. The weights for all factors is assumed to be equal (=0.2). This means that no factor has priority over the others.

The results show that scenario #3 has performed better than the others. As it is expected scenario #1, which had no rationale behind, is the worst.

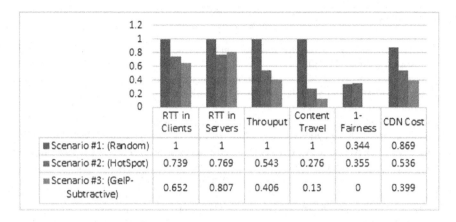

	RTT in Clients	RTT in Servers	Throuput	Content Travel	1-Fairness	CDN Cost
■ Scenario #1: (Random)	1	1	1	1	0.344	0.869
■ Scenario #2: (HotSpot)	0.739	0.769	0.543	0.276	0.355	0.536
■ Scenario #3: (GeIP-Subtractive)	0.652	0.807	0.406	0.13	0	0.399

Fig. 5. CDN cost for the experimented scenarios

6   Conclusions

In this paper we reviewed and discussed common metrics for evaluating Content Delivery Network services. Furthermore, we introduced some other metrics for this purpose including fairness, Content Travel and finally an overall Cost Function to attain a big picture of CDN performance.

In order to compare the metrics in action we designed three simulation scenarios for Replica Server Selection problem. Key measures were extracted from the simulation results. The experiments showed that investigating and improving performance of CDNs is not limited to simply optimizing latencies. Depending on scenario, different factors should be taken into account to analyze performance of these services.

7   Motivating Scenario and Benefits for Organizations

In the past years, owners of large-scale web applications have been seeking solutions to reduce the latency of their services which is inevitably caused by massive requests. Content Delivery Networks offer a solution for this issue. CDN vendors and researchers, consequently, have been working hard to come up with new ideas for improving service qualities. In this path, measurement of quality has relied mostly on the latency and delay which clients experience. However, there are plenty of factors which impact the performance of CDNs. As the volume and variety of contents being transmitted over the Internet increases, CDNs themselves might not work efficiently enough. This imposes extra costs for CDN vendors and consequently for application owners. Investigating the performance in CDNs from different angles can help organizations utilize their resources while delivering high quality services. The metrics discussed in this paper can be employed by CDN stakeholders to achieve clearer pictures about the performance of these systems.

References

1. Vakali, A., Pallis, G.: Content delivery networks: status and trends. IEEE Internet Comput. **7**(6), 68–74 (2003)
2. Pathan, A.-M.K., Buyya, R.: A taxonomy and survey of content delivery networks. Grid Computing and Distributed Systems Laboratory, University of Melbourne, Technical report, 4 (2007)
3. Buyya, R., Pathan, M., Vakali, A.: Content Delivery Networks. LNEE, vol. 9. Springer, Heidelberg (2008). https://doi.org/10.1007/978-3-540-77887-5
4. Fiadino, P., D'Alconzo, A., Casas, P.: Characterizing web services provisioning via CDNS: the case of facebook. In: 2014 International Wireless Communications and Mobile Computing Conference (IWCMC), pages 310–315. IEEE (2014)
5. Qiu, L., Padmanabhan, V.N., Voelker, G.M.: On the placement of web server replicas. In: Proceedings of the IEEE Twentieth Annual Joint Conference of the IEEE Computer and Communications Societies, INFOCOM 2001, vol. 3, pp. 1587–1596. IEEE (2001)
6. Akhtar, Z., Hussain, A., Katz-Bassett, E., Govindan, R.: DBit: assessing statistically significant differences in CDN performance. Comput. Netw. **107**, 94–103 (2016)
7. Hours, H., Biersack, E., Loiseau, P., Finamore, A., Mellia, M.: A study of the impact of DNS resolvers on CDN performance using a causal approach. Comput. Netw. **109**, 200–210 (2016)
8. Calder, M., Flavel, A., Katz-Bassett, E., Mahajan, R., Padhye, J.: Analyzing the performance of an anycast CDN. In: Proceedings of the 2015 ACM Conference on Internet Measurement Conference, pp. 531–537. ACM (2015)
9. Chen, F., Sitaraman, R.K., Torres, M.: End-user mapping: next generation request routing for content delivery. ACM SIGCOMM Comput. Commun. Rev. **45**, 167–181 (2015)
10. Sidiropoulos, A., Pallis, G., Katsaros, D., Stamos, K., Vakali, A., Manolopoulos, Y.: Prefetching in content distribution networks via web communities identification and outsourcing. World Wide Web **11**(1), 39–70 (2008)
11. Ariyasinghe, L.R., Wickramasinghe, C., Samarakoon, P.M.A.B., Perera, U.B.P., Prabhath Buddhika, R.A., Wijesundara, M.N.: Distributed local area content delivery approach with heuristic based web prefetching. In: 2013 8th International Conference on Computer Science & Education (ICCSE), pp. 377–382. IEEE (2013)
12. Krishnan, R., Madhyastha, H.V., Srinivasan, S., Jain, S., Krishnamurthy, A., Anderson, T., Gao, J.: Moving beyond end-to-end path information to optimize CDN performance. In: Proceedings of the 9th ACM SIGCOMM Conference on Internet Measurement Conference, pp. 190–201. ACM (2009)
13. Yu, M., Jiang, W., Li, H., Stoica, I.: Tradeoffs in CDN designs for throughput oriented traffic. In: Proceedings of the 8th International Conference on Emerging Networking Experiments and Technologies, pp. 145–156. ACM (2012)
14. MaxMind LLC. GeoIP (2010)
15. Jain, R., Chiu, D.-M., Hawe, W.R.: A Quantitative Measure of Fairness and Discrimination for Resource Allocation in Shared Computer System, vol. 38. Eastern Research Laboratory, Digital Equipment Corporation Hudson, MA (1984)

16. Veness, C.: Calculate distance and bearing between two latitude/longitude points using Haversine formula in Javascript. Movable Type Scripts (2011)
17. Jafari, S.J., Naji, H.: GeoIP clustering: solving replica server placement problem in content delivery networks by clustering users according to their physical locations. In: 2013 5th Conference on Information and Knowledge Technology (IKT), pp. 502–507. IEEE (2013)

Social

Toward Unified Cloud Service Discovery for Enhanced Service Identification

Abdullah Alfazi[1(✉)], Quan Z. Sheng[2], Ali Babar[1], Wenjie Ruan[1], and Yongrui Qin[3]

[1] School of Computer Science, The University of Adelaide,
Adelaide, SA 5005, Australia
{abdullah.alfazi,Ali.babar,wenjie.ruan}@adelaide.edu.au
[2] Department of Computing, Macquarie University, Sydney, Australia
michael.sheng@mq.edu.au
[3] School of Computing and Engineering, University of Huddersfield,
Huddersfield, UK
y.qin2@hud.ac.uk

Abstract. Nowadays cloud services are being increasingly used by professionals. A wide variety of cloud services are being introduced every day, and each of which is designed to serve a set of specific purposes. Currently, there is no cloud service specific search engine or a comprehensive directory that is available online. Therefore, cloud service customers mainly select cloud services based on the word of mouth, which is of low accuracy and lacks expressiveness. In this paper, we propose a comprehensive cloud service search engine to enable users to perform personalized search based on certain criteria including their own intention of use, cost and the features provided. Specifically, our cloud service search engine focuses on: (1) extracting and identifying cloud services automatically from the Web; (2) building a unified model to represent the cloud service features; and (3) prototyping a search engine for online cloud services. To this end, we propose a novel Service Detection and Tracking (SDT) model for modeling Cloud services. Then based on the SDT model, a cloud service search engine (CSSE) is implemented for helping effectively discover cloud services, relevant service features and service costs that are provided by the cloud service providers.

Keywords: Service discovery · Cloud service · Classification
Service identification

1 Introduction

Cloud computing has been growing rapidly in the past few years. It is a relatively new computing paradigm that has the capability to deliver several services on demand. In cloud computing, users are able to share a large pool of computing resources over the Internet with modest cost. Regardless of the computing

© Springer International Publishing AG, part of Springer Nature 2018
A. Beheshti et al. (Eds.): ASSRI 2015/2017, LNBIP 234, pp. 149–163, 2018.
https://doi.org/10.1007/978-3-319-76587-7_10

resources' quantity, location, and time, users can access the desirable computing resources [2]. In the area of cloud services, many research efforts have been conducted to handle security [10], privacy [9], and trust management [7], but cloud service discovery is still encountering challenges in terms of finding appropriate services to cloud users on the World Wide Web. With cloud computing, service discovery faces new challenges on the Internet due to a number of reasons. Firstly, cloud services offer different service functions, e.g., processing data, building business logics, and supporting infrastructure capabilities. Secondly, recent research has found that only 2% cloud service providers publish their services following the Web Services Description Language (WSDL). And the rest providers publish their services without considering any standards to describe their services and resources [8]. This has made cloud service discovery very challenging. Compared with Web services discovery, Web services in general use standard languages, such as the Web Services Description Language (WSDL), Unified Service Description Language (USDL), to expose their interfaces. Thirdly, the variety of Service Level Agreements (SLAs) between cloud service users and cloud service providers increases the difficulty of discovering cloud services.

Discovering service is widely considered an essential problem in many research areas such as ubiquitous computing, mobile networks, peer-to-peer (P2P) services, and service oriented computing [6,14]. In the past decade, service discovery has been a very active research area, particularly in Web services [13]. However, for cloud services, challenges need to be reconsidered and solutions for effective cloud service discovery are very limited.

To find a cloud service on the World Wide Web, a potential user normally relies on a general-purpose search engine to find a suitable cloud service. However, using such kind of search engine for this purpose is a tedious task because the search results provide large quantity of irrelevant cloud service search results, including news, blogs, journal papers, wiki, and articles, etc. This is because the term "Cloud" is a very general and widely used terminology. Therefore, the difficulty of discovering cloud services on the World Wide Web arises as a big and challenging issue. For example, we can easily see that cloud is one of the most important and popular terminologies in websites about meteorology. Moreover, many websites talking about cloud service are not necessary the provider of any cloud service. Some businesses also have nothing to do with cloud computing but they may use cloud in their names or service descriptions (e.g., cloud9carwash[1]). Figure 1 shows the first 100 search results from a current general-purpose search engine (Google or Bing) using different Keywords, such as cloud service, cloud storage, cloud service provider, cloud hosting, cloud software, cloud platform or cloud infrastructure to search for cloud services. Furthermore, general search engines are very weak in providing details about cloud service features (e.g., cloud service type, process limitation, storage maximums, memory capacity, and so on). Considering all these limitations of general-purpose search engines, in this

---

[1] http://www.cloud9carwash.com/.

work, we aim to design a cloud service search Engine to alleviate the aforementioned issues.

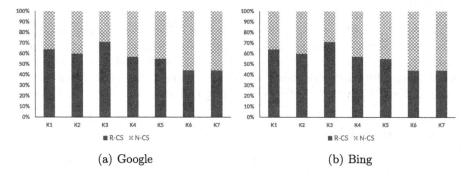

(a) Google   (b) Bing

Fig. 1. The first 100 searching results from two most popular search engines (Google and Bing) using different keywords, such as cloud service, cloud storage, cloud service provider, cloud hosting, cloud software, cloud platform and/or cloud infrastructure to search cloud services

In this paper, we focus on the design and implementation of a cloud service search engine (CSSE). CSSE helps distinguish between cloud services and other services available on the Internet. Furthermore, CSSE provides more details of a service and its features which can support cloud service search users on how to identify an appropriate cloud service towards their needs. The two main components of CSSE include (i) a cloud service identifier and (ii) a cloud service feature extractor. This identifier helps identify cloud services during the process of cloud service discovery and the process of determining a cloud service features. Moreover, the cloud service identifier can automatically identify cloud service by utilizing a classification method. Then, the feature extractor determines/extracts a cloud service's features using a cluster method and a novel approach, called Service Tracking and Detection (SDT), to detect and track other services. Finally, we can extract cloud service's features that can be used to facilitate the searching process. In a nutshell, the contributions of our work are as follows:

- We design and develop a cloud service search engine to provide highly accurate cloud service search results and provide useful details about cloud services' features, which can facilitate cloud service selection from search users.
- The cloud service identifier is built by utilizing cloud service features extracted from real cloud service providers.
- Inspired by the Topic Detection and Tracking [1], we propose a novel Service Detection and Tracking (SDT) methodology for the detection of cloud services.
- We build a unified model to expose the cloud service's features to a cloud service search user to ease the process of searching and comparison among a large amount of cloud services.

– We conduct extensive experiments to validate our proposed approach. The results demonstrate the applicability of our approach and its capability of effectively identifying and extracting cloud services' features from the World Wide Web.

The remainder of the paper is organized as follows. Section 2 reviews the related work. Section 3 presents our search engine (CSSE) architecture, including details of cloud service identification and extraction of cloud service features. Section 4 provides an implementation and our experimental study of our CSSE search engine. Finally Sect. 5 offers concluding remarks.

2   Related Work

Nowadays, the most popular approach for discovering cloud service refer ontology. Youseff et al. [16] classify cloud computing based on its components, consisting of five layers: the applications, the software environment, the software infrastructure, the software kernel, and the software hardware. Each layer contains one or more services depending on the level of abstraction. Further, each layer relies on computing concepts to measure limitations and strengths. Another attempt involves building an ontology based on the cloud business ontology model. Kang and Sim [4] propose a cloud service discovery system that uses an ontology-based approach to discover cloud services close to users' requirements. However, cloud service providers still need to register at the discovery system in order to publish their cloud services. Furthermore, their work relies on software agents to perform reasoning tasks (e.g., similarity reasoning, equivalent reasoning and numerical reasoning). Yoo et al. [15] select a cloud service that best meets a user's requirements by using a cloud ontology based on resource services. The authors use the similarity computing degree of virtual cloud service physical resources to determine the best cloud service for users. Dastjerdi et al. [3] propose an approach that uses ontology-based discovery for QoS-aware deployment of appliances on IaaS providers. This approach support end user to meet their needs from range of IaaS providers based on QoS preferences. However, the ontology design only find the suited IaaS providers for end users. Furthermore, the ontology does not support PaaS and SaaS providers.

Ma et al. [5] propose ontology-based resource management of cloud providers. This cloud computing ontology defined the concepts that described their relations. However, the ontology has to meet cloud service requirement and has been conducted in simulated environment. Rodríguez-García et al. [11,12] exploit an automatic general ICT domain that can be used to discover the cloud services best matching user needs. The authors use semantic annotation in order to improve the cloud service discovery results. From cloud service descriptions, semantic content can be extracted by using the annotation platform. Then, the semantic content can be used by the semantic search engine to assist users in finding those services that meet with their requirements and expectations.

In summary, these works did not consider the problem of how to use the cloud service web content to automatically identify cloud service. Moreover, they did not provide adequate details about features of cloud services on the Internet. To alleviate these issues, in this paper we aim to design and implement a cloud service search engine to provide highly accurate cloud service search results and provide useful details about cloud services' features, which can facilitate cloud service selection from search users.

3   Overview Cloud Service Search Engine

In this section, we first introduce our cloud service search engine (CSSE), then spotlight on describing our approach on cloud service identification and building cloud service profile.

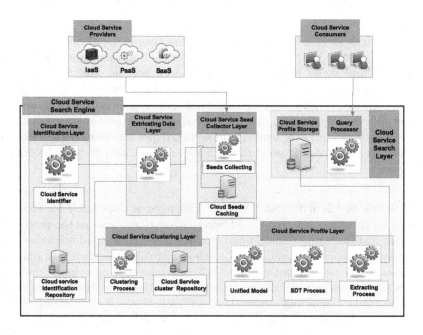

Fig. 2. Cloud service directory

3.1   CSSE Architecture

Figure 2 depicts the main components of the cloud service search engine (CSSE), which consists of six major layers: namely (1) *Cloud Services Seeds Collection Layer*, (2) *Cloud Services Extracting Data Layer*, (3) *Cloud Services Identification Layer*, (4) *Cloud Services Cluster Layer*, (5) *Cloud Services profile Layer* and (6) *Search Engine User Layer*.

Cloud Services Collector Layer: This layer is responsible for collecting possible cloud service seeds (i.e., the cloud services' URLs) in real environments. We initially collect cloud service seeds using two approaches. Firstly, we develop the cloud service source collector module that is able to collect cloud services automatically by crawling Web portals and indexes on search engines, such as Google, Bing, and Baidu. Secondly, we develop the cloud service seed inquiry based module that has the capability to inquire a cloud service and determine whether this cloud service has been cached in cloud service seeds repository. This inquiry can be done by both cloud service customers and cloud service providers. Furthermore, if the cloud service users inquire about a seed registered in the system, the system can return the inquiry result directly. Otherwise, the seed will be sent to the Cloud Services Extracting Data Layer for obtaining the essential details that can determine if the seed provides the cloud service.

Cloud Services Extracting Data Layer: This layer is responsible for extracting essential content in the cloud service source such as description, keywords, text content and hyper links. The cloud services' content lead to support of building automation cloud service identifier. The cloud services' content can be achieved automatically by filtering the cloud service source (i.e., cloud service source html homepage to text). Then the cloud services' content is sent to Cloud Services Identification Layer while cloud service hyper links sources can be sent to Cloud Service Cluster Layer if the source pass the Cloud Services Identification Layer.

Cloud Services Identification Layer: This layer is responsible for identifying cloud service provider. The Cloud Services identifier contains the process of identifying features to determine whether a given source is cloud service or not. This processing relies on classification method to realize the identification. The identification can be updated automatically after identifying a new cloud service provider to enhance identifying knowledge. Furthermore, the identifier only focuses on cloud computing which does not include cloud mobile computing. However, our cloud service directory can avoid the lack of success in identifying a cloud service source. Because it allows cloud service provider to register their services in our system, these cloud service sources can be added and can be recognized by the identification as a new cloud service provider.

Cloud Services Clustering Layer: This layer is responsible for clustering cloud service providers. The cloud service clustering is able to collect to the most similar cloud service into clusters based on clustering method. The clusters are built depend on two features which are cloud services' text and cloud services' hyper-links. Firstly, using cloud services' text can lead to finding the most similar cloud services into one cluster. Secondly, cloud service hyper-links can lead to detecting the exact services the cluster provide. This clustering approach is able to decrease the distance during detecting the service and tracking.

Cloud Services Cloud Profile Layer: This layer is responsible for generating cloud service profile based on the following processes:

1. *Modelling*: this process is responsible for building cloud service model. the model is built based on the service features. In addition, we observe several cloud services to identify the service features such as type, price, capacity. Moreover, this model is used to find the service in a cluster by investigating about the features. The process begins by selecting a cloud service provider and determine the service features that provide. Then, we build JSON model for this service. The JSON model includes many details about the cloud service which are the cloud service features. More details can be shown in Sect. 3.4.
2. *Detecting and Tracking*: this process is responsible for detecting and tracking other cloud services based on service feature model. This processing can search for the service inside the cluster by taking the JSON model which is built for the service and track this model. The process of detecting and tracking can investigate the whole cloud service websites to find the service. After we find the service we directly build the cloud service model for the cloud service.
3. *Extracting and Storing*: this process is responsible for extracting and storing the cloud service JSON model. The details of cloud services can be received from Detecting and Tracking process. Then, we can store this details in JSON model to support in building a cloud service search engine. We update this process weakly to discover any different in the cloud service features.

Search Engine User Layer: This layer provides a Web interface for users to search cloud services. A user can simply specify a searching keyword for finding cloud services. She can also specify other constraints (e.g., categories like IaaS) to narrow down the searching scope. Our system will contact the cloud service profile repository. If it is found in the repository, the detailed information (e.g., access link, features, description) of satisfied cloud services will be returned to the user.

3.2   Cloud Service Identification

In this section we demonstrate our approach to identify real cloud service providers. The proposed approach is a task that uses both information retrieval and machine learning techniques to identify cloud services. The approach of identifying task consists of number of steps. Firstly, we aim to build documents corpus which is cloud service sources. Therefore we assemble a large collection of cloud services providers' homepage and other homepage are highly related to cloud service but they are not real cloud services. This documents corpus is generated from the cloud services' homepage $S = \{s_1, ..., s_n\}$. Moreover, it exploits 5882 real cloud service and 5000 not cloud services to build classification method. Then, a document matrix is built to include the documents and is vectorized each document using the following weighting function $t = tf/(tf - td)$ where tf

denotes the term frequency, $tf - td$ the other total terms appear in the documents $s = \{t_1, ..., t_n\}$. Since we achieve highly dimension of terms, we try to reduce the dimensionality of the terms by using Latent Semantic Analysis (LSA) which is implemented using randomized Singular Value Decomposition (SVD) to build the document matrix. After we have built the document matrix we consider each term that uses weighted function as features. Finally, we utilize the cloud service text features to apply the classification method. We use k-Nearest Neighbor Classification which uses a Given data matrix of cloud services' terms $T = \{t_1, ..., t_n\}$ with K classifier and t vector $s \in S$. This classifier can find the K nearest class to cloud service vector s. The classification method can be helpful in distinguish between cloud service providers and non cloud services.

3.3   Cloud Service Clustering

Since using cloud service text features can be used to support identifying cloud service, identifying the cloud service features is a totally different task and need to extract new features and using different techniques. Therefore, we use clustering approach to find the service features by adding the cloud services' web page hyper-links as features. The cloud services hyper-links features are used to support in building cloud service profile features. In addition, we consider each hyper-link occurring in cloud serviced home page as features to build the clusters. This clustering can assign each cloud service provider as nearest as possible to ease discovering the service type and its features. The process of clustering consists of two methods. In the beginning, the clusters are built based on the term vectors that are weighted by term frequency. After we cluster the cloud services' terms. Then, we use the cloud service hyper-link $s = \{h_1, ..., h_n\}$ as features weighted by *Term Frequency* that shows in cloud services home page. Then, we apply K-Means which gives a number of clusters K that desirables and improved iteratively the Euclidean distance between each data point and the centroid nearest to it in our experiments. This processing is able to decrease the distance during applying Service Detection and Tracking process because it shows that the similar type of cloud service more frequently appear in the same cluster.

3.4   Cloud Service Profile

In this section we demonstrate the process of generating cloud service profile. The cloud service profile process will detect a service and tracking cloud services. The process consists of three phases, including Cloud Service Modelling, Service Detection and Tracking and Cloud Service Extracting and Storing. Algorithm 1 describes the cloud service profile processes.

Cloud Service Modelling: Cloud service modelling is embedded in cloud service features. This cloud service features have been achieved by observing several of cloud services in real environments. In addition, the cloud services features are

---

Algorithm 1. Cloud Service Profile Algorithm

Input: A set of cloud service sources belong to a cluster $\mathbb{C} = \{S_1, S_2, \ldots\}$, HF vectors $\overline{s_1}, \overline{s_2}, \ldots, \overline{s_{|C|}}$ for each cloud service source in $\mathbb{C}$, the number of nearest cloud service is K, the target cloud service source S_t

Output: $\mathbb{NS}$: a subset which contains K neerest cloud service sources of S_t from $\mathbb{C}$

    $\mathbb{NS} \leftarrow \emptyset$;

    while $\mathbb{C}$ is not empty **do**

        $\mathbb{NS} \leftarrow \emptyset$;

        Add S_t to sub set cluster $\mathbb{NS}$;

        Remove S_t from $\mathbb{C}$;

        for each $S_i \in \mathbb{C}$ **do**

            Compute $cosine(S_t, S_i)$ based on HF vectors $\overline{s_{S_t}}$ and $\overline{s_j}$ for cloud service sources S_t and S_j;

            Add S_i to subset $\mathbb{NS}$;

            Sort $\mathbb{NS}$ based on similarity score

            Pick up top K cloud service sources in $\mathbb{NS}$

        end for

    end while

Table 1. Cloud service features

Constant features	Variable features
Cloud providers	Cloud service CPU name
Cloud service name	Cloud service CPU capacity
Cloud service URL	Cloud service memory capacity
Cloud service HTML tag	Cloud service storage capacity
Cloud service HTML ID tag	Cloud service storage type
Cloud service HTML class tag	Cloud service price

different from service to service. For example, VPS features are totally different from storage features but they might share some common features see Fig. 3. However, we add some of constant features for all cloud service types that are provided by cloud service providers. Table 1 shows constant features and variable features.

Service Detection and Tracking: In the *Topic Detection and Tracking* (TDT) a topic is defined as a seminal event or activity, along with all directly related events and activities [1]. In order to replace the cloud service instead of topic, a cloud services is defined as a set of utilities that can provide several services. In addition, this services can be shared with several of providers. Therefore, the Service Detection and Tracking is a novel approach has been built to discover a service then track the same type of service over punch of cloud service

```
CSPN  : Godaddy

CSN   : VPS

CSPURL : godaddy.com/pro/managed-vps

CSPHTML : DIV
                                          CSPN  : Dropbox
CSPHTMLID : plans plan-container plan-
                                          CSN   : Storage
CSPHTMLclass : null
                                          CSPURL : www.dropbox.com/business/pricing
CSMemeory : 1GB RAM
                                          CSPHTML : DIV
CSStorage : 40GB
                                          CSPHTMLID : plans-table__pricing
CSprice : 43.99/mo
                                          CSPHTMLclass : null
CSBandwidth : unlimited
                                          CSStorage : 1TB
CSSystem : Linux
                                          CSprice : 11.58/mo

                                          CSUsers : 1
```

(a) Cloud Service VPS Godaddy   (b) Cloud Service Storage Dropbox

Fig. 3. Cloud service modelling

providers. The service detection and tracking is able to compare the features of different services. For example, if we pick up a service from a cluster and we detect this service is VPS then we will track this service inside the cluster based on cosine similarity score of hyper-links features because we assume this is VPS cluster. However, the service tracking is not easy task because each cloud service providers describe its service under different hyper-links. However, we observe many cloud services describe their service features under hyper-links such as plan, price, features or the name of service. Therefore, when we track a service we target to investigate those four hyper-links if they are available on cloud services' homepage, otherwise we can manually discover the cloud service.

Cloud Service Extracting and Storing: The aim of this processing is to extract cloud service features from cloud services inside the cluster. Therefore, we search for this cloud service features $s = \{f_1, ..., f_n\}$ inside the cluster then we start collect the cloud services' features. Our searching method uses initial point to search inside cloud service page which can be the plan, price, features or the name of service. This initial can be determined depend on the features that we already made. For example, if we search about VPS, we can investigate about VPS features such as memory capacity, storage capacity, CPU type, price and operating system. In addition, if we find these features we can add it to JSON model otherwise it become null.

4   Evaluation

4.1   Dataset: CSCE 2013

We use real-world cloud service sources metadata of the 5,883 valid cloud services and 5,000 valid non-cloud services in our evaluation. This data was chosen because it has been verified by our previous research work [8]. This dataset can easily provide labeling for our classification model. In our work, these Web sources of cloud services and non-cloud services have been processed in two phases. In the first phase, cloud service sources were fetched as HTML file. Then, cloud service hyper-links were extracted. In the second phase, cloud service sources were filtered to obtain only the cloud services sources text. In our experiments, we removed the HTML tags and non-English cloud services in the cloud services sources. To eliminate and filter the HTML tags, we used the HTML Parser[2]. Next, we eliminated non-English cloud services metadata using a language detection library[3]. Finally, the text features of the cloud service and non-cloud service sources only contain English language cloud services. Moreover, we discarded any cloud service sources with less than 30 terms to enhance our identification process. Then, we filtered the cloud services sources metadata and finally obtained 4,397 cloud services sources and dismissed 845 cloud services source text descriptions. Our final dataset comprises a total of 4,397 cloud services sources and 4,030 non-cloud services which has been divided into (i) 75% training data to build cloud service features model and (ii) 25% to test cloud service features. By using cloud services features, we ran the experiments to generate cloud service identifying model effectively. Then, we conducted the second experiment to show our model can effectively predict and detect cloud service.

4.2   Identifying Cloud Services

Based on our classification model, we ran the system to generate our cloud services identification by using the K-Nearest Neighbour. Firstly, we built cloud service corpus that contain 3,297 real cloud services and another non-cloud service corpus that includes 3,023 non-cloud services. Then, we achieved 987,457 terms from cloud service document matrix with high sparsity. However, after we removed the term sparsity the cloud service document matrix is still high dimension. Therefore, we used Latent Semantic Analysis (LSA) to reduce the dimension cloud document matrix and built our term features based on LSA concept. We used different number of K concepts and we ran our classification method. In the beginning, we ran the experiment with small number of K concepts and we gradually increase the K concepts. Figure 4 show the accuracy of term features using various k-nearest neighbor. In addition, it obtained high accuracy if we increase the k in k-nearest neighbor which achieved 86% with 6-nearest neighbor and increase the K concepts. In addition, we can see that the 500 concepts are obtained high accuracy with 6-nearest neighbor. However, we can notice that increasing the K of concepts can lead to decrease the identifying process because increasing of terms drives our identification to increase the noise data.

We also conducted an experiment to identify cloud services for proving the precision and recall of our proposed cloud service identifier. In this experiment

---

[2] http://htmlparser.sourceforge.net.

[3] https://code.google.com/p/language.

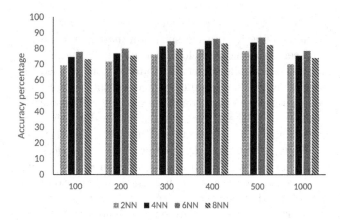

Fig. 4. Term features classification accuracy (%) using k-nearest neighbor classification, with LSA dimension reduction cloud service.

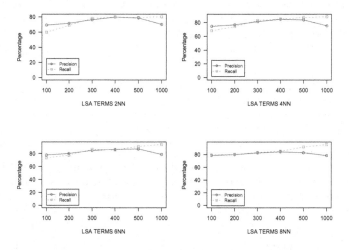

Fig. 5. The precision and recall using k-nearest neighbor classification, with LSA dimension reduction cloud service

(see Fig. 5 for the results), we used LSA terms that extracted from cloud service corpus then we run k-nearest neighbor model to determine the precision and recall. Moreover, the precision represents the percentage rate of distinguishing between cloud service or non-cloud service, whilst recall represents the percentage of cloud services identified. At the beginning, the experiment is started with 100 LSA terms then we increase the number respectively. We can see high relation between the number of LSA terms and precision and recall. we find that the increasing the number of LSA terms can reduce out model precision but it lead to increase the recall percent. Further more, we find that increasing the K number can lead to increase the recall sharply.

4.3 Cloud Service Profile

In order to determine the service, we ran our cloud profile algorithm to detect and track the service. This algorithm can search for a specific service over punch of cloud service providers. To ensure the accuracy of the results, we have labeled the cloud services sources manually before we ran our algorithm. Then, we compared our algorithm with manual processing. Figure 6 shows the precision result of cloud profile algorithm. We can see that if we increase the number of cloud service sources we increase the difficulty of detecting the service features because the precision is decrease. However, we find that service which are popular in

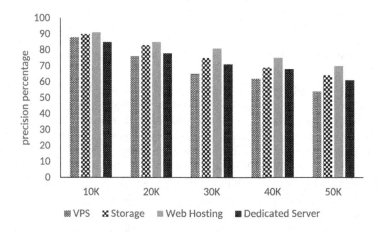

Fig. 6. Cloud service profile

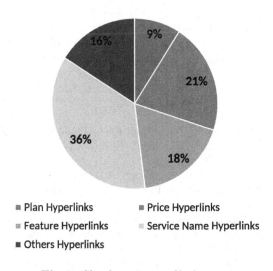

Fig. 7. Cloud service profile features

real environments such as cloud VPS and Web Hosting can be found precisely by our algorithm. Furthermore, we observed that some cloud service providers show their service features under alternative hyper-links such as plan, features and price.

Figure 7 shows that where mostly we can find that the cloud service features inside the cloud services. From Fig. 7 we found the 36% of cloud service describe their services under the service name hyper-links while 21% describe under the features hyper-links. More over, 18% of cloud service providers described their services under price hyper-link while only 9% of cloud services used plan hyper-links to describe their services. However, 18% of cloud service providers describe their services under specific name for the service which leads to difficulty in finding the service and its features.

5 Conclusions

With the growing adoption of cloud computing, efficiently finding relevant cloud services for customers is becoming a critical research issue. Unique characteristics of cloud services such as lack of standardization, diverse and dynamic services at different levels, make cloud services discovery a very challenging task. In this paper, we have conducted a comprehensive analysis of the cloud services currently available on the Web. We have developed a cloud service search engine that collects, extracts, and identifies cloud services. We have also provided details about cloud service features. Based on the cloud service identifier information, we have provided in-depth statistical analysis including the accuracy on cloud providers under current search engine and the relationship between a cloud service and its Web page profile. These results offer an overall view on the current status of cloud services in the World Wide Web. The most intriguing finding is the fact that cloud service web pages play a significant role in discovering cloud services and applications. Furthermore, we have proposed a novel approach to extract the service features based on our Service Detection and Tracking model which significantly increases the accuracy of identifying the service features.

References

1. Allan, J.: Topic Detection and Tracking: Event-Based Information Organization. The Information Retrieval Series, vol. 12. Springer, New York (2012). https://doi.org/10.1007/978-1-4615-0933-2
2. Armbrust, M., Fox, A., Griffith, R., Joseph, A.D., Katz, R., Konwinski, A., Lee, G., Patterson, D., Rabkin, A., Stoica, I., et al.: A view of cloud computing. Commun. ACM **53**(4), 50–58 (2010)
3. Dastjerdi, A.V., Tabatabaei, S.G.H., Buyya, R.: An effective architecture for automated appliance management system applying ontology-based cloud discovery. In: Proceedings of 10th IEEE/ACM International Conference on Cluster, Cloud and Grid Computing (CCGrid 2010), pp. 104–112 (2010)

4. Kang, J., Sim, K.M.: Cloudle: an ontology-enhanced cloud service search engine. In: Chiu, D.K.W., Bellatreche, L., Sasaki, H., Leung, H., Cheung, S.-C., Hu, H., Shao, J. (eds.) WISE 2010. LNCS, vol. 6724, pp. 416–427. Springer, Heidelberg (2011). https://doi.org/10.1007/978-3-642-24396-7_33

5. Ma, Y.B., Jang, S.H., Lee, J.S.: Ontology-based resource management for cloud computing. In: Nguyen, N.T., Kim, C.-G., Janiak, A. (eds.) ACIIDS 2011. LNCS (LNAI), vol. 6592, pp. 343–352. Springer, Heidelberg (2011). https://doi.org/10. 1007/978-3-642-20042-7_35

6. Meshkova, E., Riihijärvi, J., Petrova, M., Mähönen, P.: A survey on resource discovery mechanisms, peer-to-peer and service discovery frameworks. Comput. Netw. **52**(11), 2097–2128 (2008)

7. Noor, T.H., Sheng, Q.Z.: Trust as a service: a framework for trust management in cloud environments. In: Bouguettaya, A., Hauswirth, M., Liu, L. (eds.) WISE 2011. LNCS, vol. 6997, pp. 314–321. Springer, Heidelberg (2011). https://doi.org/ 10.1007/978-3-642-24434-6_27

8. Noor, T.H., Sheng, Q.Z., Ngu, A.H., Dustdar, S.: Analysis of web-scale cloud services. IEEE Internet Comput. **18**(4), 55–61 (2014)

9. Pearson, S., Benameur, A.: Privacy, security and trust issues arising from cloud computing. In: Proceedings of IEEE Second International Conference on Cloud Computing Technology and Science (CloudCom 2010), pp. 693–702 (2010)

10. Ren, K., Wang, C., Wang, Q.: Security challenges for the public cloud. IEEE Internet Comput. **16**(1), 69–73 (2012)

11. Rodríguez-García, M.A., Valencia-García, R., García-Sánchez, F.: Creating a semantically-enhanced cloud services environment through ontology evolution. Future Gener. Comput. Syst. **32**, 295–306 (2014)

12. Rodríguez-García, M.Á., Valencia-García, R., García-Sánchez, F., Samper-Zapater, J.J.: Ontology-based annotation and retrieval of services in the cloud. Knowl.-Based Syst. **56**, 15–25 (2014)

13. Segev, A., Sheng, Q.: Bootstrapping ontologies for web services. IEEE Trans. Serv. Comput. **5**(1), 33–44 (2012)

14. Wei, Y., Blake, M.B.: Service-oriented computing and cloud computing: challenges and opportunities. IEEE Internet Comput. **14**(6), 72–75 (2010)

15. Yoo, H., Hur, C., Kim, S., Kim, Y.: An ontology-based resource selection service on science cloud. In: Ślęzak, D., Kim, T., Yau, S.S., Gervasi, O., Kang, B.-H. (eds.) GDC 2009. CCIS, vol. 63, pp. 221–228. Springer, Heidelberg (2009). https://doi. org/10.1007/978-3-642-10549-4_26

16. Youseff, L., Butrico, M., Da Silva, D.: Toward a unified ontology of cloud computing. In: Proceedings of 2008 Grid Computing Environments Workshop (GCE 2008), pp. 1–10 (2008)

Predicting Issues for Resolving
in the Next Release

Shien Wee Ng[(✉)], Hoa Khanh Dam[(✉)], Morakot Choetkiertikul[(✉)],
and Aditya Ghose[(✉)]

University of Wollongong, Wollongong, Australia
{swn881,hoa,mc650,aditya}@uow.edu.au

Abstract. Deciding which features or requirements (or commonly referred to as *issues*) to be implemented for the next release is an important and integral part of any type of incremental development. Existing approaches consider the next release problem as a single or multi-objective optimization problem (on customer values and implementation costs) and thus adopt evolutionary search-based techniques to address it. In this paper, we propose a novel approach to the next release problem by mining historical releases to build a predictive model for recommending if a requirement should be implemented for the next release. Results from our experiments performed on a dataset of 22,400 issues in five large open source projects demonstrate the effectiveness of our approach.

Keywords: Software as a Service (SaaS) · Next release problem
Software analytics

1 Introduction

Successful software products must continually evolve over time (Lehman's laws of software evolution [9]), which is realized through a series of software releases. A release is a new version of an evolving product characterized by a collection of newly implemented functionalities, bug fixes or modifications of existing functionalities – all of which are commonly regarded as *issues* if the software project is managed using an issue tracking system (e.g. JIRA). Determining issues to be resolved in the next release is challenging for large and complex software projects. Different practitioners are involved in the planning for a release, i.e. the determination of which issues to be resolved for the next release, considering the cost, resource constraints, customer values, and various other factors. This is commonly known as the *next release problem (NRP)* [2,13] in requirement engineering.

Existing approaches tend to model NRP as an optimization problem. The implementation of a requirement (or issue) increases customer values but requires some cost. Hence, those existing approaches search for the optimal set of issues to be implemented for the next release of a software product. There may

© Springer International Publishing AG, part of Springer Nature 2018
A. Beheshti et al. (Eds.): ASSRI 2015/2017, LNBIP 234, pp. 164–177, 2018.
https://doi.org/10.1007/978-3-319-76587-7_11

be a single criteria (e.g. maximizing customer value [2]) or multiple criteria (e.g. maximizing customer value and minimizing cost [13]) for the optimality of a solution. This search-based software engineering problem is known as NP-hard (non-deterministic polynomial-time hardness) and most of existing approaches leverage evolutionary techniques to find the optimal solutions.

State-of-the-art NRP techniques however have not leveraged historical data from previous releases. As a software product evolves rapidly, many releases are generated over time (in the sprit of continuous delivery to retain competitive edge). Historical releases form a valuable knowledge which can be mined to extract insights to inform decisions in planning for future releases. We propose an approach to leverage the historical data on previous releases and build a machinery to recommend which new issues should be resolved for the next release using existing machine learning techniques. In addition, existing NRP techniques were evaluated on small datasets (in the order of ten to hundreds of real issues) or on artificially created issues. A data-driven approach to the NRP however requires much larger datasets of real issues.

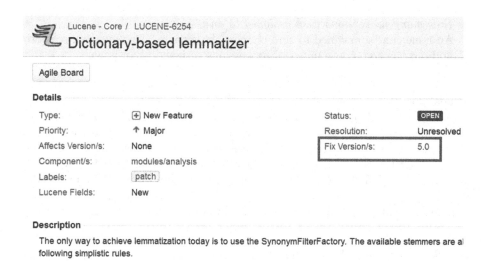

Fig. 1. An example of an issue assigned with a fix version

Many software projects today are managed through an issue tracking system such as JIRA and Bugzilla. Versions are points-in-time for a project, which help the team schedule and organize their releases (i.e. release planning). Issues are assigned to a version, indicating that those issues are scheduled to resolve for that version (i.e. a release). In JIRA, when an issue is opened, the "Fix Version(s)" field is used for specifying the version the team plan to fix this issue in. Figure 1 shows an example of a new feature request recorded as issue LUCENE-6247 in the Apache Lucene project. This issue is scheduled to be resolved in version 5.0.

The first contribution of this paper is a study to understand how release planning is done in open source settings. We study the use of the "Fix Version(s)" field in a number of large open source projects that use JIRA for issue tracking and release management. Specifically, we seek to answer the following questions:

1. *How many issues were assigned a fix version?*
   Answering this question helps us understand if assigning a fix version to an issue is a common practice of release planning in open source settings.
2. *When was an issue assigned to a fix version?*
   This question seeks to understand the common time when people start planning for the version in which an issue is resolved.
3. *How frequently was the fix version of an issue changed?*
   Issues can be initially assigned to a version, and later reassigned to another version. We would like to know the frequency of such changes throughout the lifecycle of issues.
4. *Who assigned the fix version?*
   With this question, we want to investigate who usually takes the role of release planning.
5. *How many fix versions were assigned to an issue?*
   An issue can be assigned to zero or more fix versions. This question seeks to find out the common number of fix versions assigned to an issue.

The second contribution of this paper is a predictive model which recommends whether an issue should be resolved for the next release. Our model employs Random Forests [3], a machine learning ensemble method which is effective in many prediction tasks in software engineering [4,8]. Following the notions of the next release problem, our model uses information associated with an issue which reflect the effort/cost of resolving it, the degree of interests in having the issue resolved, and the customer (i.e. the reporter) importance. Our prediction model trained using Random Forest was able to achieve on average 72% precision, 70% recall, 71% F-measure, and 81% area under the ROC curve (AUC).

2 A Study of "Fix Version(s)"

2.1 Dataset

This section describes our study of the use of the "Fix Version(s)" field in five large open source projects, namely Apache Hadoop Common, Apache Jackrabbit Content Repository, Apache Lucene - Core, JBoss Developer Studio, and Mulesoft Mule. Issues from all of these projects are recorded in the JIRA issue tracking system. We used the Representational State Transfer (REST) API[1] provided by JIRA to query and collected the issue reports from those projects.

For each project, we collected all the *closed* issues which were recorded in its issue tracking system until the time when this study was conducted. We then

---

[1] https://docs.atlassian.com/jira/REST/latest/.

Table 1. Dataset

Project	# dates	# collected issues	# valid issues
Hadoop	2005-07-24 to 2016-03-17	10,863	6,841
Jackrabbit	2004-09-16 to 2015-10-22	3,860	2,790
JBoss	2007-03-16 to 2016-03-24	3,141	2,258
Lucene	2001-10-09 to 2016-03-14	7,110	4,826
Mule	2004-03-22 to 2016-03-14	8,924	5,685
Total		26,788	22,400

filtered out issues that were closed due to being marked as duplicate, invalid or "wontfix". For instance, we collected 10,863 closed issues in Hadoop from 2005-07-24 and 2016-03-17. After the filtering process, 6,841 issues remains in our dataset. Table 1 summarizes the number of issues collected from the five projects. In total our dataset consists of 22,400 issues from the five projects.

2.2 How Many Issues Were Assigned to a Fix Version?

We found that most of the valid issues across the five open source projects were assigned with a fix version. In fact, 98% of the issues in Mule had a version assigned to it. This number is 88% in Lucene, 90% in Jackrabbit, 92% in JBoss, and 94% in Hadoop. Our findings suggest that assigning a fix version to issues is a common practice of release planning in the open source projects that use JIRA. The active use of the "Fix Version(s)" field within and across projects indicate the validity of the fix versions for our study.

2.3 When Was an Issue Assigned to a Fix Version?

Fix version(s) can be assigned to an issue at different stages in the issue's life. While an issue is still open, the fix version assigned to the issue indicates a target, i.e. the team aims to resolve the issue when that version is released. On the other hand, when an issue is resolved or closed, the "Fix Version/s" field conveys the version(s) that the issue was resolved in. For example, issue HADOOP-3816[2] in project Apache Hadoop was initially assigned to version 0.18.0 when the issue was created. However, at the time the issue was closed, it was associated with version 0.19.0, indicating that it was actually resolved and shipped with version 0.19.0 (instead with version 0.18.0).

We processed the change logs of all the issues in our dataset to identify when issues were *first* assigned to a fix version. We observed different patterns in the projects from our findings (see Fig. 2). In Lucene and JBoss, a large number of issues (47% and 57%) was assigned to a fix version at the time when the issues were created. On the other hand, the majority of issues in Jackrabbit (40%) and

---

[2] https://issues.apache.org/jira/browse/HADOOP-3816.

Mule (47%) did not have a fix version assigned when they were created, but within the five days after that. Across the five projects, there is a small portion of issues which were first assigned a fix version between 6 to 10 days after their creation. 32% of the issues in Hadoop were not assigned to a fix version 10 days after creation.

2.4   How Frequently Was the Fix Version of an Issue Changed?

An issue can be initially assigned to a fix version, and then at a later stage reassigned to another version. Again, by processing the change log of each issue, we counted the number of times the fix version of the issue were changed. Table 2 shows the distribution of the number of changes to the fix version of all issues in the five projects. The result shows that the majority of the issues have been assigned at least one fix version.

Changes which are done to the fix version field may be due to the changes in release planning [6]. Other factors may include mistakes done by an individual and issue not being able to be resolved by a designated deadline. Figure 3 shows an example of mistakes done by an individual in the assignment of fix version to the issue JCR-3665 of the Apache Jackrabbit project. The issue was initially

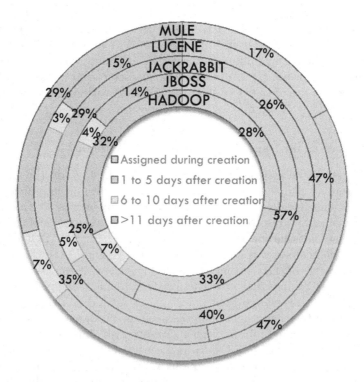

Fig. 2. The distribution of the time (with respect to the creation time) when an issue was first assigned with a fix version

Table 2. The distribution of the number of times the fix version of an issue was changed

Project	min	median	mean	max	std
Hadoop	1	1	1.4	11	0.83
Jackrabbit	1	1	1.5	8	0.77
JBoss	1	1	1.9	14	1.49
Lucene	1	1	1.4	15	0.84
Mule	1	1	1.7	11	1.10

assigned to fix version 2.7.1 and was changed to fix version 2.7.2. Upon realizing that the issue was indeed part of fix version 2.7.1, changes was made again to reassign fix version 2.7.2 back to its initial target, i.e. fix version 2.7.1.

2.5   Who Assigned the Fix Version?

Each issue may involve a number of participants such as the person who created the issue (i.e. the reporter), the developer who was assigned to resolve the

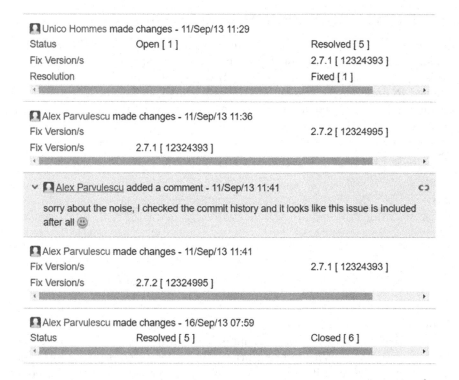

Fig. 3. Screenshot showing a mistake done by an individual on the fix version of an issue

issue (i.e. the assignee), or other people in the team. Those stakeholders may also participate in planning which version an issue should be resolved in. Our study has found that in Jackrabbit, Lucene, and Mule the issue reporter play a dominant role in release planning for the issues they reported. For example, 63% of the updates made to the "Fix Version(s)" field of all the collected issues in Lucene were done by the reporters. In some other projects (Hadoop and JBoss), the other team members have done this task most often. In all the five projects, the assignees rarely updated the "Fix Version(s)" field (Table 3).

Table 3. The distribution of who assigned fix versions to issues

Project	Reporter	Assignee	Someone else
Hadoop	34%	8%	58%
Jackrabbit	42%	19%	39%
JBoss	40%	18%	42%
Lucene	63%	17%	20%
Mule	41%	26%	33%

2.6   How Many Fix Versions Were Assigned to an Issue?

An issue can be assigned to zero or more versions, indicating that the team aims to multiple targets. In most of the five projects, we found that the majority of the issues (71% in Jackrabbit, 87% in JBoss and Hadoop, 73% in Mule) were assigned to only one fix version. On the other hand, in Lucene issues assigned with more than one versions are the majority, constituting 51%.

Fig. 4. Screenshot showing multiple fix versions assigned to an issue

In cases where issues were assigned to multiple fix versions, we have found that the team was concurrently maintaining multiple branches of a product (product variations). When a new feature was implemented or a bug was fixed, they sometimes wanted it to be released with a newer version of those product variations. For example, issue JCR-3949 in Apache Jackrabbit was a bug which affected five existing versions 2.4.5, 2.6.5, 2.10.1, 2.8.1, and 2.11.3 (see Fig. 4).

The Jackrabbit team planned to fix this bug and released the fix in the next versions of those previous releases, e.g. release 2.4.6 is the next version of release 2.4.5. Note that these versions can be either external or internal releases.

3 Next Release Recommendation

The second part of our work is to build a machinery which recommends whether an issue should be resolved for the next release. This machinery is built as a predictive model which is trained using historical releases and issues. We used the same dataset from the above study (Sect. 2.1) for both training and testing. The predictive model is built as a classification which determines if an issue is resolved for the next version (the *true* class) or not (the *false* class). We employed Random Forests (RF), a randomized ensemble of decision trees. Random Forests [3] is a significant improvements of the decision tree approach by generating many classification and regression trees, each of which is built on a random resampling of the data, with random subset of variables at each node split. Tree predictions are then aggregated through voting. We trained 100 classification trees using the *randomeforest-matlab*[3] package for Matlab.

For the training and testing of our predictive model, we need to label each issue (true or false) in our dataset (i.e. ground truths). We do so by obtaining the fix version(s) assigned to each issue, and check if at least of these versions was the next release (with respect to the time when it was assigned with the issue), then we label the outcome of this issue as *true* (and *false* otherwise). To determine if a version V was the next release or not, we obtained the time when it was assigned to the issue, and get the released version U that was after and closest to the point in time. If V and U are the same version, then V was in fact the next release.

Our predictive model has a number of predictors which are features we extracted from an issue. These features are relevant in the reasoning about the selection of an issue for the next release. These features are also generic. This means that we will be able to extract the same set of features from data in different software projects. These software projects can be using JIRA as their issue tracking system or any other existing issue tracking systems. We divide those features into three group: one reflecting the effort/cost of resolving an issue, one reflecting the degree of interests in having an issue resolved, and one reflect the customer (in this case the reporter) importance. These are generally the factors considered in the next release problem [2,13] (Table 4).

The first group includes the issue type and two textual features derived from the title and description of an issue. Each issue is assigned a *type* (e.g. Task, Bug, New feature, Improvement, and Documentation) which indicates the nature of the task associated with resolving the issue (e.g. fixing a bug or implementing a new feature). Implementing a new feature might require more effort than fixing bug. For example, in project Moodle "New Feature" issues were on average assigned to 26 story points, while "Bug" issues were assigned to 11 story points.

---

[3] https://code.google.com/archive/p/randomforest-matlab/.

Table 4. Features of an issue

Feature	Description
Type	Issue type
Priority	Issue priority
Votes	The number of votes for an issue
Watchers	The number of people who are watching an issue
No. of comments	The number of comments
Issue links	The number of dependencies of an issues (including blocking)
Readability and word length	Readability and the length of title + description
Reporter reputation	Reflect the reporter importance
Remaining time	The time between the prediction time and the next release date (i.e. how many dates left)

We also extract the *length* and the *readability* index of the title and the description of an issue. Previous studies (e.g. [7]) have shown that issue reports that are easier to read are fixed faster. The length is measured in terms of the number of words in the title and description, while we used Gunning Fox [10] to measure the readability index.

The second group of features concern the degree of interests drawn by an issue. First, the issue's *priority* presents the order in which an issue should be attended with respect to other issues. Issues with a higher priority may be scheduled to be resolved first, and thus assigned with sooner releases. JIRA allows stakeholders to vote for a particular issue, which is a form of expressing their preference for that issue to be resolved or completed. JIRA also allows to watch an issue, subscribing for notifications of any updates relating to that issue. Thus, the number of *votes* and *watchers* of each issue are extracted. Furthermore, highly interested issues tend to attract more activities such as comments. Thus, we also extract the number of *comments* posted to an issue. We note that all of these numbers were extracted up to the point where a prediction is made. For example, although the final number of comments posted on an issue is 10, there were only 4 comments made at Day 3 since the issue was created. If we want to make a prediction at Day 3, then we use 4 as the input (rather than 10). This is to avoid the leaking phenomenon in which "future" information was used to build a prediction model.

In the next release problem, the customer's importance to the company is an essential factor in prioritizing requirements from different customers. In the open source context, we model this as the reputation of the person who reported an issue. Previous studies have used the reporter reputation to predict whether a new bug report will receive immediate attention or not [7], or found that bugs reported by low reputation people are less likely to be reopened [14], or used issue reporter's reputation to predict the delay in resolving an issue [4]. For our model, we use Hooimeijer's submitter reputation [7] as follows:

$$reputation(D) = \frac{|opened(D) \cap fixed(D)|}{|opened(D)| + 1}$$

The reputation of a reporter D is measured as the ratio of the number of issues that D has reported and resolved to the number of issues that D has reported plus one.

Finally, there are interdependencies between issues, which is an important factor that needs to consider in selecting issues for the next release. For example, in order to implement a new functionality requested in an issue, one requires the existence of another functionality requested in another issue, then both issues need to be in the same release or the latter should be put in the earlier releases than the former. To reflect this nature, we extract the number of links (e.g. blocking, related to, etc.) an issue has with other issues. Our future work would investigate to leverage the actual nature of the links (as done with using the networked classification in previous work [5]).

4   Evaluation

4.1   Experimental Setting

The predictions of the next release have been made at three different prediction times, day 0, day 6, and day 11 from the issue's creation date, e.g. predictions for an issue created on January, 1 2015 will be done at January, 1, 6, and 11 2015. We treated the predicting of the next release as binary classification i.e. the *true* class means an issue that has been resolved for the next release, the *false* class, in contrast, is an issue that has not been resolved for the next release. Table 5 shows the number of issues in each class (*True* and *False*) across three prediction times. We noted that the label of an issues (i.e. true and false) can be changed corresponding to prediction times. For example, issue *HADOOP-11301* in the Hadoop project was created on November, 12 2014. This issue falls into the *False* class in the day 0 and 6 prediction. In the day 11 prediction, this issue turns into the *True* class because it has been assigned to the release version 2.7.0 which the release date is on April, 04 2015. Note that the extraction of the features is also associated to the prediction times.

We used 10-fold cross validation which an issue i^{th} in every ten issues is included in fold i^{th}. We acknowledged that the number of issues in both classes are imbalance (class imbalanced). There are only 20%–38% of issues fall into the true class. To avoid a bias of classifiers to predict the majority class, we do so by randomly selecting negative samples (i.e. the false class) as the same number of issues in the true class in each prediction. For example, in the Hadoop project, there are 1,336 true-issues at day 0 prediction. We randomly selected 1,336 false-issues for our experiments. We employed Random Forests to train our classifiers to predict whether an issue is resolved for the next release. We obtained 100 binary classification trees using the Random Forests for Matlab (see footnote 3).

4.2   Performance Measures

The false samples are not of interest in predicting next release. Reporting the average of precision/recall across classes is likely to overestimate the true performance. The evaluation focus on the performance of predicting the true class. The confusion matrix is then used to store the correct and incorrect predictions made by a classifier. For example, if an issue is classified as *true* when it is *true*, the classification is a true positive (tp). If the issue is classified as *true* when actually it is *false*, then the classification is a false positive (fp). If the issue is classified as *false* when it is in fact *true*, then the classification is a false negative (fn). Finally, if the issue is classified as *false* and it is in fact *false*, then the classification is true negative (tn). The values stored in the confusion matrix are used to compute Precision, Recall, and F-measure to evaluate the performance of the predictive models:

– Precision: The ratio of correctly predicted *true* issue over all the issues predicted as *true* issue. It is calculated as:

$$Prec = \frac{tp}{tp + fp}$$

– Recall: The ratio of correctly predicted *true* issue over all of the actually *true* issue. It is calculated as:

$$Re = \frac{tp}{tp + fn}$$

– F-measure: Measures the weighted harmonic mean of the precision and recall. It is calculated as:

$$F - measure = \frac{2 * Prec * Re}{Prec + Re}$$

– Area Under the ROC Curve (AUC) is used to evaluate the degree of discrimination achieved by the model. The value of AUC is ranged from 0 to 1 and random prediction has AUC of 0.5. The advantage of AUC is that it is insensitive to decision threshold like precision and recall. The higher AUC indicates a better predictor.

4.3   Results

Table 6 shows the predictive performance in terms of precision, recall, F-measure, and Area under ROC curve (AUC) across the three different prediction times. The prediction at day 0 and day 6 achieved the highest F-measure – it achieves 0.72 F-measure averaging across all projects. In the Hadoop project, Random forests achieves the highest precision and F-measure – it achieves 0.78 precision and 0.77 F-measure (averaging across the three prediction times), while the highest recall of 0.76 is achieved in the Lucene and Mule projects. Note that all projects and all prediction times achieve AUC greater than 0.5. From the results made at 3 different prediction times, we conclude that predictions made at a later date does not improve the overall performance of the classifier. This in return tells us that predictions on whether an issue is to be resolved for the next release can be done upon the creation of the issue (day 0).

Table 5. Experimental settings

Project	Day 0		Day 6		Day 11		#issues
	True	False	True	False	True	False	
Hadoop	1,336	5,097	1,354	5,079	1,370	5,063	6,433
Jackrabbit	875	1,635	983	1,527	979	1,531	2,510
JBoss	691	1,397	735	1,353	733	1,355	2,088
Lucene	1,640	2,600	1,793	2,447	1,826	2,414	4,240
Mule	2,084	3,463	2,067	3,480	2,054	3,493	5,547

Table 6. Experimental results

Project		Day 0	Day 6	Day 11	Project		Day 0	Day 6	Day 11
Hadoop	Prec	0.74	0.81	0.79	Jackrabbit	Prec	0.70	0.67	0.67
	Re	0.69	0.78	0.79		Re	0.69	0.67	0.67
	F	**0.71**	**0.80**	**0.79**		F	0.69	0.67	0.67
	AUC	0.81	0.89	0.87		AUC	0.79	0.75	0.74
JBoss	Prec	0.69	0.68	0.69	Lucene	Prec	0.77	0.75	0.72
	Re	0.61	0.59	0.54		Re	**0.79**	**0.75**	**0.72**
	F	0.65	0.63	0.61		F	0.78	0.75	0.72
	AUC	0.81	0.79	0.78		AUC	0.87	0.84	0.81
Mule	Prec	0.73	0.72	0.72					
	Re	**0.76**	**0.76**	**0.75**					
	F	0.75	0.74	0.73					
	AUC	0.83	0.82	0.82					

5 Related Work

Since the next release problem (NRP) was formally introduced by Bagnall et al.
[2], there has been a range of interests on addressing this problem. Bagnall
et al. considers it as a constraint optimization problem. Each requirement is
associated with a customer's value and a certain cost of implementing it. There
are also interdependencies between requirements such as one requirement being
a prerequisite of another. Hence, the requirements are selected such that the
customer values are maximized under the constraint that the cost is kept under
a given threshold. A number of search-based techniques (e.g. using backbone
multi-level search as in [12] have been proposed to tackle this problem. Zhang
et al. [13] later approached the NRP as a multi-objective optimization problem
in which two (conflicting) objectives are considered: maximizing the customer
values and minimizing the cost. The solutions are then presented as a Pareto-
optimal front. Evolutionary techniques (e.g. genetic algorithms) are the common

approach that have been used. In contrast with existing work, our approach to the NRP leverage data mining (i.e. mining historical releases and machine learning (i.e. building a predictive model for selecting issues to be resolved for the next release).

The approach proposed here is relevant to the field of release engineering. Release engineering as defined by Adams and McIntosh [1] is the process which involves bringing individual code contributions from a developer's workplace to the end user in the form of software releases. Release engineering can be further broken down into six different phases, code change integration, continuous integration, build system specifications, infrastructure-as-code, deployment and release. Throughout the lifecycle of a project, different tasks are to be performed by release engineers, i.e. personnel involved in the development, maintenance and the organization's release infrastructure [1]. Our approach utilizes the historical information available from issue repositories of open sourced projects. This is to provide insights to release engineers in determining if an issue is to be resolved by the next release.

6   Conclusions and Future Work

In this paper, we have presented the results from an empirical study on the use of the "fix version" field for release planning in five large open source projects. In these projects, our findings suggest that assigning fix version to issues is a common practice in those projects (and possibly those using the JIRA tracking system). Our study also found that most of the issues were assigned a fix version at the time they were created and most of them changed only once. We also found that reporters played a dominant role in release planning.

The NRP is a special case of the release planning problem [11] which deals with decisions related to selecting and assigning features to a sequence of consecutive releases. Our approach can be extended to address the release planning problem by doing multi-class classification (instead of binary classification) where each class represents a version. One of our future work involves investigating this approach. We will also look into using different machine learning algorithms (e.g. SVM, Logistic Regression) to build a classifier and identify the best performing algorithm.

References

1. Adams, B., McIntosh, S.: Modern release engineering in a nutshell - why researchers should care. In: 2016 IEEE 23rd International Conference on Software Analysis, Evolution, and Reengineering (SANER), vol. 5, pp. 78–90, March 2016
2. Bagnall, A.J., Rayward-Smith, V.J., Whittley, I.: The next release problem. Inf. Softw. Technol. **43**(14), 883–890 (2001)
3. Breiman, L.: Random forests. Mach. Learn. **45**, 5–32 (2001)
4. Choetkiertikul, M., Dam, H.K., Tran, T., Ghose, A.: Characterization and prediction of issue-related risks in software projects. In: Proceedings of the 12th Working Conference on Mining Software Repositories (MSR), pp. 280–291. IEEE (2015)

5. Choetkiertikul, M., Dam, H.K., Tran, T., Ghose, A.: Predicting delays in software projects using networked classification. In: Proceedings of the 30th IEEE/ACM International Conference on Automated Software Engineering (ASE), pp. 353–364 (2015)
6. Choetkiertikul, M., Dam, H.K., Tran, T., Ghose, A.: Predicting the delay of issues with due dates in software projects. Empir. Softw. Eng. 1–41 (2017)
7. Hooimeijer, P., Weimer, W.: Modeling bug report quality. In: Proceedings of the 22 IEEE/ACM International Conference on Automated Software Engineering (ASE), pp. 34–44. ACM Press, November 2007
8. Kocaguneli, E., Menzies, T., Keung, J.W.: On the value of ensemble effort estimation. IEEE Trans. Softw. Eng. **38**(6), 1403–1416 (2012)
9. Lehman, M.M.: On understanding laws, evolution, and conservation in the large-program life cycle. J. Syst. Softw. **1**, 213–221 (1984)
10. McCallum, D.R., Peterson, J.L.: Computer-based readability indexes. In: Proceedings of the ACM '82 Conference, pp. 44–48. ACM (1982)
11. Ruhe, G., Saliu, M.O.: The art and science of software release planning. IEEE Softw. **22**(6), 47–53 (2005)
12. Xuan, J., Jiang, H., Ren, Z., Luo, Z.: Solving the large scale next release problem with a backbone-based multilevel algorithm. IEEE Trans. Softw. Eng. **38**(5), 1195–1212 (2012)
13. Zhang, Y., Harman, M., Mansouri, S.A.: The multi-objective next release problem. In: Proceedings of the 9th Annual Conference on Genetic and Evolutionary Computation, GECCO 2007, pp. 1129–1137. ACM, New York (2007)
14. Zimmermann, T., Nagappan, N., Guo, P.J., Murphy, B.: Characterizing and predicting which bugs get reopened. In: Proceedings of the 34th International Conference on Software Engineering (ICSE), pp. 1074–1083. IEEE Press, June 2012

Trust and Privacy Challenges in Social Participatory Networks

Haleh Amintoosi[1,3], Mohammad Allahbakhsh[2,3(✉)], Salil S. Kanhere[3],
and Aleksandar Ignjatovic[3]

[1] Ferdowsi University of Mashhad, Mashhad, Iran
amintoosi@um.ac.ir
[2] University of Zabol, Zabol, Iran
allahbakhsh@uoz.ac.ir
[3] The University of New South Wales, Sydney, Australia
{haleha,mallahbakhsh,salilk,ignjat}@cse.unsw.edu.au

Abstract. Trust and privacy in social participatory sensing systems
have always been challenging issues. Trust and privacy are somehow
interconnected and interdependent concepts, and solutions that take into
account both of these two parameters simultaneously will result in better people evaluation in the context of social participatory networks. In
this paper, we propose a trust and privacy aware framework for recruiting workers in social participatory networks which controls and adjusts
the privacy and trustworthiness of workers accordingly. The proposed
method employs the reputation scores gained by a worker to adjust the
privacy settings from which the worker can benefit. This interdependency
helps requesters find more suitable workers. The simulation results show
the promising behavior of the proposed framework.

1 Introduction

Social participatory networks, as a means for enlisting human in online tasks,
have grown in popularity in past few years. Ushahidi (http://ushahidi.com) is
an example of such networks, which recruits people as workers, to participate in
online tasks or report events and incidents through multiple channels, including
SMS, email, Twitter, and the World Wide Web. Social participatory networks
enable individuals and organizations, as service requesters, to leverage an abun-
dant workforce to accomplish tasks such as describing a photo, proofreading a
text, etc.

The success of a typical social participatory network depends on overcoming
several challenges. The first challenge is recruiting sufficient number of well-
suited workers, i.e., those who satisfy the task's requirements. An indicator for
this suitability is worker's performance in a past series of similar tasks. Without assurance about the suitability of workers, verifying the validity of received
contributions may be difficult.

The second challenge is evaluating the trustworthiness of contributions in an
effort to weed out low fidelity/quality data. The open nature of social networks

© Springer International Publishing AG, part of Springer Nature 2018
A. Beheshti et al. (Eds.): ASSRI 2015/2017, LNBIP 234, pp. 178–190, 2018.
https://doi.org/10.1007/978-3-319-76587-7_12

which allows everyone to contribute, while valuable for motivating workers, facilitates erroneous and untrusted data preparation. For instance, following the devastation incurred due to Hurricane Sandy in the US in October 2012, social media was flooded with misinformation and fake photos (see http://news.yahoo.com/10-fake-photos-hurricane-sandy-075500934.html). While some of these were easy to identify as fake data, several others were initially thought to be true. This clearly highlights the need for a trust system which is responsible for performing necessary validations both from the perspective of data trustworthiness and also the reliability of data contributors. The third challenge is providing a secure and privacy-aware environment to contribute data. Social participatory networks have always been subject to misbehaviour and malicious activities due to the inherent openness. Workers may be dishonest, have insufficient skills and expertise or biased interests. A common approach to detect such activities is considering the reputation score as evaluation criteria. Reputation score is a metric reflecting the overall quality of a worker from the community's point of view [1], and is computed based on the information such as the history of the worker's past behaviour. Access to more information about a worker will inherently result in a more accurate estimation of his reputation. On the other hand, availability of such information depends on the worker's privacy settings. Although several reputation systems are proposed, the correlation between reputation and privacy has not been efficiently investigated in literature.

In order to address the above-mentioned challenges, we propose a framework that takes into account the reputation score and quality metrics of workers while taking care of their privacy. This framework proposes to re-adjust privacy settings of workers, when they lose or gain reputation. This framework consists of several components. The first component is the Recruitment Module, which is responsible for addressing the challenge of recruiting sufficient well-suited workers. This module leverages friendship relations to identify suitable candidates among friends and Friends of Friends (FoFs) and recruit them via the most credible routes. The second component is the Trust Module, which is responsible for addressing the challenge of assessing contribution trustworthiness. For each received contribution, the trust module separately evaluates the quality of contribution and the trustworthiness of the worker, and combines them to arrive at a trustworthiness score for the contribution. To allow for better selection of well-suited workers, the Reputation Module calculates a reputation score for each worker by using the Google PageRank [2] algorithm. Finally, the Privacy Module is responsible for preparing a privacy aware environment to cooperate. In fact, the privacy module creates a correlation between reputation and privacy by enabling the system to adjust the workers' privacy settings according to their reputation scores. This enables the requester to observe more information about the worker, to better judge the worker's abilities and skills. Note that the privacy adjustment is only performed for those who have accepted to contribute to a task. It is done on a specific set of quality-related information and is based on the worker's permission granted to the system at the time of registration.

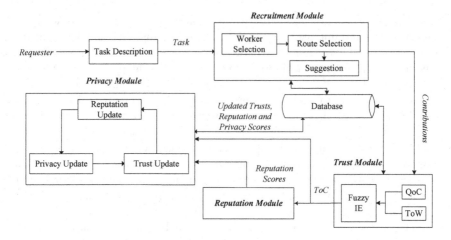

Fig. 1. Framework architecture

2   The Proposed Framework

2.1   Overview

We represent a typical social participatory network as a graph with a set of nodes representing social network members and a set of edges representing relationships between them. Each member has a profile that contains his attributes and information. Some attributes represent the member's personal information such as name and address. Others include the settings and outcome of member's social behavior. Examples are the member's reputation score, the history of his previous transactions, the pairwise trust scores and the privacy settings that the member adjusts for his sensitive information to identify its accessibility level.

As mentioned above, for a subset of profile information, the system is able to re-adjust the privacy settings according to the alteration of member's reputation score. We refer to this subset as reputation-aware attributes. Location is an example of reputation-aware attribute. The privacy settings for a person's location attribute can be adjusted in a way that provides access ranging from a fine-grained level such as precise location (latitude, longitude) to a coarse-grained description such as city or state.

2.2   Architecture

Figure 1 illustrates the overall architecture of our proposed framework. The social network serves as the underlying publish-subscribe infrastructure for worker recruitment. We assume that all the information about the social network structure and its members (i.e., their profile information and social relations) are kept in a database. The database is responsible for sharing the information amongst all framework components. Whenever a requester advertises a task (including the specification of the task's main requirements such as required expertise or location), a set of workers may apply to contribute. Requester can utilize the recruitment module to select suitable workers. Provided contributions are then evaluated by the trust module and a trust rating is assigned to each contribution. Based on it, the pairwise trust rank between the requester and worker and the worker's reputation score are calculated in reputation module. The privacy module then updates the worker's privacy settings accordingly. More details about the functionality of individual modules are provided in the following.

2.3   The Recruitment Module

The recruitment module consists of three components: The worker selection component crawls the social graph up to L levels (friends and FoFs) to determine eligible workers who can fulfill the task's requirements. Next, route selection component traverses the social graph to find the best route from requester to each of eligible workers. The best route will be the route with highest trustworthiness and highest privacy preservation. To do so, a credibility score, which is the combination of the trust score and privacy score of the route, is calculated. In case of multiple routes, the route with the highest credibility is chosen. Those eligible workers for whom, the credibility of the route is greater than a predefined threshold are considered as selected workers. Periodically (where a period typically spans a certain number of tasks), the suggestion component provides each requester with a list of well-behaved workers for further recruitment. More details about the recruitment module can be found in [3].

2.4   The Trust Module

The trust module is responsible for maintaining and evaluating a comprehensive trust rating for each contribution. There are two aspects that need to be considered: (1) Quality of Contribution (QoC) and (2) Trustworthiness of Worker (ToW). As mentioned before, the database contains the required information about workers. When a contribution is received by the trust module, the effective parameters that contribute to these aspects are evaluated and then combined to arrive at a single quantitative value for each. In order to quantify QoC, a group of parameters must be evaluated such as: relevance to the campaign, fulfilment of task requirements, etc. To quantify ToW, a set of personal and social parameters should be evaluated. Personal parameters are the worker's expertise, his timely behavior, and his locality. Social parameters are the friendship duration between the requester and the worker, and the timegap between their consecutive interactions. These parameters are combined to arrive at a single value for ToW. The two measures QoC and ToW then serve as inputs for the fuzzy inference system, which computes the final objective Trustworthiness of Contribution (ToC). More details on the calculation of ToC can be found in [4].

2.5   The Reputation Module

As mentioned above, the trust module assigns an objective trust rating (denoted by ToC) to each contribution. In addition to the system's objective assessment, the requester subjectively evaluates the trustworthiness of contributions. The result of this subjective evaluation is denoted by RE (Requester Evaluation). We assume that RE has a value in the range of $(ToC - \mu, ToC + \mu)$, where $\mu = 1 - \rho_r$ and ρ_r is the requester's reputation score. RE has a value in the range of $[0, 1]$. The reputation module leverages ToC, RE and ρ_r to update the pairwise trust ranks between the requester and worker, using Eq. 1.

$$\tau_{rw} = \begin{cases} \tau_{rw} + |ToC + \rho_r \times RE| : ToC > \theta_1 \\ \tau_{rw} + |ToC - \rho_r \times RE| : ToC < \theta_2 \end{cases} \tag{1}$$

where τ_{rw} is the pairwise trust between the requester r and the worker w, and constants θ_1 and θ_2 are application specific thresholds. In experimentations, we consider $\theta_1 = 0.7$ and $\theta_2 = 0.35$.

Once a reasonable number of contributions are received, the reputation module calculates the reputation scores of workers. We follow the Google PageRank model for calculating the reputation scores in which, the pairwise trust ranks between requesters and workers are leveraged. More details on the calculation of pairwise trusts and reputation scores can be found in [5].

2.6   The Privacy Module

Privacy preservation is a serious concern in social participatory networks and several solutions have been proposed aiming at providing the maximum possible privacy for the workers [6]. Although privacy preservation is crucial to the success of a social network, sometimes workers misuse these privacy preservation options to gain unfair benefits. They may provide low quality or fake contributions, and at the same time, utilize the system's privacy settings to avoid being uniquely identified. By unique identification, we mean the disclosure of the real-world identity of a person, i.e. his real name; real address, telephone number, etc. This is different from the disclosure of the identity of members in most social networks. Although the majority of profiles in social networks are created with the name of people, there is no proof of identification to assure that the person behind that profile is exactly the person he claimed to be. So, it is reasonable to claim that the real-world identity of members is hidden in almost all social networks.

In the following, we provide an example of such privacy setting abuse. Amazon online market (www.amazon.com) hides the sensitive information such as the real identity and location of the people who write reviews on products, due to privacy reasons. Note that information such as real name, address, phone number, e-mail address and a valid credit card must be provided by the members at the time of registration. According to an article in The New York Times in February 2004 [7], a glitch in the Canadian Amazon web site revealed the real identity of a number of reviewers. The revealed information showed that a notable portion of reviews on books were written by their own authors, publishers or competitors. In fact, they misused the identity shield option of Amazon to impersonate another person. These fake reviews may easily mislead buyers into purchasing these products. This is an obvious example of hiding behind the system's privacy settings.

In almost all online social networks, the privacy settings are either fixed or under the complete control of users, and there is no correlation between a member's behavior, reflected in his reputation score, and the visibility of his information. The lack of such interdependency leads to the problems such as the example outlined above. In particular, problem arises because the sensitive information of the reviewer is kept private by the system and any changes in his reputation score does not lead to the disclosure of his private information. To the best of our knowledge, none of the existing work in the area of reputation management in research prototypes and social networking sites considers such correlation.

One possible solution to such an issue is to adopt a mechanism in which, the worker's privacy settings can be dynamically adjusted by the system based on his reputation score. Note that these changes only affect reputation-aware attributes and the disclosure of which does not compromise the worker's privacy. This will deter workers from misbehaving as it can lead to adversely affect their reputation and consequently, threaten their privacy. For this to work, workers must grant the privacy adjustment permission to the system at the time of registration for contributing in a task.

2.7   Reputation and Privacy Correlation

The main idea behind the functionality of privacy module is to adjust reputation score and privacy settings of the workers interdependently. To do so, we adjust the worker's privacy settings based on his current reputation score. Such an adjustment may result in hiding or disclosing more sensitive information about the worker. In order to adjust privacy settings and reputation scores, we propose an algorithm that leverages the above mentioned modules, as follows:

1. For each requester-worker pair, calculate the pairwise trusts (τ_{rw}).
2. For each worker w, calculate the reputation score (ρ_w).
3. For each requester-worker pair, adjust the privacy settings (Q_{wr}) (details in the following).
4. Re-calculate (τ_{rw}).
5. End.

The first two steps are performed by the trust and reputation modules. In the following, we will explain the third step with more details.

2.8   Privacy Settings Update

Once reputation scores are calculated, the pairwise privacy settings between the requester and workers are updated accordingly. The adjustment of pairwise privacy settings between the requester r and the worker w is based on the worker's reputation score (ρ_w). In particular, although the worker is able to pre-set the privacy settings of his reputation-aware information at his desired level, the ability to retain these settings on the intended level depends directly on the worker's reputation score. In other words, a reputable worker will have the privacy settings closer to his desired level in comparison with a worker with lower reputation. The adjustment of privacy settings is done based on the following rule: If the reputation score of the worker (ρ_w) is decreased, we re-adjust the privacy settings of his reputation-aware information to lower levels. On the contrary, if he gains reputation, we re-adjust the privacy settings to higher levels up to the worker's desired levels.

Assume that Q_{wr} is the set of current privacy scores of worker w for reputation-aware information, as observed by the requester r. Privacy scores represent the numerical values of their corresponding privacy settings. Similarly, assume that U_{wr} denotes w's desired privacy scores, as observed by r. We first compute the amount of change in the worker's reputation score as follows:

$$\delta_w = \frac{\rho_w^{j+1} - \rho_w^j}{\rho_w^j} \qquad (2)$$

In Eq. 2, ρ_w^j and ρ_w^{j+1} are the worker's reputation scores calculated in two consecutive iterations. Assume that $newQ = (1 + \delta_w) \times Q_{wr}$. Then, the updated privacy scores are calculated as:

$$Q_{rw} = \begin{cases} newQ : newQ < U_{wr} \\ U_{wr} \quad\ : \text{otherwise} \end{cases} \qquad (3)$$

As reflected in Eq. 3, when $newQ$ exceeds the user-defined privacy scores of the worker, his privacy preferences are selected to prevent enforcing restrictions higher than worker's desired privacy scores.

3   Experimentation and Evaluation

To undertake the preliminary evaluations outlined herein, we chose to conduct simulations. We developed a custom Java simulator for this purpose. The data set that we use for our experiment is the real web of trust of Advogato.org [8], which is a web-based community of software developers in which, site members rate each other in terms of their trustworthiness. The result of these ratings is a rich web of trust, which comprises of 14,019 users and 47, 347 trust ratings.

Whenever a task is launched, one of the Advogato users is selected to be the requester. The worker selection component traverses the Advogato graph beginning from the requester until level L (L = 3) to find suitable workers. Next, the route selection component finds the best routes. Tasks are then exchanged and trust server calculates ToC for each receiving contribution. Pairwise trust scores along the routes are then updated based on the ToC achieved. The worker's reputation score and his privacy settings are then updated accordingly. We run the simulation for 30 and 60 rounds, each round consisting of launching 30 tasks.

As mentioned before, the privacy adjustment is done for reputation-aware attributes. For simplicity, we assume that the reputation aware attributes consist of two attributes: workers' locality and the history of his previous contributions. Then, for each attribute, we set the accessibility level based on its privacy score. As for history of contribution, if the privacy score is 1, the accessibility will be zero, meaning that nothing from the history of worker's previous contributions is accessible to the requester. If the score is 0.8, then the requester has access to the history of the previous 6 months, and so on. Similar settings have been done for the locality, ranging from access to the exact location to coarser dimensions. Moreover, for each worker, we randomly assign a value between 0.6 and 0.8 to his desired privacy score (U_{wr}).

In order to observe the performance of the system in the presence of noise, we artificially create situations in which, the quality of produced contributions for a set of workers reduces for a period of time. Our goal is to observe whether the system is able to rapidly detect such behavioural change and demonstrate a reasonable reaction accordingly. The duration of behavioural change has been set to be between the 10th and 20th rounds. During this transition period, the QoC of the 2000 workers has been artificially reduced to an amount less than 0.2. We investigate the number of workers during the simulation. We expect to see that the proposed framework is able to rapidly eliminate these workers from the set of eligible workers.

In order to evaluate the performance of our proposed architecture, we assumed four different settings, based on the different methods leveraged in framework modules. Specifically, we compare the following:

– AVG-NP: Averaging is used to combine ToW and QoC, resulting in the ToC, and the privacy settings are not updated.
– FUZZY-NP: The same as AVG-NP except that ToC is calculated through leveraging fuzzy inference engine to combine ToW and QoC.
– FUZZY-P: The same as FUZZY-NP except that the privacy settings are also updated.

As mentioned before, a ToC rating is calculated for each contribution in the trust module, and those with ToC lower than a predefined threshold (which is set to 0.5) are revoked from further calculations. We consider the overall trust as the evaluation metric. The overall trust of a campaign is defined as overall $\frac{\sum_{i:1}^{n} ToC_i}{n}$ in which, n is the number of non-revoked contributions. Greater overall trust demonstrates better ability to achieve highly trustable contributions and revoke untrusted ones. Overall trust has a value in the range of $[0, 1]$.

As explained before, the worker selection component determines a set of eligible workers. A subset of eligible workers, known as selected workers, consists of those for whom, the credibility score of the route is greater than a predefined credibility threshold (set to 0.6). Relevant to this selection process, we define the notion of participation score as the ratio of selected workers to eligible workers. Greater value of participation score demonstrates that the recruitment strategy is better able to recruit more suitable workers using optimum routes. Participation score has a value in the range of $[0, 1]$.

Figure 2 demonstrates the evolution of average overall trusts for all methods. As this figure shows, the third method is able to achieve higher overall trust than

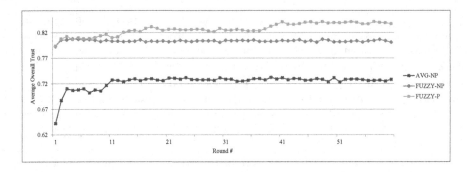

Fig. 2. Evolution of average overall trust

the other methods. This clearly shows that ToC calculation via fuzzy inference engine and updating the privacy settings result in recruiting highly qualified workers and thus, obtaining trustworthy contributions.

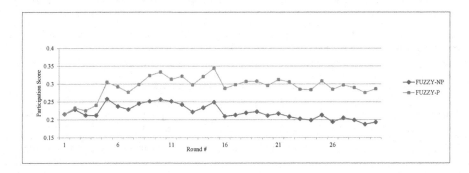

Fig. 3. Evolution of participation score

Figure 3 depicts the evolution of participation score for the second and third methods which, as mentioned above, differ in not updating/updating the privacy settings. As this figure shows, updating the privacy settings results in recruiting more suitable workers. Worker selection process in both methods is limited to L levels (L = 3). But since the third method takes worker's privacy into account, it results in the selection of a vast range of suitable workers. This improvement is better understood when combined with the results in Fig. 2. In other words, updating the privacy scores results in recruiting greater number of workers and at the same time, achieving highly trustable contributions.

Figure 4 depicts the evolution of number of workers in the presence of noise. As this figure shows, the number of workers encounters a decrease in the transition period (i.e., between the 10th and 20th rounds). However, the third method is able to eliminate those workers who produce low quality contributions sharply and then retain back to an acceptable level. This is due to the correct adjustment

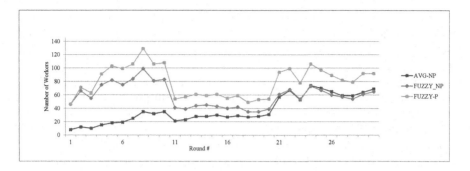

Fig. 4. Evolution of number of workers in the presence of noise

of fuzzy rules and also the correct update on privacy settings which results in fast detection and elimination of malicious workers.

4 Related Work

Social networks have attracted the attention of various research groups ranging from application developers to data mining researchers and crowdsourcing systems. In particular, social networks can serve as an underlying substrate for recruiting social network members as workers to participate in crowdsourcing tasks. Several pieces of research show that the huge amount of data generated by crowd workers, contains facts, processes and events [30] that seriously need to be analyzed [25–29]. But, beside all these challenges, the quality of the contributions is one of the most important issues that needs to be investigated.

In order to obtain quality outcome from social network members, a number of trust related approaches have been presented which aim at evaluating the quality and trustworthiness of contributions [9–12]. Authors in [11] presented an extensive overview of existing trust systems that can be used to derive measures of trust and reputation for Internet transactions. Also in [1], a survey on quality control approaches has been presented which describes and classifies the state-of-the-art according to the quality dimensions and factors both in task design time and run time. In [13], the problem of extracting useful knowledge form social network datasets is explored where privacy concerns restrict the accurate analysis of these networks. It also proposed three trust score computation algorithms, based on the k-anonymity and generalization models. In [14] provide a survey on trust evaluation in E-Commerce. Amintoosi and her colleagues have proposed a trust-based privacy-aware framework for selection of participants in social participatory sensing systems [12]. Authors in [15] propose to address the issue of modelling and quantification of trust, particularly in different contexts.

Privacy preservation is another challenge in the success of social participatory networks. Due to the large amount of sensitive personal data in social networks, various security and privacy challenges arise. In a study on more than 4,000 Facebook users, the members' willingness to reveal large amounts of personal information have been quantified and observed that while personal data is generously provided, limiting privacy preferences are hardly used [16]. In fact, only a small number of members change the default privacy preferences, which are set to maximize the visibility of users' proles. In a similar research conducted on risk taking, trust and privacy concerns in Facebook and MySpace [17], it has been suggested that social networking sites inform potential users that risk taking and privacy concerns are potentially important concerns before individuals sign-up and create profiles. In [18], it has been shown how one can exploit a social network with mixed proles to predict the sensitive attributes of users. Authors in [19] study role of factors such as personality of member, sensitivity of information and the context in which information is revealed on the willingness of people to reveal their private information. Moreover, Sicari and her colleagues study trust and privacy challenges in Internet of Things [20]. In [21], researchers study how the concepts of trust and privacy evolves, and how the users express concerns about sharing their information in online social networks. Ye and colleagues investigate the impact of big data characteristics on the concept of trust and privacy in big data era [22].

In order to evaluate the privacy settings in social participatory networks, a framework to compute the privacy score of a social network user has been proposed in [23], which has taken into account the privacy settings of users with their profile items and developed mathematical models to estimate the sensitivity and visibility of profile items.

In [24], authors examined the nature of the relationship between privacy, trust and self-disclosure in online communities and indicated that privacy and trust at a situational level interact such that high trust compensates for low privacy, and vice versa.

The proposed methods so far, while some of them such as [23, 24] study the relationship between trust and privacy, none of them proposes how to change them accordingly, or how to make users compensate for their misbehaviour or change of their reputation scores, which is the main contribution of this paper.

5   Conclusion and Future Directions

In this paper we aim at addressing one of the trust and privacy issues in the context of social participatory networks, particularly, the interdependency between the workers' reputation scores and their privacy settings. More precisely, when a worker loses reputation, it will be fair to re-adjust her privacy settings and reveal some of her non-critical information. This will not only deter low reputation workers from misbehaviour, but it will protect requesters from being harmed by letting them know more about low quality workers.

However, this interdependency and modification of privacy settings can raise some challenges that need more investigations. The first challenge is to find optimum initial values for privacy settings. Changing the workers' privacy settings directly impact the worker's chance to be recruited. Thus, finding optimum privacy settings is challenging and depends on factors such as the type of the task, the underlying social network, the worker's personal preferences, etc.

The second challenge may arise because of conflicts between the social network privacy preservation system and updates in worker's privacy settings. The recruitment platform may decrease the worker's privacy settings. This reduction, however may lead to the privacy leakage, if combined with other public information available in worker's profile.

Resolution of privacy attacks is another challenge. In this work, we have not considered privacy attacks. However, social networks are subject to different types of attacks such as collusion, Sybil attacks, etc., which need to be investigated.

References

1. Allahbakhsh, M., Benatallah, B., Ignjatovic, A., Motahari-Nezhad, H.R., Bertino, E., Dustdar, S.: Quality control in crowdsourcing systems: issues and directions. IEEE Internet Comput. **17**(2), 76–81 (2013)
2. Page, L., Brin, S., Motwani, R., Winograd, T.: The PageRank citation ranking: bringing order to the web. Stanford InfoLab, Technical report (1999)
3. Amintoosi, H., Kanhere, S.S.: A trust-based recruitment framework for multi-hop social participatory sensing. In: 2013 IEEE International Conference on Distributed Computing in Sensor Systems (DCOSS), pp. 266–273. IEEE (2013)
4. Amintoosi, H., Kanhere, S.S.: A trust framework for social participatory sensing systems. In: Zheng, K., Li, M., Jiang, H. (eds.) MobiQuitous 2012. LNICST, vol. 120, pp. 237–249. Springer, Heidelberg (2013). https://doi.org/10.1007/978-3-642-40238-8_20
5. Amintoosi, H., Kanhere, S.S.: A reputation framework for social participatory sensing systems. Mob. Netw. Appl. **19**(1), 88–100 (2014)
6. Wu, X., Ying, X., Liu, K., Chen, L.: A survey of privacy-preservation of graphs and social networks. In: Aggarwal, C., Wang, H. (eds.) Managing and Mining Graph Data. ADBS, vol. 40, pp. 421–453. Springer, Boston (2010). https://doi.org/10.1007/978-1-4419-6045-0_14
7. Harmon, A.: Amazon glitch unmasks war of reviewers. N. Y. Times **14**(8) (2004)
8. Levien, R., Aiken, A.: Attack-resistant trust metrics for public key certification. In: USENIX Security (1998)
9. Allahbakhsh, M., Ignjatovic, A., Benatallah, B., Beheshti, S.-M.-R., Foo, N., Bertino, E.: An analytic approach to people evaluation in crowdsourcing systems. arXiv preprint arXiv:1211.3200 (2012)
10. Allahbakhsh, M., Ignjatovic, A., Benatallah, B., Beheshti, S.-M.-R., Foo, N., Bertino, E.: Detecting, representing and querying collusion in online rating systems. arXiv preprint arXiv:1211.0963 (2012)
11. Jøsang, A., Ismail, R., Boyd, C.: A survey of trust and reputation systems for online service provision. Decis. Support Syst. **43**(2), 618–644 (2007)
12. Amintoosi, H., Kanhere, S.S., Allahbakhsh, M.: Trust-based privacy-aware participant selection in social participatory sensing. J. Inf. Secur. Appl. **20**, 11–25 (2015)
13. Dai, C., Rao, F.-Y., Truta, T.M., Bertino, E.: Privacy-preserving assessment of social network data trustworthiness. Int. J. Coop. Inf. Syst. **23**(02), 1441004 (2014)
14. Zhu, Y., Yan, Z.: A survey on trust evaluation in e-commerce. In: Proceedings of the 9th EAI International Conference on Mobile Multimedia Communications, MobiMedia 2016, pp. 130–139. ICST (Institute for Computer Sciences, Social-Informatics and Telecommunications Engineering), ICST, Brussels, Belgium (2016)

15. Cho, J.-H., Chan, K., Adali, S.: A survey on trust modeling. ACM Comput. Surv. **48**(2), 28:1–28:40 (2015)
16. Gross, R., Acquisti, A.: Information revelation and privacy in online social networks. In: Proceedings of the 2005 ACM Workshop on Privacy in the Electronic Society, pp. 71–80. ACM (2005)
17. Fogel, J., Nehmad, E.: Internet social network communities: risk taking, trust, and privacy concerns. Comput. Hum. Behav. **25**(1), 153–160 (2009)
18. Zheleva, E., Getoor, L.: To join or not to join: the illusion of privacy in social networks with mixed public and private user profiles. In: Proceedings of the 18th International Conference on World Wide Web, pp. 531–540. ACM (2009)
19. Bansal, G., Zahedi, F.M., Gefen, D.: Do context and personality matter? Trust and privacy concerns in disclosing private information online. Inf. Manag. **53**(1), 1–21 (2016)
20. Sicari, S., Rizzardi, A., Grieco, L., Coen-Porisini, A.: Security, privacy and trust in Internet of Things: the road ahead. Comput. Netw. **76**, 146–164 (2015)
21. Ostherr, K., Borodina, S., Bracken, R.C., Lotterman, C., Storer, E., Williams, B.: Trust and privacy in the context of user-generated health data. Big Data Soc. **4**(1), 2053951717704673 (2017)
22. Ye, H., Cheng, X., Yuan, M., Xu, L., Gao, J., Cheng, C.: A survey of security and privacy in big data. In: 2016 16th International Symposium on Communications and Information Technologies (ISCIT), pp. 268–272, September 2016
23. Liu, K., Terzi, E.: A framework for computing the privacy scores of users in online social networks. ACM Trans. Knowl. Discov. Data (TKDD) **5**(1), 6 (2010)
24. Joinson, A.N., Reips, U.-D., Buchanan, T., Schofield, C.B.P.: Privacy, trust, and self-disclosure online. Hum. Comput. Interact. **25**(1), 1–24 (2010)
25. Beheshti, S., Venugopal, S., Ryu, S.H., Benatallah, B., Wang, W.: Big data and cross-document coreference resolution: current state and future opportunities. CoRR, vol. abs/1311.3987 (2013). http://arxiv.org/abs/1311.3987
26. Beheshti, S., Nezhad, H.R.M., Benatallah, B.: Temporal provenance model (TPM): model and query language. CoRR, vol. abs/1211.5009 (2012)
27. Beheshti, S., et al.: A systematic review and comparative analysis of cross-document coreference resolution methods and tools. Computing **99**(4), 313–349 (2017)
28. Beheshti, S.-M.-R., Benatallah, B., Sakr, S., Grigori, D., Motahari-Nezhad, H.R., Barukh, M.C., Gater, A., Ryu, S.H.: Process Analytics: Concepts and Techniques for Querying and Analyzing Process Data. Springer, Cham (2016). https://doi.org/10.1007/978-3-319-25037-3
29. Beheshti, S.-M.-R., Benatallah, B., Motahari-Nezhad, H.R., Sakr, S.: A query language for analyzing business processes execution. In: Rinderle-Ma, S., Toumani, F., Wolf, K. (eds.) BPM 2011. LNCS, vol. 6896, pp. 281–297. Springer, Heidelberg (2011). https://doi.org/10.1007/978-3-642-23059-2_22
30. Allahbakhsh, M., Arbabi, S., Motahari-Nezhad, H.R., Benatallah, B.: Big data analytics using cloud and crowd. CoRR, vol. abs/1604.04749 (2016). http://arxiv.org/abs/1604.04749

Application

Relating SOA Governance to IT Governance and EA Governance

George Joukhadar[1(✉)] and Fethi Rabhi[2]

[1] School of Information Systems and Technology Management,
University of New South Wales, Sydney, Australia
g.joukhadar@student.unsw.edu.au
[2] School of Computer Science and Engineering,
University of New South Wales, Sydney, Australia
f.rabhi@unsw.edu.au

Abstract. Service-Oriented Architecture (SOA) governance is considered a key success factor when using a service-oriented approach for aligning IT to business. However, some organizations misinterpret the role of SOA inside the organization and there is scarce empirical evidence about how SOA governance is applied in practice. This research paper will study the position of SOA governance in relation to Information Technology (IT) governance and Enterprise Architecture (EA) governance inside the organization. Semi-structured interviews were conducted with experts in the field. The findings illustrate how organizations initially considered SOA governance as a separate entity; they recently started seeing the relationships between SOA governance, IT governance, Enterprise Architecture governance and corporate governance. In this paper, different views and opinions are presented; nevertheless, they all lead to the conclusion that SOA governance need to be considered at a higher level inside the organization and organizations should not treat SOA governance as a separate entity from and IT governance and EA governance.

Keywords: Corporate governance · IT governance · EA governance
SOA governance · Governance framework

1 Introduction

Service-Oriented Architecture (SOA) "is a strategy for constructing business-focused software systems from loosely coupled, interoperable building blocks (called services) that can be combined and re-used quickly, within and between enterprises, to meet business needs" [1]. Most organizations face significant challenges implementing SOA [2]. Governance is considered the key factor for successful SOA implementation [3], however, it does not guarantee success [1].

In a business environment, IT governance and SOA governance are treated as separate entities. Even though most researchers agree that SOA governance is a subset of IT governance, known IT governance frameworks such as ITIL and COBIT do not address SOA specific challenges [2, 3]. Some researchers argue that IT governance and SOA

© Springer International Publishing AG, part of Springer Nature 2018
A. Beheshti et al. (Eds.): ASSRI 2015/2017, LNBIP 234, pp. 193–202, 2018.
https://doi.org/10.1007/978-3-319-76587-7_13

governance have little in common. Others consider SOA governance as a subset of IT governance; some others consider that SOA governance extends from IT governance to corporate governance. Moreover, very few SOA and SOA governance research articles address the connections with Enterprise Architecture (EA) and its governance. This research paper will clarify the relationship of SOA governance to IT governance by investigating the opinion of experts in the relevant field. Section 2 of this research paper provides a background on IT governance and SOA governance as presented in the literature before discussing and presenting the research problem. Section 3 addresses the methodology used to address the research problem. The last two sections address the findings and future work respectively.

2 Background of the Study

A literature review for relevant work in the field of SOA, SOA governance and IT governance pertinent to this research study has been carried out. This section defines important terms and keywords used and outlines the research problem.

2.1 Definitions

Governance is about bringing the right people to the table to have the right conversation with the right process and best information available [4]. It helps to ensure that organizations build the right services, in the right way, at the right time [5]. Governance is different from management and leadership.

Corporate governance is the system by which organizations are directed and controlled. It consists of sub-governance like financial governance, human resource governance, IT governance, risk governance, etc. Corporate governance means establishing and enforcing how a group of people agrees to work together to achieve organizational objectives [6].

According to the IT Governance Institute, "**IT governance** is the responsibility of executives and the board of directors, and consists of the leadership, organizational structures and processes that ensure that the enterprise's IT sustains and extends the organization's strategies and objectives" [7]. In their book 'IT governance', Weill and Ross [8] define governance as "specifying the decision rights and accountability framework to encourage desirable behavior in the use of IT", and they describe IT governance as the "most important factor in generating business value from IT". IT governance deals with the structures, processes and relational mechanisms involved in IT decision making, and highlights IT's business supportive, or business driving [9].

Larrivee [10] defines **SOA governance** "as the guidelines by which we would use SOA to produce the expected results of delivering information from back office applications." While Niemann [11] argues that SOA governance focuses on the smooth adoption and successful operation of an SOA as the Enterprise Architecture (EA) in a company and claims that the overall goals are SOA compliance and the guarantee of reusability and standardization throughout the system. SOA governance is seen by [12, 13] as a continuous process that constantly 'mediates' between business requirements and the operational reality in an SOA system; its goal is to strengthen IT-Business alignment.

2.2   Relationship Between Corporate Governance and IT Governance

Corporate governance issues can no longer be solved without considering IT due to the business dependency on IT. Corporate governance should therefore drive and set IT governance. At the same time, IT can influence strategic opportunities as outlined by the enterprise and can provide critical input to strategic plans. That mean, IT governance should be seen as a driver for corporate governance as it enables the enterprise to take full advantage of its information if implemented properly. Therefore, IT governance and corporate governance should not be considered as pure distinct disciplines, and IT governance needs to be integrated into the overall governance structure of the enterprise. More precisely, IT governance should be considered as corporate governance applied to IT. IT is an integral part of the business and IT governance is an integral part of corporate governance [14].

2.3   Relationship Between SOA Governance and IT Governance

SOA governance provides executives with the visibility and control necessary for IT governance to be able to increase the business agility of their organizations, and it allows them to interconnect brittle legacy IT infrastructure [15]. Some researchers see SOA governance as a subset of IT Governance that only focuses on the lifecycle of services and composite applications in an organization's SOA [13, 16]. Others, argue that in SOA world, successful governance can help accelerate SOA adoption and encourage the use of SOA best practices for an organization [17]. Some others consider that there is a common misconception that SOA governance is governance of an SOA and this indicates a fundamental misunderstanding of the role of SOA [15]. Bloomberg [15] argues that when an enterprise adopts SOA, it should approach the organization of all of its IT assets from a service-oriented perspective. As such, service orientation provides a broad organizing principle for all aspects of IT in the company — including IT governance. Therefore SOA governance is IT governance in the context of SOA, rather than governance of SOA [15], it extends corporate governance and IT governance and it was created as an extension or a specialization to traditional governance with a special mission of delivering business value using the SOA style [12]. In conclusion, SOA governance promises to augment the IT governance process, while mitigating its risks, and facilitating the dialogue between business and IT users.

2.4   Governance Frameworks Current State

The literature review shows a lack around the relationship between SOA governance and IT governance. Most researchers put aside IT governance while studying SOA governance [2]. Nevertheless, recent years have witnessed few studies that have based their SOA governance frameworks on existing IT governance frameworks and stated the need to complement SOA governance and IT governance frameworks. However, these studies are narrow and are not based on strong empirical data.

In the area of IT governance, a number of existing frameworks cover all aspects of IT and they provide structures, action scope, guidelines, reference processes, and best practices, etc. [13]. However, they lack applicability concerning SOA specific challenges, e.g., SOA lifecycle, SOA roadmap and SOA maturity challenges [11, 16]. Hence, in order to meet SOA governance requirements, researchers claim that existing IT governance frameworks need to be extended [11, 13]; or either SOA governance should build upon and perhaps extend existing IT and operational governance [5]. For example, COBIT - which is a widely accepted control framework for IT governance - has served as a basis for many of the proposed SOA governance approaches [11, 18, 19]. However, COBIT (version 4.1) does not completely cover SOA. It addresses evaluation processes, governance structure and control mechanisms, but does not support some important SOA governance aspects such as service lifecycle, service portfolio management, SOA roadmap and SOA maturity [2].

2.5   The Research Problem

From the literature survey, we see many gaps. Firstly, there is not enough research on the integration of SOA governance frameworks within IT governance frameworks. Moreover, there are conflicting claims and inconsistencies in the literature concerning the role of SOA governance during SOA adoption. The research of Weill and Ross [8] showed that good IT governance has clear business benefits, "still the lack of such governance did not mean game is over" [5]. According to Woolf [5, 13] research studies and articles have shown it is not the case for SOA or SOA governance. SOA must be governed in order to realize the potential of a service-based approach. Simultaneously empirical research found that in everyday businesses, organizations are using IT governance frameworks, like COBIT, to deal with SOA [18].

There are little empirical evidence on the implications and usage of the SOA governance frameworks and how these frameworks are actually working in the most effective way. However, there is so much that is not known and not researched and there are many claims made in the literature that are not substantiated by empirical evidence. As a result, there is confusion about the role and usage of SOA governance in the organization. To the best of our knowledge, no publication exists which qualitatively studies the relationship between IT governance and SOA governance, and compares the impact of different IT and SOA governance frameworks. Therefore, there is a need to enhance the business and technical meaning of IT governance and SOA governance and the relationship between them. The purpose of this research study is to help understanding the relationship between SOA governance and IT governance. For this reason, we need to know if IT and SOA governance efforts are well integrated with overall corporate governance arrangements in the organization and how effective are IT and SOA governance arrangements within the organization [20–22]. This proposed research could well provide executives with some guidelines on how to practice effective governance (directing and controlling of IT resources).

3   Research Methodology and Design

This paper is based on a research study about SOA governance in practice. The study uses an interpretive qualitative research methodology based on semi-structured interviews as a first phase and in-depth field-study in the second phase. This paper is based on the first phase of the research.

The first phase of this research study involves conducting interviews with experts who have experience with SOA governance in multiple companies and who participated in several SOA projects. Twenty-eight interviews were conducted including three pilot interviews. The role of the interviews is to acquire a broad view of SOA governance issues at the time the study is done. The interviewees were selected and recruited through professional networks of SOA/IT governance experts. The interviews took the form of face-to-face personal interviews, online interviews or phone interviews. The questions were open-ended where responses were questioned and discussed further. Consequently, the respondents were able to clarify both the questions and the answers. The interviews focused on the relation between corporate governance, IT governance and SOA governance and extensively on the aspects of the governance frameworks used in practice.

The majority of the participants had a decision-making role or a consultancy role in the organizations they worked for and their experience with service management and SOA varies from four to more than twenty-five years. They have worked with a minimum of two organizations and on different SOA projects in different sectors: telecommunication, government, financial services, information technology and services, education, IT healthcare, computer software and software services and products. The participants have occupied the roles of Systems Analyst, Project Manager, Technical Architect, Enterprise Architect, Chief Architect, Chief Technology Officer, SOA Architect, SOA Consultant, etc. At the time of the interviews, the participants were located in Australia, South Africa, Canada, USA, South America, MEA, UK, Europe and India.

Data analysis is conducted during and after each phase. The interview transcripts are being analyzed using Thematic Analysis. Coding in Thematic analysis helps the researcher to build a systematic account of what has been observed and recorded [23].

4   Findings

4.1   Relationship Between IT Governance and SOA Governance

Most participants agree that SOA governance is not only a sub-set of IT governance, but it gives organizations visibility and control over their SOA development and deployment via establishment of policies, controls, and enforcement mechanisms; it also allows the organization to be supportable long term. However, there were different opinions on how to extend this definition into the business domain and how to position SOA governance within the organization.

Participant 5 sees that the definition could be extended depending on how to define the boundaries of SOA governance; i.e. where it runs into Centre of Excellence as well how to define the mechanism. While according to participant 6, SOA governance is about packaging up systems, allowing systems and processes to talk to each other's and how they are aligned using an Enterprise Service Bus (ESB). Importantly participant 8 claims that IT governance can exist without SOA governance but poorly and often, that is what happens. This is because there is varying degrees of maturity across organizations Australian and international about their IT governance. Participant 13 sees that SOA governance drives the business; it is not a set of rules but a decision making process; therefore it is more about the approach taken and that approach is based on the culture change that is developed inside the organization.

From a different perspective, participant 11 concludes that SOA governance has to be considered part of corporate governance and its change management has to span outside of IT. "SOA governance is a way of doing corporate governance that involves IT and business people working together to determine what they are trying to achieve, what are the roles and responsibilities that need to occur in order for that to create the business capabilities that they are trying to do". Participant 11 supports their claim by saying that the corporate governance is responsible for delivering a vision and SOA is responsible to achieve that vision. This requires change from a business side as much as it requires deployment of different emerging technology.

On the other hand, participants 7, 15, 16, 19 and 26 consider that SOA governance is also around Enterprise Architecture, which focuses on controlling part of the architecture components within the organization. Participant 7 argues that the Enterprise Architecture department should be responsible for the SOA governance framework. The full picture according to participant 15 and 19 is as follows: corporate governance followed by IT governance and then Enterprise Architecture (EA) governance where SOA is a part of EA governance. According to participant 16, EA and SOA "go hand in hand"; however, organizations need to have IT governance in place and they should drive their SOA governance off that IT governance framework. Participant 26 sees SOA governance is an extension of both IT governance and Enterprise Architecture governance because IT governance and EA governance are actually both supporting the business therefore aligning the business objectives and business goals together gives a better chance of realizing SOA benefits.

Participants 14 and 17 take a middle perspective between the different views presented above, participant 17 claims that "EA should be part of the conversations; a lot of vendors don't mention it because they don't have a good answer for it." Similarly, participant 14 divides SOA governance in two branches: SOA governance itself and the service governance and claims that Enterprise Architecture defines how services are operated.

In summary, participants of this research study agree that SOA governance is not only the governance of SOA - a set of procedures and policies adapted within the organization – but also it is also a matter of leverage tools that help to enforce and guide these procedures. Therefore, SOA governance extends to IT governance, EA governance and corporate governance. We conclude that the participants have different views on SOA governance positioning within the organization; however, none of the participants mentioned that their way is the only way. Fourteen participants claim that there is more than one way for doing SOA governance and that depends on the organization's attributes (size, culture, needs, goals, location, etc.). The problem these days is not where to place SOA governance within the organization; however, it is extremely important for organizations to understand the role of SOA governance; the challenge is to be able to respond quickly because "organizations have been asked to govern things that they never would have thought of before" according to participant 8; therefore organizations need to be able to implement governance increasingly and more rapidly.

4.2 Governance Frameworks Used by Participants

In response to the question if organizations use IT/EA governance frameworks to govern SOA, most participants argue that major organizations are aware and use IT and EA governance frameworks: ITIL, COBIT, TOGAF, etc. (participants 7 and 8) as well as other SOA governance frameworks from vendors: IBM, Oracle, the Open Group, etc. (participants 14 and 16) or custom-build frameworks (participants 4, 6 and 9). Participant 8 claims that IT and SOA governance frameworks were seen as separate things up until 5 years ago. It is now agreed by many participants that IT and SOA governance frameworks need to be used simultaneously by organizations, but it is still not the case in some organizations. For this reason, both IT governance framework and SOA governance framework are complimentary and need to be set up properly within the organization according to participant 9. Nevertheless, organizations have to see the difference between IT and SOA governance framework; the difference is where they connect and where they fit into each other; that is mainly through applications according to participant 7.

It is important to note that ITIL is seen more entrenched then COBIT by participant 8, and is the most used IT governance framework according to most participants of this research. ITIL is used to evaluate and assess what IT capabilities and services organizations need to put in place. It certainly becomes a reasonably pervasive standard in terms of assessing the requirements and capabilities for IT service functions and it is a comprehensive library of processors and protocols, according to participant 6. Participant 11 indicates that both ITIL and COBIT have evolved from an Enterprise Architecture point of view i.e. managing IT within an enterprise and across an enterprise to minimize its cost. "They are considered a cost minimizer not a benefit maximizer."

Most participants of this research study believe that existing IT and EA governance frameworks do not cover SOA governance. Participant 11 claims, "TOGAF is inadequate in terms of what its framework can do because it does not deal with cross boundary issues. ITIL is too narrow but it is very good when it comes to change management." For this, organizations need to use an SOA governance framework as well as IT governance framework. Participant 7 for example recommends the OSIMM model from the Open Group for assessing the maturity level. "It is always additional to the IT governance framework or other Enterprise Architecture frameworks which they use." However, participant 19 claims that some organizations are using either ITIL or COBIT to govern SOA, but the success depends on how much effort they want to put into it. "This is because these frameworks are generic and the vendors' frameworks have made a stab beyond that by making it more specific to their technologies".

From that perspective, some participants see that IT governance frameworks are typically more mature than SOA governance frameworks. In some anomalous situations (e.g. systems integration tasks), some organizations have decided to take in more repeatable scalable type approach; therefore organizations have built themselves some methodology for SOA governance as stated by participants 4 and 6. Some participants also claim to build their own SOA governance framework either from scratch or around one of the vendors approach, while it is noted by all participants that none of the IT or SOA governance frameworks have been taken off the shelf. "They are used as frameworks to guide the things that we should be doing" according to participant 6.

Participant 8 expresses their beliefs about vendor-based SOA governance frameworks that "they tend to be very product centric and they are very much driven around; their stack is also aging; they are not keeping up with some of the newer trends that are very prevalent in the more of the open source tools". Participant 8 adds, "They are also seen as a bit of a Novena". They are seen as a great thing in principle, but their practices are very hard to achieve and even harder to maintain. Therefore, many of the services that tend to be developed around large organizations are duplicated.

In conclusion, it has been noted by many of the participants that the framework is not their objective; they rely on the years of expertise that people have. For example, participant 7 built their own SOA maturity roadmap against the OSIMM framework. Similarly, participants 4, 8, 9, 14 and 16 and 19 had to either customize vendor-based frameworks, built their own, or even do both.

4.3　Mechanisms Used to Select the Framework

Most of the participants interviewed agree that experience and communication are the main bases when selecting or building a governance framework. According to participant 5, discussion with the people who have the key decision in the organization is the mechanism used to select and customize the framework. While according to participants 6, 9 and 13, the knowledge of experts is the main mechanism, and the experience of the organization around formalization play an important role in studying the organizations' position in terms of SOA. Similarly, some organizations choose their governance framework "because they selected a certain IT vendor for their SOA architecture and their SOA technical equipment" according to participant 19.

5　Conclusion and Future Work

Participants of this research agree that organizations misinterpret the role of SOA and SOA governance in the organization; however, it is noticeable that during the last few years, organizations started to see the implication of implementing IT governance, EA governance and SOA governance simultaneously.

None of the participants claims that the selected governance framework has ever been problematic or could be a source of failure for SOA implementation because there is always the opportunity to make modifications depending on the organizational needs and requirements. Most participants agree that SOA governance should be the responsibility of the governance board, and the decision-making mechanisms should be made outside the IT department considering IT advice and involvement. At the same time, careful thought should be given to who need to be involved in the decision-making.

As mentioned above, this paper focuses on the relationship between IT governance and SOA governance as seen by practitioners. Additionally, this research study will address the major aspects of the governance frameworks used in practice. Future work of Phase I will focus on the importance and practical usage of SOA governance aspects. When Phase I is completed, two organizations will be selected for Phase II – a field research study: one organization that has been successful with SOA governance and another one that attempted to implement SOA governance. This second phase will allow having direct, in-depth contact with organizational participants, particularly through interviews and direct observations of activities. Data collection in this phase relies on observing, listening to members, taking notes, getting involved sometimes, and running field interviews. Comparing and contrasting the results of the two phases will provide grounding for the development of substantive theoretical claims regarding the relationship between IT governance and SOA governance and the importance and role of the SOA governance aspects.

References

1. Weir, L.A., Bell, A.: Oracle SOA Governance 11g Implementation. Packt Publishing Ltd., Birmingham (2013)
2. Hojaji, F., Shirazi, M.R.A.: A design science approach to develop a new comprehensive SOA governance framework. Int. J. Manag. Inf. Technol. (IJMIT) **4**, 33 (2012)
3. Hassanzadeh, A., Namdarian, L., Elahi, S.: Developing a framework for evaluating service oriented architecture governance (SOAG). Knowl.-Based Syst. **24**, 716–730 (2011)
4. Grant, K., Hackney, R., Edgar, D.: Strategic Information Systems Management. Course Technology, Cengage Learning, Hampshire (2010)
5. Falkl, J., Laird, R.G., Kreger, H., Carrato, T.: IBM advantage for SOA governance standards. IBM developerWorks (2009)
6. ANAO: Corporate Governance in Commonwealth Authorities and Companies - Discussion Paper. Australian National Audit Office (1999)
7. ITGI: Control Objectives for Information and Related Technology (CoBIT) 4.1. IT Governance Institute (2007)
8. Weill, P., Ross, J.W.: How Top Performers Manage IT Decision Rights for Superior Results. Harvard Business School Press, Cambridge (2004)
9. Simonsson, M., Johnson, P., Ekstedt, M.: The effect of IT governance maturity on IT governance performance. Inf. Syst. Manag. **27**, 10–24 (2010)
10. Larrivee, B.: SOA: no governance needed. Or is it? AIIM E-DOC **21**, 24–25 (2007)
11. Niemann, M., Janiesch, C., Repp, N., Steinmetz, R.: Challenges of governance approaches for service-oriented architectures. In: 3rd IEEE International Conference on Digital Ecosystems and Technologies, pp. 600–605 (2009)
12. Holley, K., Palistrant, J., Graham, S.: Effective SOA Governace. On Demand Business. IBM (2006)
13. Woolf, B.: Introduction to SOA governance. developerWorks (2006). http://www.ibm.com/developerworks/library/ar-servgov/
14. Jordan, E., Musson, D.: Corporate Governance and IT Governance: exploring the board's perspective (2004)
15. Bloomberg, J.: SOA Governance: Reengineering IT Governance. ZapThink (2004)

16. Laningham, S.: What is SOA governance? A chat with SOA governance integration lead, Gil Long. Spotlight on IBM software solutions (2007). http://www.ibm.com/developerworks/podcast/spotlight/st-070307atxt.html

17. High, J.R., Krishnan, G., Sanchez, M.: Creating and maintaining coherency in loosely coupled systems. IBM Syst. J. **47**, 357–376 (2008)

18. Luthria, H.: The organizational diffusion of service-oriented computing: investigating the realization of business value from service-oriented architectures. Ph.D. thesis - Information Systems, Technology and Management - The Australian School of Business. Doctor of Philosophy. University of New South Wales, Sydney Australia (2009)

19. Niemann, M., Eckert, J., Repp, N., Steinmetz, R.: Towards a generic governance model for service-oriented architectures. In: Americas Conference on Information Systems (AMCIS). AIS Electronic Library, Toronto (2008)

20. Bieberstein, N., Bose, S., Fiammante, M., Jones, K., Shah, R.: Service-Oriented Architecture (SOA) Compass: Business Value, Planning, and Enterprise Roadmap. IBM Press, Upper Saddle River (2006)

21. Josuttis, N.M.: SOA in Practice - The Art of Distributed System Design. O'Reilly Media, Sebastopol (2007)

22. Keen, M., Adamski, D., Basu, I., Chilcott, P., Eames, M., Endrei, M., Fagalde, B., Raszka, R., Seabury, S.D.: Implementing Technology to Support SOA Governance and Management. IBM Redbooks, Indianapolis (2007)

23. Ezzy, D.: Qualitative Analysis: Practice and Innovation. Allen & Unwin, Crows Nest (2002)

Semantic Textual Similarity as a Service

Roghayeh Fakouri-Kapourchali[1], Mohammad-Ali Yaghoub-Zadeh-Fard[2(✉)], and Mehdi Khalili[1]

[1] Payame Noor University, Tehran, Iran
fakouri.r19@gmail.com, m.khalili@pnu.ac.ir
[2] University of New South Wales, Kensington, Australia
m.yaghoubzadehfard@unsw.edu.au

Abstract. Ensembling well performing models has been proved to outperform individual models in semantic textual similarity task; however, employing existing models still remains a challenge. In this paper, we tackle this issue by providing a service oriented system to index a text similarity model using RESTful services. We also propose a baseline approach, based on an effective penalty-award weighting schema and word-level edit distance, in which pairs of sentences are divided into two main categories based on the number of substitution, insert, and delete required to convert the first sentence to the second one. It is debated that, when the word-level edit distance is very small, it is wiser to measure dissimilarity than similarity. Using knowledge bases along with common natural language processing tools, the proposed method tries to enhance the accuracy of measuring similarity between two sentences. We compared the proposed method with existing approaches, and we found that it produces promising results. Our source code is freely available on GitLab.

Keywords: Semantic textual similarity · Sentence similarity
Text similarity · Service oriented design

1 Introduction

Measuring similarity between two pieces of text is a fundamental task for many natural language processing (NLP) tasks. Information retrieval (IR) systems aim to find the most similar documents to a given query, virtual assistants seek for the most similar utterances and corresponding commands for a user's request [11], and plagiarism detection systems are in quest of finding copies and poorly paraphrased text pieces [18].

Even though it may seem a trivial task for humans to calculate textual similarity, it is still a challenging problem in Natural Language Understanding (NLU). Word matching is the traditional approach but barely are such systems capable of detecting the similarity between phrases such as "short notice" and "in the blink of an eye." Since each model has its own cons and pros, it has been noticed that most of the top-ranked groups in Semantic Textual Similarity (STS) competition employed an ensemble of some other models and algorithms

© Springer International Publishing AG, part of Springer Nature 2018
A. Beheshti et al. (Eds.): ASSRI 2015/2017, LNBIP 234, pp. 203–215, 2018.
https://doi.org/10.1007/978-3-319-76587-7_14

to enhance their accuracy [12]. Ensembling takes a lot of affords since it requires data scientists to look for various papers, algorithms, and open-source software which are written in many different programming languages. Because of the wide usages of textual similarity systems and the fact that ensembling models are more promising, it is of the paramount importance to host existing models and algorithms.

The contribution of this paper is two-fold: we (1) propose a simple architecture for hosting textual similarity APIs, and (2) introduce a novel approach based on a penalty-award system, which is also freely available for the public, by employing knowledge resources, corpus statistics, and some heuristics. Our approach is based on the idea that measuring dissimilarity is easier and accurate than measuring similarity between two sentences with a small edit distance.

2 Concepts

Semantic Textual Similarity (STS), introduced in SemEval[1]-2012, aims to measure the degree of semantic equivalence between two sentences. Given two sentences, STS assigns a score between 0 and 5, with 5 indicating exact equivalence and 0 meaning unrelatedness of the sentences. Table 1 gives a brief description of five integer scores and their examples.

Table 1. STS score interpretation

Score	Description
0	Sentences are taking about different topics
1	Sentences are inequivalent but on the same topic
2	Sentences are inequivalent but share some details
3	Sentences are roughly equivalent with some differences in important information
4	Sentences are virtually equivalent with some differences in unimportant details
5	Sentences are completely interchangeable without missing any information

Sentence Pair is a pair of sentences being measured. It could also be a pair of words, pieces of text, or even documents. Dealing with text with various lengths is by itself a big challenge, and requires different approaches. For example, a simple dictionary or word embedding techniques [20,24] can be used to measure semantic similarity between words, but for longer pieces of text the approach needs some curations [16].

Word-Level Edit Distance (WLED), is the minimum number of word-level edit operations (delete, insert, and substitution) required to transform one

---

[1] International Workshop on Semantic Evaluation.

sentence to another. For example, given the cost of all operations equals to one, WLED of the following sentence pair is 2:

- I own a pretty car.
- I have a car.

because changing "own" to "have" and eliminating "pretty" will eventuate in having the second sentence in the above-mentioned sentence pair.

Word Similarity Types is defined between words as presented in Table 2. These types allow us to define more relations between words than just having a binary relationship.

Table 2. Word similarity type

Type	Description
1	Words are exactly the same
2	Both words are in another's synonym set
3	Only one of the words is in another's synonym set
4	Words have the same sequence of Latin letters and numbers
5	One of the words is abbreviation of another or it is part of the abbreviation of the other word
6	Synonym sets of two words have intersections
7	Words are antonyms
8	Words have the same sequence of Latin letters
9	At least one of the words is in another's related-word set
10	There is not any relationship between words

3   System Architecture

Semantic textual similarity, which has applications in machine translation, summarization and many similar tasks, has recently become a hot topic among researchers. As a result, in quest of finding accurate and reliable results, STS became one of the primary tasks of SemEval since 2012 providing various datasets for both monolingual and cross-lingual sentences making supervised STS a reality.

By the advent of this task, every year, several teams take participate in this challenge and provide various to measure semantic similarity of sentence pairs. These solutions can be classified in three groups as follows [5]: Vector Space Model, Text Alignment, and Machine Learning Algorithms. To achieve a better accuracy, it is usual to take the advantages of all above mentioned approaches, and it is also of paramount importance to pre-process sentences and normalized them before taking any steps forward. Therefore, as it is depicted in Fig. 1, there are at least two types of required tools for a STS system: (1) text preprocessors

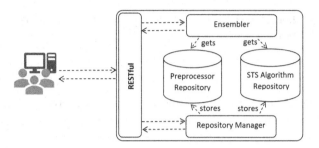

Fig. 1. System architecture

(2) STS algorithms which are handled by Ensembler and Repository Manager in the proposed architecture (see Fig. 1).

The current design does not include repositories for knowledge bases, dictionaries, and datasets. It is assumed that each algorithm (web API) has a built-in set of datasets, word embedding, and knowledge resources. Even though these types of resources are not included in our system, they are very beneficial since they can be employed by researchers to facilitate the access to high-quality datasets and knowledge resources without the hassle of searching; we leave this for our future work.

Repository Manager is in charge of adding new preprocessors and algorithms to the system. In this architecture, entries are nothing but web APIs including their parameters, unique names, category, type of sentence pair (word, sentence, paragraph, and document), and meta-data. For a similarity algorithm, we need to store its name, accepted languages, similarity score range (usually between 0 and 1), and built-in API parameters such as keys. At the moment, our system only supports a fixed schema for APIs, but for the later works we will work on making it flexible by adding parameter mappings. Repository manager also provides an API for users to search for existing similarity algorithms and preprocessors.

Ensembler is in charge of processing users' requests by applying the preprocessors and algorithms in the request. Required parameters. Ensembler returns a list of scores with corresponding meta-data for each score (such as algorithm name and score range.) Along with these set, it calculates a semantic similarity value for the given sentence pair by a guilt-in regression model trained on available datasets and algorithms in the system. The main reason for offering a set of measures is to provide a platform which does the much of feature engineering, and scientists can focus on selecting features and models instead.

We also defined a default semantic similarity measure along with some common preprocessing functions in our prototype[2] which are described in the following sections.

---

[2] https://gitlab.com/mysilver/semantic-text-similarity.

4   Built-in Preprocessors

While the system architecture allows adding pre-processors as web APIs, it has several built-in preprocessors: Case Converter, Sentence Orderer, and Tokenizer.

Case Converter converts the letter of a given text to a proper sentence-case. Uppercase and title-case sentences do not properly parsed with most NLP tools which make this preprocessor necessary for many algorithms.

Sentence Orderer sorts two sentences in a sentence pair by their lengths. Since most of algorithms employ machine learning methods and consequently features obtained from the two sentences, ordering sentences can be a simple but useful normalization. This idea stems from the fact that sometimes features are based on a single sentence, and in the training process, a feature for different training samples should be in the same position. For example, imagine we have following features: (1) length of first sentence (2) length of second sentence. Without ordering sentences, for all training samples the values of these features could be interchangeable and incomparable.

Tokenizer includes realizing idioms and phrases in sentences in our system. By definition, an idiom is a group of words having a special meaning which is not deducible from individual words. As the definition goes, we cannot understand the meaning of an idiom by looking at its individual words. For instance, in the sentence "in the blink of an eye", "in the blink of an eye" is a saying that should not match with "eye blink."

5   Built-in Semantic Similarity Method

The main idea in our methodology is to divide pairs of sentences into two different categories which should be treated differently: (1) sentence pairs with a small WLED, and (2) the rest of sentence pairs. The common sense indicates that, in the first category, dissimilar words play more significant roles in measuring text similarity than similar ones. To make this point clearer, let's consider following sentence pair:

- He was never invited to the party.
- He was invited to the party.

The only difference in these sentences is having an extra word "never" in the first sentence. Having the knowledge about the rule of never in the sentence and the fact that it is the only difference between two sentences, we are able to detect that these two sentences are opposite. Therefore, it is easier to consider differences than similarities. However, our observations indicate that as the number of differences increases, it is better to look on the bright side and consider similarities. This idea leads us towards a divide-and-rule scenario:

1. Semantic similarity when WLED is small
2. Semantic similarity for the rest of sentences

However, we need to define "small". Calculating WLED values depends on the defined operations costs. However, we assign a cost of 1 for each operation and consider threshold of 1 for determining small and big WLEDs.

5.1   Text Similarity for Small WLED

As we mentioned earlier, when there are only a few differences in the two sentence, it is recommended to concentrate just on the differences. This paper focuses on following sentence pairs which have WLED values of 0 or 1. Considering the range, we are left with three states:

– There is no different between sentences (WLED = 0)
– One of the sentences has one word more
– In the same position, two sentences have different words

The word-level edit-distance of zero indicates that two sentences are identical, and without any assessment they have the maximum level of similarity.

In the second case, the sentences are exactly the same if the extra word is omitted from its sentence. To determine level of similarity between two sentences, the role of extra word plays a significance role. Contemplating on various scenarios, we suggest checking the rules presented in Table 3 in see which one applies first. It is worth noting that these rules are priorities from top to down. For example, in the second rule, we know that the extra word is not changing the sentiment of its sentence.

Table 3. Similarity score when one of the sentences has one word more

Score	Rule/example
1	The extra word changes the sentiment of sentence *"They are friends"* and *"They are not friends"*
5	The extra word is a stop-word *"The fishermen disappointed"* and *"Fishermen are disappointed"*
3	The extra word is a noun *"A man is playing a flute"* and *"A man is playing a bamboo flute"*
4	The extra word is a verb *"A man is playing the cello"* and *"A man seated is playing the cello"*
4	The extra word is an adjective *"A young child is riding a horse"* and *"A child is riding a horse"*
5	The extra word is an adverb *"Equip specifically with furniture"* and *"Equip with furniture"*

Table 4. Similarity score when two sentences have different words in the same position

Score	Type	Example
5	2	*"Introductory portion of a story"* and *"Introductory section of a story"*
5	3	*"Rabbit is running from an eagle"* and *"Hare is running from an eagle"*
5	4	*"We are all friends with @helen"* and *"We are all friends with Helen"*
4	6	*"To vibrate in a different pattern"* and *"To vibrate in a definite pattern"*
1	7	*"Enemies will return soon"* and *"Friends will return soon"*
3	8	*"I will be in Spain on 2th Jan"* and *"I will be in Spain on 4th Jan"*
3	9	*"The man is playing the guitar"* and *"The girl is playing the guitar"*

The third state happens when two sentences have different words in the same position and the rest of two sentences are the same; comparison of those words and determining similarity type of words can give us how similar two sentences is in this case. Heuristic assigned scores for each case when based on word similarity type is presented in Table 4. For the case of having the last word-similarity type, it is possible to assign a similarity based on the knowledge about stop-words, sentiment analysis, and part of speech tags of words.

5.2 Text Similarity for Bigger WLED

As previously mentioned, as operation cost of editing increases, the role of similar words grows as well. In order to measure similarity of such sentences, we focus on similarities and penalize differences. Our similarity function considers two factors:

- Similarity of first sentence words to those of second sentence
- Similarity of sentiments of two sentences

Equation 1 is a top level view of how we calculate similarity of two sentences. In this equation, $core_{align}$ and $score_{sentiment}$ calculate similarity of words and sentiments of sentences s and s'. Since we have two different approaches towards sentence pairs based on their WLED, it is necessary to scale similarity score between 0 to 5. Using Eq. 2, similarity score can be converted to its appropriate class; where $score$ comes from Eq. 1 and Max is the maximum score can be yield using Eq. 1. This helps us to use both methods in as single similarity function (or a feature in machine learning models) simultaneously.

$$Sim(s, s') = score_{align}(s, s') + score_{sentiment}(s, s', score_{align}(s, s')) \quad (1)$$

$$Class(score) = 5|score + Max|/(2Max) \quad (2)$$

Word Alignment, the task of finding translation relationships between two pieces of text in natural language processing, is one of the most popular approach in finding textual similarity. Here we employ a greedy similarity function using word alignment in Eq. 3.

$$score_{align}(s, s') = \frac{1}{|s|} \sum_{t \in s} \max_{t' \in s'}\{sim(t, t')\} \tag{3}$$

According to Eq. 3, similarity of $s = \{t_1, t_2, ..., t_{|s|}\}$ and $s' = \{t'_1, t'_2, ..., t'_{|s|}\}$ equals to mean of word alignments. We also need a similarity function to measure how much two words are similar. We have three factors in measuring word similarity: (1) inverse document frequency (idf) of first word, (2) first word part of speech (POS) score [30,31], and (3) similarity type score of two words. *idf* is a widely used coefficient in text processing systems to mitigate the impact of high-frequency words; the second factor gives a coefficient for POS tags, and the third factor is based on word similarity type defined in Table 2. To calculate similarity of two words, we suggest Eq. 4:

$$sim(t, t') = idf(t) \times \begin{cases} reward(pos(t)) \times wsts(t, t') & wst(t, t') \leqslant threshold \\ penalty(pos(t)) \times wsts(t, t') & \text{otherwise} \end{cases} \tag{4}$$

where *wsts* stands for *word similarity type score*; we have assumed that *word similarity types (wst)* are ranked in order of significance and those ranked below *threshold* have a positive role as opposed to the rest. Function *wsts* also assigns a coefficient for the word similarity type for t and t'. Moreover, *reward* and *penalty* are functions of part-of-speech, and for a given part-of-speech return a proper score.

Sentiment Similarity is defined as a function of s, s', and their word alignment score as presented in Eq. 5:

$$score_{sentiment}(s, s', score) = \begin{cases} r(Max - |score|) & equal sentiments \\ p(Max - |score|) & \text{otherwise} \end{cases} \tag{5}$$

where *score* has been calculated by $score_{align}$, *Max* is the maximum possible value for $score_{align}$, r is a coefficient to reward sentimentally equal sentence, and p is to penalize dissimilar sentences regarding their sentiments. The idea behind sentiment scoring is the fact that semantically similar sentences are supposed to be also sentimentally equal. The final similarity value is the sum of sentiment and word alignment scores.

6   Implementation

We implemented our method using regression and enriched it with a few features (e.g. ngram, Levenshtein distance [22], Jaccard coefficient, and KullbackLeibler divergence [15]) along with WLED based feature we introduced.

We obtained Stanford CoreNLP toolkit [17] to analysis natural languages and performed lemmatization, part of speech tagging, sentiment analysis, parsing, and named entity recognition. Natural language understanding also requires having knowledge about relations among words. Knowledge resources such as WordNet [21] and BabelNet [23] provide invaluable information needed for measuring semantic similarity. In this paper, we obtained WordNet, Collins English online dictionary, and Roget's Thesaurus [19] to find synonyms, antonyms, and related words for each of words in a sentence.

7   Evaluation and Comparison

In order to train and test the proposed model, we downloaded the standard datasets available on SemEval website and tested using the datasets released from 2015 to 2017. The past datasets used for developing purposes and parameter configuration.

During the developing time, we manually defined *Reward* and *penalty* functions (provided in Table 5), and left the parameter optimization for our future work; *wsts* is also defined as Table 6 with t (in Eq. 4) tuned to 5^3. Finally, r and p in Eq. 5 are set to 0 and 0.05 respectively.

Table 5. Part-of-speech coefficients

Function/POS	Nouns	Verbs	Adjectives	Adverbs	Unknown
Reward	5	5	3	1	4
Penalty	−14	−8	−2.5	−0.5	−6

Table 6. Similarity type coefficients

Similarity type	1	2	3	4	5	6	7	8	9	10
Coefficients	1.3	1.3	1.3	1.2	1	0.6	1	0.5	0.5	1

After setting variables and preparing datasets, we compared our model with top results available on SemEval special page containing competition results in 2015 to 2017.

The results of evaluation for 2015 datasets are presented in Table 7. We have compared our models (WLED and Enriched WLED with other features) with top-4 teams named as DLS@CU [28], ExBThemis [14], Samsung [13], and NeRoSim [5]. Even though the WLED model is not among top results, it shows an acceptable performance. The common sense indicates that using this feature along with those employed in top-results can be very effective.

---

[3] It means only word similarity Type 1 to 5 positively contribute to the semantic similarity of two sentences.

Table 7. Evaluation results for datasets in 2015 [2]

Dataset/Team	Enriched WLED	WLED	NeRoSim	Samsung	ExBThemis	DLS@CU
Answers-forums	0.7078	0.5677	0.6940	0.6589	0.6946	**0.7390**
Answers-students	0.7734	0.6984	0.7446	**0.7827**	0.7784	0.7725
Belief	0.7431	0.6145	**0.7512**	0.7029	0.7482	0.7491
Headlines	0.8224	0.7814	0.8077	**0.8342**	0.8245	0.8250
Images	**0.8709**	0.8258	0.8647	0.8701	0.8527	0.8644
Mean correlation	0.7980	0.7241	0.7849	0.7920	0.7942	**0.8015**

Table 8. Evaluation results for datasets in 2016 [4]

Dataset/Team	Enriched WLED	WLED	NaCTeM	MayoNLP	UWB	Samsung Poland
Answer-answer	0.6601	0.5977	0.6143	0.6024	0.6426	**0.6625**
Headlines	0.8158	0.7729	0.7726	0.8046	0.7802	**0.8194**
Plagiarism	0.8233	0.7643	0.8050	0.8148	0.8182	**0.8303**
Postediting	**0.8769**	0.7987	0.8484	0.8286	0.8177	0.8751
Question-question	0.7293	0.7305	0.7471	0.6937	0.7466	0.7465
Mean correlation	**0.7812**	0.7315	0.7487	0.7561	0.7573	0.7781

Table 9. Evaluation results for datasets in 2017 [12]

Dataset/Team	Enriched WLED	WLED	BIT	ECNU	DT_TEAM	RTV
English-to-English	0.8384	0.7404	0.8400	0.8518	0.8536	**0.8547**

In the same way, the proposed method was compared to 2016 datasets and top-rank teams (Samsung Poland NLP [26], UWB [10], MayoNLP [1], and NaCTeM [25]); the results are available in Table 8. In these datasets Enriched WLED model outperforms all teams.

As opposed to prior years, it is not easy to outperform participants in 2017. Evaluating our models by using 2017-dataset, we found ourselves ranked 5 by having a correlation of 0.8384 for Enriched WLED and 0.7403 for WLED. The best result for this dataset has a correlation of 85.47. Even though our system worked quite well but we are not among the top three results. There are several reasons behind the performance improvement in this year: (1) top ranked teams used deep learning techniques, and (2) they employed ensembling of well-performed techniques [12]. Moreover, Enriching WLED model by a few basic features also indicates that ensembling is very effective in STS. This observation suggests to have a system to index numerous textual similarity functions as we provided in Sect. 3 (Table 9).

8   Related Work

Semantic textual similarity solutions can be classified in three groups as follows [5]: Vector Space Model, Text Alignment, and Supervised Machine Learning Algorithms. However, top-ranked models usually are an ensemble of various approaches [12]. A detailed evaluation of prior STS participants, algorithms, and systems can also be found in comparative studies in [2–4, 12].

To the extent of our knowledge, there are only a few open source projects for determining semantic similarity of sentences. To the extent of our knowledge, DKPro Similarity [6] is the best system available and it provides many simple but not very advanced features. TakeLab's top performing system [29] from SemEval 2012 is freely available for Python, and DLS@CU's word alignment system [27] (the top performing team in SemEval 2014) is another open-source Python code. Unfortunately, newly implemented systems are not available for the public, and data scientists need to implement their own versions which is both time-consuming and costly.

Beside having open-source software systems, there are also a few web APIs to measure textual similarities. RxNLP Text Similarity API[4] is an static version of such system which only supports 3 basic similarity measures (cosine, dice, and Jaccard). Dandelion Text Similarity API[5] also provides an endpoint to measure semantic similarity of short pieces of text. The output of this endpoint is just a number between 0 to 1 and they do not provide a list of features. Given the importance of measuring textual similarity and its wide range applications, to the extent of our knowledge, there is not any comprehensive web API providing an easy endpoint to calculate advanced textual similarity measures.

9   Conclusion

In this paper, we proposed a novel edit-distance based feature for measuring semantic similarity of two sentences and then investigated its effectiveness. We discussed the reason why we should have a system to gather textual similarity APIs and proposed an architecture for such a system. As our future works, we will work on the semantic similarity API repository system, and gather related APIs and algorithms. This is a big challenge since there only a few basic web APIs and most of the algorithms must be implemented manually. Another challenge is to motivate STS scientists to provide compatible APIs for the public to mitigate the hassle of measuring textual similarity. We believe this can be solved by advertising scientific works. Adding new features (especially those powered by deep learning), benefiting from NLP tasks such as word sense disambiguation and coreference resolution [7–9], parameter optimization, and applying deep learning techniques are other tasks to enrich our System in future.

---

[4] http://www.rxnlp.com/api-reference/text-similarity-api-reference/.

[5] https://dandelion.eu/docs/api/datatxt/sim/v1/.

References

1. Afzal, N., Wang, Y., Liu, H.: MayoNLP at SemEval-2016 task 1: semantic textual similarity based on lexical semantic net and deep learning semantic model. In: SemEval@ NAACL-HLT, pp. 674–679 (2016)
2. Agirre, E., Banea, C., Cardie, C., Cer, D.M., Diab, M.T, Gonzalez-Agirre, A., Guo, W., Lopez-Gazpio, I., Maritxalar, M., Mihalcea, R., et al.: SemEval-2015 task 2: semantic textual similarity, English, Spanish and Pilot on interpretability. In: SemEval@ NAACL-HLT, pp. 252–263 (2015)
3. Agirre, E., Banea, C., Cardie, C., Cer, D.M., Diab, M.T, Gonzalez-Agirre, A., Guo, W., Lopez-Gazpio, I., Maritxalar, M., Mihalcea, R., Rigau, G., Wiebe, J.: SemEval-2014 task 10: multilingual semantic textual similarity. In: SemEval@ COLING, pp. 81–91 (2014)
4. Agirre, E., Banea, C., Cer, D.M., Diab, M.T., Gonzalez-Agirre, A., Mihalcea, R., Rigau, G., Wiebe, J.: SemEval-2016 task 1: semantic textual similarity, monolingual and cross-lingual evaluation. In: SemEval@ NAACL-HLT, pp. 497–511 (2016)
5. Banjade, R., Niraula, N.B., Maharjan, N., Rus, V., Stefanescu, D., Lintean, M.C., Gautam, D.: NeRoSim: a system for measuring and interpreting semantic textual similarity. In: SemEval@ NAACL-HLT, pp. 164–171 (2015)
6. Bär, D., Zesch, T., Gurevych, I.: DKPro similarity: an open source framework for text similarity. In: Proceedings of the 51st Annual Meeting of the Association for Computational Linguistics: System Demonstrations, Sofia, Bulgaria, pp. 121–126. Association for Computational Linguistics, August 2013
7. Beheshti, S.-M.-R., Benatallah, B., Venugopal, S., Ryu, S.H., Motahari-Nezhad, H.R., Wang, W.: A systematic review and comparative analysis of cross-document coreference resolution methods and tools. Computing **99**(4), 313–349 (2017)
8. Beheshti, S.-M.-R., Nezhad, H.R.M., Benatallah, B.: Temporal provenance model (TPM): model and query language. CoRR, abs/1211.5009 (2012)
9. Beheshti, S.-M.-R., Venugopal, S., Ryu, S.H., Benatallah, B., Wang, W.: Big data and cross-document coreference resolution: current state and future opportunities. CoRR, abs/1311.3987 (2013)
10. Brychcin, T., Svoboda, L.: UWB at SemEval-2016 task 1: semantic textual similarity using lexical, syntactic, and semantic information. In: SemEval@ NAACL-HLT, pp. 588–594 (2016)
11. Campagna, G., Ramesh, R., Xu, S., Fischer, M., Lam, M.S.: Almond: the architecture of an open, crowdsourced, privacy-preserving, programmable virtual assistant. In: Proceedings of the 26th International Conference on World Wide Web, pp. 341–350. International World Wide Web Conferences Steering Committee (2017)
12. Cer, D., Diab, M., Agirre, E., Lopez-Gazpio, I., Specia, L.: SemEval-2017 task 1: semantic textual similarity-multilingual and cross-lingual focused evaluation. arXiv preprint arXiv:1708.00055 (2017)
13. Han, L., Martineau, J., Cheng, D., Thomas, C.: Samsung: align-and-differentiate approach to semantic textual similarity. In: SemEval@ NAACL-HLT, pp. 172–177 (2015)
14. Hänig, C., Remus, R., De La Puente, X.: ExB themis: extensive feature extraction from word alignments for semantic textual similarity. In: SemEval@ NAACL-HLT, pp. 264–268 (2015)
15. Kullback, S., Leibler, R.A.: On information and sufficiency. Ann. Math. Stat. **22**(1), 79–86 (1951)

16. Le, Q., Mikolov, T.: Distributed representations of sentences and documents. In: Proceedings of the 31st International Conference on Machine Learning (ICML 2014), pp. 1188–1196 (2014)
17. Manning, C.D., Surdeanu, M., Bauer, J., Finkel, J.R., Bethard, S., McClosky, D.: The Stanford coreNLP natural language processing toolkit. In: ACL (System Demonstrations), pp. 55–60 (2014)
18. Maurer, H.A., Kappe, F., Zaka, B.: Plagiarism-a survey. J. UCS **12**(8), 1050–1084 (2006)
19. Mawson, C.O.S.: Roget's thesaurus of english words and phrases (1976)
20. Mikolov, T., Sutskever, I., Chen, K., Corrado, G.S., Dean, J.: Distributed representations of words and phrases and their compositionality. In: Advances in Neural Information Processing Systems, pp. 3111–3119 (2013)
21. Miller, G.A.: WordNet: a lexical database for English. Commun. ACM **38**(11), 39–41 (1995)
22. Monge, A.E., Elkan, C., et al.: The field matching problem: algorithms and applications. In: KDD, pp. 267–270 (1996)
23. Navigli, R., Ponzetto, S.P.: BabelNet: building a very large multilingual semantic network. In: Proceedings of the 48th Annual Meeting of the Association for Computational Linguistics, pp. 216–225. Association for Computational Linguistics (2010)
24. Pennington, J., Socher, R., Manning, C.: Glove: global vectors for word representation. In: Proceedings of the 2014 Conference on Empirical Methods in Natural Language Processing (EMNLP), pp. 1532–1543 (2014)
25. Przybyła, P., Nguyen, N.T.H., Shardlow, M., Kontonatsios, G., Ananiadou, S.: NaCTeM at SemEval-2016 task 1: inferring sentence-level semantic similarity from an ensemble of complementary lexical and sentence-level features. In: Proceedings of the 10th International Workshop on Semantic Evaluation (SemEval 2016), pp. 614–620 (2016)
26. Rychalska, B., Pakulska, K. Chodorowska, K., Walczak, W., Andruszkiewicz, P.: Samsung Poland NLP team at SemEval-2016 task 1: necessity for diversity; combining recursive autoencoders, WordNet and ensemble methods to measure semantic similarity. In: SemEval@ NAACL-HLT, pp. 602–608 (2016)
27. Sultan, M.A., Bethard, S., Sumner, T.: DLS@CU: sentence similarity from word alignment. In: SemEval@ COLING, pp. 241–246 (2014)
28. Sultan, M.A., Bethard, S., Sumner, T.: DLS@CU: sentence similarity from word alignment and semantic vector composition. In: SemEval@ NAACL-HLT, pp. 148–153 (2015)
29. Šarić, F., Glavaš, G., Karan, M., Šnajder, J., Bašić, B.D.: TakeLab: systems for measuring semantic text similarity. In: Proceedings of the Sixth International Workshop on Semantic Evaluation (SemEval 2012), Montréal, Canada, pp. 441–448. Association for Computational Linguistics, 7–8 June 2012
30. Yaghoub-Zadeh-Fard, M.A., Minaei-Bidgoli, B., Rahmani, S., Shahrivari, S.: PSWG: an automatic stop-word list generator for Persian information retrieval systems based on similarity function pos information. In: 2015 2nd International Conference on Knowledge-Based Engineering and Innovation (KBEI), pp. 111–117, November 2015
31. Yaghoub-Zadeh-Fard, M.A., Rahmani, S., Kashefi, O., Minaei-Bidgoli, B.: An efficient set of parts of speech in Persian information retrieval systems (1394)

Logistics and Supply Chain Management Investigation: A Case Study

Ngoc Hong Tam Dao[1], Jay Daniel[2(✉)] , Stephen Hutchinson[3],
and Mohsen Naderpour[4]

[1] International College of Management, 151 Darley Road, Manly, NSW 2095, Australia
[2] Derby Business School, The University of Derby, Kedleston Road, Derby, DE22 1GB, UK
J.Daniel@derby.ac.uk
[3] Ubisoft Australia, 14 Mountain Street, Ultimo, NSW 2007, Australia
Stephen.Hutchinson@ubisoft.com
[4] Faculty of Engineering and IT, University of Technology Sydney,
15 Broadway, Ultimo, NSW 2007, Australia
Mohsen.Naderpour@uts.edu.au

Abstract. This paper investigates several aspects of logistics and supply chain management such as advantages of a full model of logistics and supply chain management. In addition, it also details a series of challenges in logistics and supply chain management in general and in the computer and video game industry in particular. It also focuses on some popular models and the common trend in logistics and supply chain management. Especially, it analyses the logistics and supply chain model of Ubisoft Australia – a computer and video game publisher. By conducting interviews and observations together with gathering company internal records, it points out some potential problems of Ubisoft Australia with the software system, communication and information flow in inbound logistic and non-conforming returns. Finally, several recommendations are made for future improvements.

Keywords: Reverse logistics · Supply chain management
Video and game industry

1 Introduction

Recently, globalization has widely spread out all over the world and brought many benefits for international business. Although global expansion offers a huge number of opportunities, it is undeniable that there are also several disadvantages. Among those challenges, fierce competition is of most concern for all business owners. Consequently, the effective logistics and supply chain management that provides the best customer services, high quality of products and cost-effectiveness has become the key factor that directly affects the survival of an organization [1]. For the computer and video game industry, according to [2, 3], it is an extremely competitive industry that evolves rapidly, which features a new generation of consoles, where technologies and new companies can appear or disappear at each generation. As a result, in order to remain profitable and competitive it is essential to have an agile, adaptable and efficient supply chain. In other

© Springer International Publishing AG, part of Springer Nature 2018
A. Beheshti et al. (Eds.): ASSRI 2015/2017, LNBIP 234, pp. 216–230, 2018.
https://doi.org/10.1007/978-3-319-76587-7_15

words, this industry requires a dynamic logistics and supply chain management providing the right services and products to the right location at the right time with the right quantity and quality for a competitive price [3].

Having realized the increasing importance of logistics and supply chain management as an effective and efficient process to maximize profitability as well as minimize the cost, Ubisoft Australia has been developing this process since the business was expanded to Australia in 2001. However, a recent review of logistics and supply chain management activities identified a number of potential problems due to several factors such as higher level of customer service requirements together with the fierce competition from rivals [23, 24]. This study aims to review the logistic and supply chain management mechanism at Ubisoft Australia, to identify the challenges, to make recommendation to reduce the limitations, and to propose suggestions for future developments. To achieve this, a combinatorial methodology is proposed and implemented in the case study environment.

The rest of the paper is organized as follows. Section 2 represents the literature review related to this study. Section 3 describes the research methodology. Section 4 provides the results and a brief discussion. Finally, Sect. 5 concludes the paper and presents some further research directions.

2   Literature Review

Logistics and supply chain process is described as a flow of activities involved, directly or indirectly, from materials sourcing to the distribution of finished products to customers [4]. In details, this process includes all parties such as material sourcing, material purchasing, inbound logistics, operations and outbound logistics to ensure that the customer's requests are received and fulfilled [5]. According to Khalili-Damghani et al. (2015), this process is mainly known as the flow of traditional logistics or the process of forward logistics. Forward logistics is divided into two phases: inbound logistics and outbound logistics. Inbound logistics includes all aspects of material sourcing, material purchasing, transporting to factories. Meanwhile, outbound logistics handles the rest of the process such as the transportation of the finished goods to warehouses or distribution centers, then from the warehouses or distribution centers to customers. In general, forward logistics has been considered as an essential fundamental of an organization operations to ensure the input and output of products or services [6].

Customer service and satisfaction are crucial for staying in the business and competing in the marketplace as well as fulfilling regulatory obligations in countries such as Australia. For this to happen, logistics and supply chain process is not limited to the forward logistic. It has expanded to the process of dealing with faulty stock which is called reverse logistics that consists of all parties involved such as faulty stock collecting, sorting, repairing, re-manufacturing and recycling [7].

Reverse logistics has been more and more popular because it has been considered as one of the effective solutions that help the companies improve customer service level and reduce the negative impacts of faulty stock on the environment [8]. Therefore, it plays an important role in gaining competitive advantages, increasing the corporate social responsibilities as well as the reputation of the companies [25]. A full model of logistics and supply chain process that integrates both forward and reverse logistics are shown in Fig. 1. It is definitely important to have a logistics model that is operational and cost effective in both forward and reverse logistics [9].

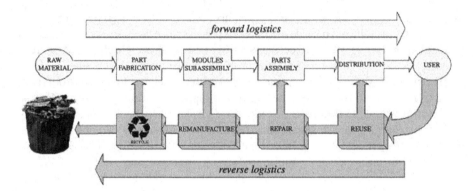

Fig. 1. Integrated forward and reverse logistics process [8].

2.1 Logistics and Supply Chain Management Challenges

The integrated model of logistics and supply chain process is a complex system that gives not only a certain number of opportunities but plenty of challenges also. Im and Deek (2011) claimed that software integration is one of the most challenging elements in the process of logistics and supply chain management [10]. It is undeniable that software integration has brought many advantages to effective control and operations of purchasing, transportation, manufacturing, inventory, and payment [11]. However, due to the integration of many functions with the involvement of many parties (the company itself, material suppliers, manufacturers and even customers), software integration has become complicated and difficult for the company's operations. Likewise, the researches of Enriquez et al. (2015) and Gambetti and Giovanardi (2013) also point out the challenges in logistics and supply chain management [12, 13]. However, they focus on other aspects that are called communication flow and information flow in global logistics and supply chain management. Poor communication leads to different problems in the supply chain such as sending wrong products and quantities to customers, missing or late deliveries which impact on delivery in full on time (DIFOT).

Another challenge in logistics and supply chain management that has been more and more of concern is faulty stock returns or reverse logistics [7]. Reverse logistics process is to deal with the collecting, handling and returning of faulty stock which increases time and cost in the supply chain. Besides the above challenges, demand forecast, network relationship building, transportation, inventory and green logistics and supply chain, in general, are also considerable problems in logistics and supply chain management in general [14].

In the computer and video game industry, the logistics and supply chain management has not been limited only to these challenges but also to some other typical challenges such as embargo issues and digital – physical distribution [15, 16]. It is usual within the video games industry to have a strict global launch date for a new product. Failure to control access to a new product can have repercussions in territories beyond our own country. Product may be destined for store, end-user customers or journalists who are reviewing the product and it is important that strict delivery guidelines are adhered to. Distributors such as Ubisoft must have a calculated and extensive control over all areas of the supply chain to ensure that street dates are adhered to. Embargos are placed on stores preventing them from selling any stock early. Attention is paid to delivery schedules to avoid having stock delivered too early thus reducing the risk of street dates being breached [17].

Another challenge that has been of concern to all game publishers in recent times is the increase in digital distribution. Although the increase of digital distribution has brought many advantages, there is a very large number of obstacles which have implied negative impacts on a retail chain, or which could even lead to the disappearance of retail outlets in the future [15]. However, it is argued that physical distribution has its own strengths which help this form of distribution continue running in the video game industry, especially the "hands-on experience" at retail outlets that the digital distribution can never have. Therefore, in the future, although the physical distribution has declined, dual distribution channels will be maintained.

2.2   Popular Logistics and Supply Chain Management Models

A 3PL model is a form of outsourcing activities that are related to logistics and distribution. The benefits that a 3PL provider can offer are a vast resource network, expertise, scalability and flexibility, continuous optimization, time and money saving. Obviously, with a 3PL provider, the company does not spend time to take care of the behind-the-scenes tasks; therefore, the company can focus on other tasks such as sales, marketing and business development [18].

Drop shipping is another method in logistics and supply chain management in which the goods are directly delivered to customers without passing through the distribution centers or warehouses. Therefore, the sellers can save time and costs for warehouse, stocks, inventory, shipping and administration fees.

In contrast with the drop shipping model, the "hub and spokes" model is enhanced with a distribution center ("hub") when the goods are consolidated before delivering to customers ("spokes"). Strategically the hub is usually at a good location that is more convenient for the product transportations from suppliers/manufacturers to the "hub" than from the "hub" to the "spokes" [5].

Under the pressure of fierce competition in the global market, companies are forced to change or think of new methods to improve their process, customer satisfaction and stay ahead in the game with their rivals. In recent times, anticipatory shipping technique has been considered as the latest approach in logistics and supply chain management patented by Amazon. This method is mainly based on Big Data and predictive analysis. In detail, based on the "previous browsing behaviors" and buying decisions of customers, Amazon can predict which items and the quantity their customers would like to buy in the near future; then they will arrange delivery to an Amazon hub in the geographically related region before their customers officially purchase these items. The key strengths of this method are faster delivery and additional sales. Although this method still has much debate about its pros and cons, it has still been considered as an innovation in logistics and supply chain management [19].

2.3   Ubisoft Australia Logistics and Supply Chain Model

Ubisoft is a world leader in creating, publishing and distributing of interactive entertainment and services, especially computer and video games. As per game revenues ranking, Ubisoft Group has become one of the top 10 public companies with a rich portfolio of world-renowned brands [20]. Through its worldwide network of business offices and studios, Ubisoft provides memorable gaming experiences across all popular platforms [21]. Ubisoft Australia is a branch of the global Ubisoft group. It is a business office with around 30 staff allocated in four teams - Marketing, Sales, Finance and Operations. The business sells products not only to retailers in Australia and New Zealand but also to online games stores.

The logistics and supply chain model of Ubisoft Australia has been considered as a typically full model with forward logistics, reverse logistics and 3PL with the combination of drop shipping and "hub and spokes" logistics model as presented in Fig. 2. The inbound flow from production is managed in conjunction with the head office team to draw stock from local factories as well as manufacturers in other parts of the world. Depending on demand volumes orders can be shipped directly from manufacturers to the retail/wholesale distribution centre or channeled through the 3PL warehouse. Stock can be cross-docked through the 3PL for urgently required orders; or stored at the warehouse until required. Utilizing the 3PLs courier partnerships, stock is transported to its required destination based on the needs of Ubisoft's customers. The orders are transported to the courier's main distribution centres before being redirected to regional DC's and depots. Finally, they are delivered to the store docks either by the courier or subcontractors. In some cases, the orders then become inducted into the retailer's supply chain for distribution to their own store network. In circumstances where customers need

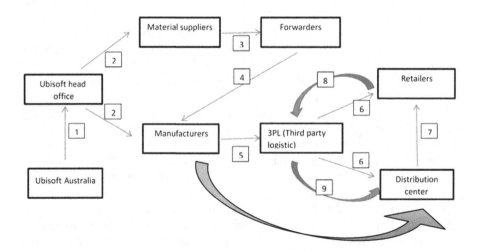

Fig. 2. Flow chart of Ubisoft supply chain.

to return stock to Ubisoft, an authorization is sought by the customer. Once this request has been approved, goods are collected from either the store or their reverse logistic warehouse using the 3PL's carrier. Once returned to the warehouse the goods are checked for conformity before reworking or destruction.

3 Methodology

The proposed methodology is a general research methodology that can be used in other domains as well as in the computer and video game industry. The methodology is organized in three phases: (1) Data collection, (2) Data analysis and (3) Suggestions that are detailed in the following sub-sections (Table 1).

Table 1. Interview questions.

Question	Description
Q1	Which aspects of Ubisoft's supply chain are you most concerned about? Please can you explain your concerns?
Q2	As a 3PL of Ubisoft, could you please let us know the advantages and disadvantages you have met when processing Ubisoft orders?
Q3	Could you please tell me more details about the stock returns and stock destruction?
Q4	How can we know that the stock destruction process was completed?

3.1 Data Collection

The research focuses on both qualitative and quantitative data. The qualitative data includes in-depth structured interviews and personally structured observations. This also paves the way for the quantitative data collection.

- **Qualitative Data**

The first in-depth interview is conducted with Ubisoft Australia operations team (one Operation Director and two Operation Coordinators) with open-ended questions regarding the aspects of logistics and supply chain system of Ubisoft Australia with more concerns and their reasons. The second in-depth interview is conducted with 3PL warehouse supervisor with open-ended questions about the advantages and disadvantages when processing Ubisoft orders and how they dealt with the stock returns.

Another source of data is structured observations about the communication and information flow of inbound logistics of Ubisoft Australia.

- **Quantitative Data**

The following quantitative data is collected:

- Stock return quantity in 2014 and 2015.
- Ubisoft terms and conditions of stock returns.
- Pictures of stock return reasons.
- Competitors' activities about stock returns.

3.2 Data Analysis

In the data analysis stage, a thematic analysis is conducted to look across all the data to identify the common issues that recur, and identify the main themes that summarizes all the views collected. This is the most common method for descriptive qualitative projects. The key stages in a thematic analysis are to:

1. Read and annotate transcripts.
2. Identify themes.
3. Develop a coding scheme.
4. Code the data.

3.3 Suggestions

This phase follows immediately behind data analysis to provide some suggestions for improvements. Suggestion is a creative process during which new concepts, models and functions of artifacts are demonstrated.

4 Results

4.1 Interviews

The results of interviews with Ubisoft Operation team and 3PL warehouse supervisor are summarized as follows:

Q1. According to Operation Coordinator 1, the software system that has been used at Ubisoft for nearly one year is very complicated and slow. It takes more time to handle the works in comparison with the old one. The software problem is also confirmed by Operation Coordinator 2 when he claimed that sometimes, the errors occurred and caused the interruption of the daily workflow. There was no choice to input the records into the system manually in order to keep the workflow running smoothly, which takes time to raise SOS-tickets to IT team at head office in France for checking and giving further instructions.

Q2. Another issue which was raised by Operation Coordinator 1 is the return authorization. At present, although Ubisoft does not have many stock returns, if this issue is not managed well, it will become an issue in the future. As a result, the increase of non-conforming returns is implied. Same as Operation Coordinator 1, Operation Director also worried about non-conforming returns and its consequences on how to maintain good customer service but not increase costs. Finally, another concern is related to embargo commitment. It is a feature of the computer and video game industry. So far, Ubisoft Australia has never had the problem with retailers about embargo commitments. According to 3PL Supervisor, her company and Ubisoft have had a long time working together so the advantages are that they have a good relationship and they are familiar with all requested procedures and documents as well as commitments with Ubisoft. With regard to disadvantage, stock returns have become a matter of most concern.

Q3. 3PL Supervisor claimed that there are several difficulties. The first issue is related to the receipt of stock returns. Some retailers, such as retailer 1, retailer 4 and retailer 5, have consolidation of stock return so it does not take a lot of time to receive the returns. However, retailer 2 is another case because its stores make independent claims and returns; therefore, it takes more time to handle the receipt of stock returns. Another issue is about the time consumed in sorting because there are many stock returns without labelling. The last issue that is also related to time-consuming is non-conforming stock returns. With these returns, it really takes time to separate, check, and report to Ubisoft the quantity in details and wait for the instructions from Ubisoft. It is related to not only time-consumption but extra cost also.

Q4. The process of stock returns and stock destruction is completed when a certificate of destruction that clearly mentions the destruction quantity is issued to Ubisoft right after the stock return destruction finishing, stated by 3PL Supervisor.

4.2 Observations

The observations show the typical flow of communication and information of Ubisoft Australia inbound logistics has seven stages as below as well as presented in Fig. 3:

1. Ubisoft Australia places a demand to Ubisoft head office in France.
2. Ubisoft head office places orders to Material/Component Suppliers and Local Manufacturers, and contacts Forwarder companies.
3. If there is no problem about materials/components, Local Manufacturers will go ahead with production.
4. If not, Local Manufacturers will contact Ubisoft head office and Ubisoft Australia.
5. Ubisoft Australia comes back to Ubisoft head office.
6. Ubisoft head office checks with Material/Component Suppliers.
7. Then Ubisoft head office updates the information to all parties (Ubisoft Australia, Forwarder companies and Local Manufacturers).

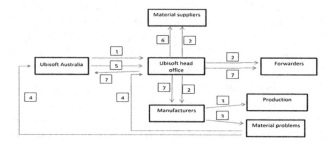

Fig. 3. Flow chart of communication in inbound logistic.

From the above communication and information flow, it is clear that Ubisoft head office has controlled all information and played the main role in communication with all parties.

4.3 Quantitative Data

- Stock return quantity in 2014 and 2015: As per internal reports of Ubisoft Australia, total stock return quantity in 2014 was 5,352 units; meanwhile, the total stock return quantity in 2015 was 14,976 units. It means the stock return quantity was nearly triple in the period from 2014 to 2015 (Fig. 4).

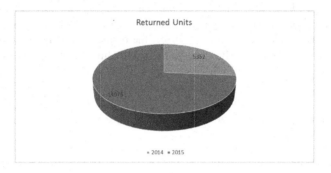

Fig. 4. Stock return quantity [22].

- Ubisoft terms and conditions of stock returns: As per terms and conditions of stock returns, Ubisoft Australia only accepts the returns of the stock with the below conditions:
  - The stock is faulty and
  - The stock is purchased from Ubisoft Australia directly, and
  - The stock carries the valid return authorization from Ubisoft Australia, and
  - All authorized returns must be sent back within 30 days of receiving the return authorization

  Overall, these terms and conditions of stock returns aim to prevent the returns of non-conforming stock.
- Stock return nonconformity evidence: Some evidence of stock returns that were collected while Ubisoft Operation team had a random check of the stock returns before destruction show some reasons for return such as "Didn't like it" or "Seven-day return". Actually "Didn't like it" return and "Seven-day return" are not promotion programs of Ubisoft Australia, but for some retailers to attract their customers. These reasons are obviously out of Ubisoft Australia terms and conditions for stock returns. In other words, it shows that the retailers do not strictly implement the Ubisoft Australia terms and conditions of stock return.
- Competitors' activities about stock returns: Through competitors' activities, all competitors have used ullage agreements with their retailers and each competitor has its own terms and conditions to deal with the problem of stock returns. In general, these terms and conditions are almost the same and they aim to limit the cost and quantity of stock returns, especially non-conforming returns. However, at present, stock returns and non-conforming returns are unavoidable.

4.4 Challenges Identified

From the data analysis, three main potential problems related to Ubisoft Australia logistics and supply chain management are determined:

- Ubisoft recently implemented a global Enterprise Resource Planning (ERP) system in the Australian subsidiary. Switching from a bespoke localized system to one designed to manage a multi-site global enterprise has impacted flows within the supply chain due to inflexibility. The reliance on technical support facilities in other countries and other time zones has led to a less responsive process of error correction and bug fixing. There have also been issues with the change management process as a result of this implementation. As is typical in new system integrations, it can take many months for the users to be comfortable with the new tool.
- Ubisoft uses the resources and buying power of its head office to drive competitive costs and service levels from major manufacturing partners. At the same time the local Ubisoft team is able to use their geographic proximity and logistics skills to coordinate reactive and personalized procedures to facilitate the efficient manufacture and delivery of goods. Sometimes there are ambiguities in the roles of the centralized office acting as both a supply partner and a head-office. Obviously, Ubisoft Australia have not shared all necessary information and not been involved in whole communication loop with all related parties to support the local manufacturers promptly, especially whenever the local manufacturers have problems with their input. Therefore, there is a very large potential of delays in production.
- Based on the current returns policy, volumes of product returned under a faulty status will inevitably increase in direct proportion to the number of units sold into retail. It is clear from examining random samples of returned goods that many of these products would fall under a category of non-conformance. In other words, Ubisoft should not be obligated to facilitate the return of these products or issue a subsequent credit.

4.5 Recommendations

Recommendation 1: It is clear that supply could be improved and obstacles more easily overcome with a greater sharing of information by the central office. Similarly offering the local office more autonomy in the decision making whilst still exercising the purchasing power over suppliers would lead to a more versatile logistics flow.

Recommendation 2: Regarding communication and information flow in inbound logistics, to avoid potential delays for production, Ubisoft Australia should be more active and involved in material delivery management as well as production control. In detail, the communication and information flow should be changed as represented in Fig. 5.

1. Ubisoft Australia sends the demand request to Ubisoft head office in France.
2. Ubisoft head office places the material orders to material suppliers, bulk orders to local manufacturers then shares information about BOM (Bill of Materials), specifying which material items are placed at which suppliers and delivery schedule of all materials with Ubisoft Australia.

3. Ubisoft Australia will follow up the rest of the process. For example, they will directly contact material suppliers to remind them of the shipment schedule to ensure the materials are shipped on-time, then they should contact forwarder company for shipment arrangement, and they should closely work with local manufacturers to update the shipment schedule of all materials/components so that the local manufacturers can arrange their production plan accordingly.
4. In case the local manufacturers have problems with material/components delays or material quality, they will contact Ubisoft Australia.
5. Ubisoft Australia has to double check with material suppliers and freight forwarder company.
6. Ubisoft Australia then updates local manufacturers with required information from material suppliers and forwarder companies.

This communication and information flow helps Ubisoft Australia work closely with all related parties and proactively solve the problems in inbound logistics instead of relying on head office in France. Therefore, the potential delays in local production can be considerably avoided.

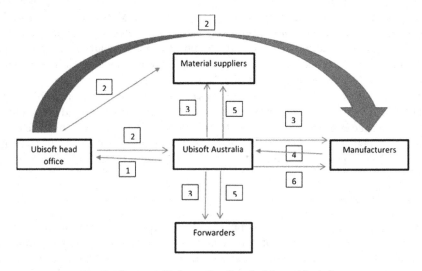

Fig. 5. Suggested information flow in inbound logistics.

Recommendation 3: With the stock returns problem, there are several ways to deal with this problem

- Instead of random checking, a suitable sampling system of returns quantity should be used to find out which ones are really defective and authorize returns. It is better to keep a regular record and reporting made of non-conforming product and that this information be shared with relevant parties including the retailers who have returned the goods.
- Refuse credit for non-conforming returns or challenge non-conforming returns (reverse credits).

- Change the model of return by return collection – repair – resale the good ones and destroy the unrepaired ones instead of destroying all returns. In some circumstances it may be possible to refurbish returned products for resale (as is the practice in the video industry) thus reducing production costs and the impact on the environment due to over-production.
- There may be opportunities to establish an ullage agreement with some retailers which would see them managing their own faulty/damaged items without returning the goods. This would see them receiving extended rebate terms as an off-set for absorbing the costs of faulty returns from their own customers. The issue with this is that the distributor never has the ability to check or derive proof of any faults in their games. On the other had it dramatically reduces the costs of the reverse logistic function.

4.6 Implications for Practice

- Software system: The software system was designed not only for Ubisoft Australia and supply chain management but for the worldwide system and other purposes also, for example, accounting and financial control. Moreover, this software system has been run for nearly one year; that is long enough to know which problems or which difficulties have been caused. Therefore, it is really necessary and urgent to re-design and upgrade the software system so that it is significantly more convenient for all related stakeholders.
- Inbound logistics: Potentials of material delays that affect bulk production can be totally avoided with a better communication and information flow. In other words, Ubisoft Australia Operation Coordinator might spend more time following all material delivery schedules, working closely with material suppliers and forwarder companies as well as local manufacturers.
- The effects of stock return on sales volume: Although the stock return was suddenly increased (5,352 units in 2014 – 14,976 units in 2015) and Ubisoft Australia has found some non-conforming returns by random checks, as per Ubisoft terms and conditions of stock return, they could refuse credit for non-conforming returns or challenge non-conforming returns (reverse credits) but they did not do this because they have been totally aware of the negative impacts on sales volume and the importance of the good relationship building with retailers. In other words, they have accepted this cost of non-conforming returns as the "cost of doing business" [22].
- Consequences of non-conforming returns: There are two kinds of non-conforming returns. The first one is faulty but returned without authorization from Ubisoft. The other one is not faulty but has implied the sales returns. At present, Ubisoft and all rivals in computer and video game industry are trying to deal with the non-conforming returns smoothly to avoid the conflicts and the negative impacts on their business relationship with the retailers. However, the solutions that they have applied cannot solve this problem thoroughly.
- For future development: To maintain the sustainable development and stay ahead in the game with their rivals, Ubisoft Australia is forced to change or think of new methods to improve their processes for cost saving and customer satisfaction.

- Software integration with retailers: Currently, Ubisoft Australia software is only integrated with local manufacturers. However, a better collaboration with retailers via software integration might avoid the sales return. Information integration such as sell-through data and stock in store currently exists between Ubisoft and some of its retailers. There is also some use of vendor managed inventory at store which is managed via a third party. With the emergence of new supply-chain focused retailers into the Australian market customer satisfaction will be improved by finding greater synergies with the retailer's supply models. It can help Ubisoft Australia to control the available stock at retailers' stores and adjust their supply. A good example of this method is the cooperation between P&G and Amazon that helps both P&G and Amazon save cost, allocate and control the stock and inventory well. This solution has also contributed to the limit of sales returns because both Ubisoft Australia and retailers have a better collaboration in demand forecasts and stock allocation as well as inventory.
- Logistics and supply chain model: At present, Ubisoft Australia uses a typically full model with forward logistics, reverse logistics and 3PL with the combination of drop shipping and "hub and spokes" logistics model. To save the cost of distribution center operations and utilize the advantages of the new trend in logistics and supply chain management, Ubisoft can consider the logistics and supply chain model with forward logistics, reverse logistics and 3PL with the combination of drop shipping and anticipatory shipping instead of "hub and spokes" logistics. This new logistics and supply chain model allows Ubisoft not only to cut cost for distribution center administration fees but to enhance a higher level of customer services also with anticipatory shipping method as the stock will be delivered faster than the old way. However, due to the embargo commitments with retailers – a key feature in the computer and video game industry – anticipatory shipping should be applied for re-orders. For the new releases, Ubisoft Australia just needs the drop shipping.

5   Conclusion and Future Work

The paper reviews several aspects of logistics and supply chain management in general and in the computer and video game industry in particular. In addition, it analyses the logistics and supply chain model of Ubisoft Australia – a computer and video game publisher. The results highlight the problems of Ubisoft Australia in the software system and communication and information flow in inbound logistic and non-conforming return areas. Finally, several recommendations are proposed to cease the problems.

This research offers several directions for future research such as the disadvantages of drop shipping, anticipatory shipping, software system integration between publishers and retailers/customers, as well as the difficulties related to a higher level of demand forecasts in the computer and video game industry in general and in Ubisoft Group - Ubisoft Australia in particular.

Acknowledgment. Authors would like to express their appreciation for the cooperation and help of Ubisoft Australia.

References

1. Linkdin. https://www.linkedin.com/pulse/roles-operations-supply-chain-managers-organization-irfan-ozduru
2. Langlotz, A.C.H., Rhode, M., Whaley, C.: Video games industry overview: an analysis of the current market and future growth trends. International Business Project 4-47 (2008)
3. Claro Tomaselli, F., Di Serio, L.C.: Supply networks and value creation in high innovation and strong network externalities industry. J. Technol. Manag. Innov. **8**, 177–185 (2013)
4. Khalili-Damghani, K., Tavana, M., Najmodin, M.: Reverse logistics and supply chains: a structural equation modeling investigation. Int. J. Ind. Eng. **22**, 354–368 (2015)
5. Minculete, G., Olar, P.: New approaches to supply chain management concept. Logistics integration of "Hub and Spoke" model. Valahian J. Econ. Stud. **5**, 21 (2014)
6. Varzandeh, J., Farahbod, K., Zhu, J.J.: Global logistics and supply chain risk management. J. Bus. Behav. Sci. **28**, 124 (2016)
7. Gu, Q., Tagaras, G.: Optimal collection and remanufacturing decisions in reverse supply chains with collector's imperfect sorting. Int. J. Prod. Res. **52**, 5155–5170 (2014)
8. Cerasis. http://cerasis.com/2015/07/20/reverse-logistics-system/
9. Lee, Y.J., Baker, T., Jayaraman, V.: Redesigning an integrated forward–reverse logistics system for a third party service provider: an empirical study. Int. J. Prod. Res. **50**, 5615–5634 (2012)
10. Mohtashami, M., Deek, F.P., Im, I.: Critical factors in collaborative software development in supply chain management. Int. J. Inf. Technol. Manag. **10**, 233–246 (2011)
11. Mccrea, B.: Supply chain execution software: a look at what's going on under the hood and shaping the supply chain execution space in 2016–and beyond. Logistics Management (Highlands Ranch, Colo.: 2002) (2016)
12. Enriquez, L.A., Castorena, O.H., Veyna, O.P.: Relationship supply chain management and information technology and communication in production processes to improve competitiveness of manufacturing SMEs in Aguascalientes. Revista Internacional Administracion & Finanzas **8**, 79–91 (2015)
13. Gambetti, R.C., Giovanardi, M.: Re-visiting the supply chain: a communication perspective. Corp. Commun. Int. J. **18**, 390–416 (2013)
14. Corominas, A.: Supply chains: what they are and the new problems they raise. Int. J. Prod. Res. **51**, 6828–6835 (2013)
15. Berman-Grutzky, M., Cederholm, A.: The obstacles and opportunities for digital distribution in the video game industry, today and tomorrow. Skolan för datavetenskap och kommunikation, Kungliga Tekniska högskolan (2010)
16. Whatculture. http://whatculture.com/gaming/9-crippling-problems-gaming-industrys-future?page=3
17. Gameskinny. http://www.gameskinny.com/5mzpa/what-exactly-is-a-game-embargo
18. Li, L., Ford, J.B., Zhai, X., Xu, L.: Relational benefits and manufacturer satisfaction: an empirical study of logistics service in supply chain. Int. J. Prod. Res. **50**, 5445–5459 (2012)
19. Forbes. https://www.forbes.com/sites/onmarketing/2014/01/28/why-amazons-anticipatory-shipping-is-pure-genius/#4b742d794605
20. Polygon. http://www.polygon.com/2015/4/20/8459589/chart-shows-which-public-companies-are-making-the-most-money-from
21. Ubisoft: Annual Report 2016 (2016)
22. Ubisoft: Stock Returns Review (2016)
23. Taghikhah, F., Daniel, J., Mooney, G.: Sustainable supply chain analytics: grand challenges and future opportunities. In: 2017 Proceedings PACIS, July 2017

24. Daniel, J., Talaei-Khoei, A.: Developing a conceptual model to evaluate green suppliers: decision making method using DEMATEL. In: 22nd Americas Conference on Information Systems, AMCIS 2016. Surfing the IT Innovation Wave (2016)
25. Taghikhah, F., Daniel, J., Mooney, G.: Profit, planet and people in supply chain: grand challenges and future opportunities. Res. Pap., pp. 1299–1313, June 2017

Author Index

Printed in the United States
By Bookmasters